A GUIDE
FOR USING THE
FOREIGN
EXCHANGE
MARKET

A GUIDE
FOR USING THE
FOREIGN
EXCHANGE
MARKET

TOWNSEND WALKER

A Ronald Press Publication

JOHN WILEY & SONS,   New York   ·   Chichester   ·   Brisbane   ·   Toronto

Library of Congress Cataloging in Publication Data:

Walker, Townsend, 1942–
  A guide for using the foreign exchange market.

  "A Ronald Press publication."
  Bibliography: p.
  Includes index.
  1. Foreign exchange. 2. International business
enterprises–Finance. I. Title.
  HG3851.W38   332.4′5   80-21975
  ISBN 0-471-06254-5

Printed in the United States of America

10 9 8 7 6 5 4 3 2 1

To
Stormy

PREFACE

This book contains the tools and the methods of analysis needed to operate in the foreign exchange and international money markets. It is designed as a learning manual and a reference. Extensive graphics make it possible to visualize problems and their solutions. Case problems and exercises are based on actual situations. A range of solution is given for each problem, so the reader learns the logic used to evaluate various options. This Guide concentrates on techniques, analysis, calculation, and explanation. It provides a way of thinking about foreign exchange problems.

The book is written from the viewpoint of the corporate treasurer whose company is engaged in international business. It is intended for people in corporate treasuries, for bankers, and for students considering either position. Foreign exchange dealers will benefit from the corporate perspective and from the calculations.

No prior knowledge of foreign exchange is assumed. Those with some knowledge will benefit from seeing the subject matter placed within a consistent framework and this will help them communicate more easily the knowledge they have.

One reason the book was written is that the material has not previously been organized in one place. Some of it has not been written at all; it is part of the oral tradition of foreign exchange market participants.

The genesis of the book was the Foreign Exchange Workshop I developed for Bank of America in London in 1977. I want to thank Glen Smith, Chris Braunlich, Stan Broderick, Rodney Fetzer, and Nicolas Wapler for their help during this time. The Workshop continues to be offered worldwide by the bank and is an intensive learning experience in foreign exchange. I am grateful to the Bank for its permission to use ideas and symbols from the Workshop in this book.

Fred Kohler taught me how to structure information about the foreign exchange market so that it can be readily learned. Beverly Mills read and edited the manuscript and is responsible for its clarity. These two people played a vital role in shaping this book and I thank them. The author alone is responsible for error.

Townsend Walker

San Francisco, California
January 1981

CONTENTS

CHAPTER ONE
EXPOSURE

"Exposure" means being open to risk. There is the risk that something good will happen, as well as the risk something unfortunate will happen. The corporation in international business is open to risk because the currency of their income is different from the currency of their expenses. Corporations make and buy products in one country and sell them in another, receive dividends from their foreign subsidiaries, borrow all over the world, invest overseas, and build power plants and airports in foreign countries.

TRANSACTION EXPOSURE

The risk these companies face is that the conversion rate between the currency of their income and the currency of their expenses changes over time. The rate that generated a profit when the transaction was initiated may be different from the rate of conversion when the money actually flows. The rate of conversion, the *exchange rate,* of two countries does change and changes from minute to minute every business day. A corporation is exposed because of these changing rates, the different currencies, and the time between fixing the price of a transaction and actually paying the money.

This type of exposure is called *transaction* exposure because it has to do with transactions—acts of buying, selling, borrowing, or lending. The other types of exposure are accounting, which deals with balance sheet

1

items, and economic, which considers the long-term operating effects of exposure to currency change. The latter types are not within the scope of this book. This book looks at different types of transaction exposure and what can be done about them.

Here are four specific exposure situations. In May the Charlston Motor Company signs a contract with the government of Tunisia to deliver 50 dump trucks. The trucks will be made in Charlston's Wisconsin plant. They will be delivered in Tunisia in September, at which time Charlston will be paid two million French francs.

Norris Tools Limited manufactures gardening tools in England's Midlands. The steel is obtained from British Steel; the wooden handles for the tools are brought from a Swedish supplier. Norris agrees to be billed in Swedish kroner since the Swedish supplier offers a better price in its own currency. Orders are placed seven to eight times a year. From the time they are ordered, the handles take a month to arrive, and the invoice is payable within 30 days.

Bailie Industries Ltd., a Toronto-based multinational, makes auto accessories in every country of North America and Western Europe. It is company policy that the subsidiaries remit dividends as soon, and as often, as local authorities will allow, but government clearance procedures are notoriously erratic. The result is that the international treasurer in Toronto comes in many mornings to find a telex on the desk stating that lire are sitting in the account in Milan, ready to be converted. A week later a telex from Vienna may advise of schillings being remitted.

In 1975 Parker & Company, a Massachusetts-based electronics firm, borrowed Swiss francs for 10 years at the attractive rate of 5%; the alternative was to borrow dollars at 14%. Parker has been repaying the loan in quarterly installments.

The common elements in all these situations of transaction exposure is that all the companies measure the results of their operations against their home currency. For Charlston, it is U.S. dollars; for Norris, pounds sterling; for Bailie, Canadian dollars; and for Parker, U.S. dollars. The companies all have inflows or outflows of money in foreign currencies. For each corporation there is a time lapse between the day that terms are agreed on and the day that a conversion between foreign currency and home currency takes place. There are three elements in transaction exposure situations—a home currency, a foreign currency, and time.

In the Bailie Industries situation it may seem that time is not a factor; the money is there now. Exposure exists, however, until the conversion to the home currency is actually made. In this instance time has been collapsed. The time between the knowledge of the currency flow and the conversion is hours, as opposed to days or months in the other situations. Norris Tools raises a different time question. From what date does the exposure exist—from the date the order is placed, or when delivery is made? It exists from the date the order is placed because from that date onward Norris is open to the risk that the value of the Swedish kroner will rise in relation to the pound, even though the company has no obligation to pay until the handles are delivered.

What is the risk in the other situations? In Charlston the risk is that the French franc falls in relation to the U.S. dollar; in Bailie, that the currencies of the dividends fall relative to the Canadian dollar; and in Parker, that the Swiss franc rises against the dollar.

Symbols are used to represent these exposure situations and to facilitate finding solutions to them. The symbols consist of balls and arrows of different shades. A ball represents a company, and the shade of the ball represents its currency, the home currency. Arrows are flows of money, and the different shades are different currencies, foreign currencies and the home currency. Unless otherwise indicated, two arrows of the same size represent the same amount of money. Time moves from left to right.

If an arrow is pointing toward the ball, money is coming in—from sales, dividends, bank loans, and so on

An arrow pointing away from the ball means that money is flowing out—as a result of payments to suppliers, repayment of bank loans, and investments

This is an outflow of a foreign currency today

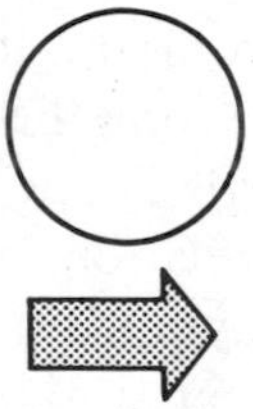

This is an inflow of one foreign currency in one month and an outflow of a different foreign currency in two months

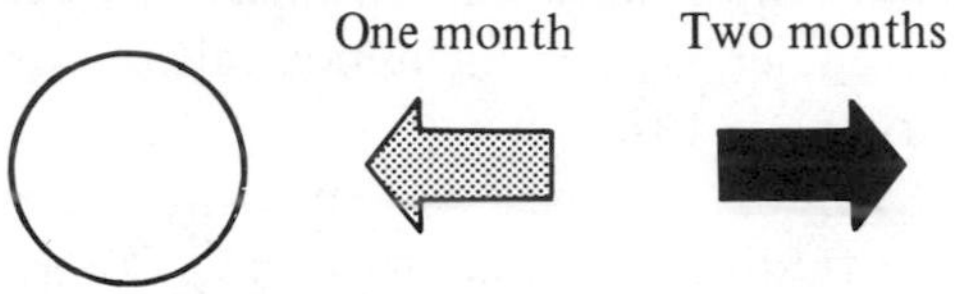

One month   Two months

The symbols are used to represent the exposure situations faced by Charlston, Norris, Bailie, and Parker. Since each company is being examined individually, the same shade is used for the home currency and the other shades represent foreign currencies.

Four months

Charlston Motor Co.

Assuming the contract is being signed today, Charlston will be receiving French francs in four months. The inflow of foreign currency is shown at four months. Because the company has an inflow of foreign currency, it is said to be *long* foreign currency.

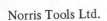

Norris places an order with the Swedish supplier and two months later pays out Swedish kroner; this is shown by the outflow at two months. Because the company has an outflow of foreign currency, it is said to be *short* foreign currency.

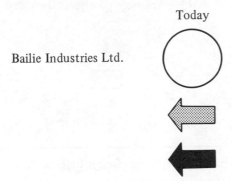

Bailie receives dividends from its subsidiaries, often learning about them the same day they are paid. This is shown by the two arrows of different shades today. Bailie is long foreign currencies.

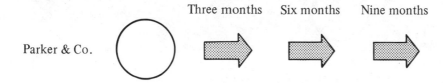

If Parker has just made a loan payment, this is what the future looks like for the company, payments of Swiss francs at quarterly intervals. This is represented by the outflows at months 3, 6, 9, and so on.

Now we can use the symbolic language to consider other possible exposures.

I.

This situation represents a company selling overseas. The customer is invoiced in the currency of the seller. There is no foreign exchange exposure because the home currency and the currency of the inflow are the same.

II.

This company is an intermediate processing firm in Belgium that buys steel ingot in France and sends specialized steel products back to France. There is no exposure in this particular time period because the foreign currency inflow equals the foreign currency outflow.

III.

This situation is typical of an international trading company. It has inflows and outflows of the same currencies at different times. The company pays for the goods before it receives the proceeds from the resale. There is a time exposure only. The company is neither long nor short the currency.

IV.

This company makes household products for the European market from its base in Ireland. It imports most of the polyvinyl chloride it uses in the process. This situation represents a payment for the plastic in Dutch guilders and lire receipts from Italian customers. There is a double exposure here; the company is long lire and short guilders. It is possible for both currencies to move in an unfavorable direction for the company.

The three key elements—home currency, foreign currency(ies), and time—are all present if a corporation has transaction exposure.

It is not always easy for a company to choose the currency it wants to have as its home currency. The currencies in which it does business may not include the currency of the country in which it is based. Here are some examples of difficult choices. An American construction firm working in the Middle East may have a large contract in Saudi riyals and source much of the equipment and labor force in Europe. The Hong Kong subsidiary of a British multinational may concentrate on making as many Hong Kong dollars as possible. This is not necessarily the same thing as making as many pounds as possible. A Greek ship owner receives all his charter income in dollars, but his expenses are in the currencies of every port the ship calls in. Some multinational companies have sizable blocks of shareholders in more than one country. Their stocks are quoted on more than one national exchange. The performance of these corporations is being evaluated by more than one nationality, each in terms of its own currency.

The criteria for chosing a home currency are the residence of the largest number of shareholders, the currency in which the company's books are kept and published, or the location of headquarters. The Greek ship owner and the American construction firm can choose their home currency on one of these bases. For the Hong Kong subsidiary objectives can be set in terms of pounds rather than Hong Kong dollars. The multinational firm with more than one constituency sometimes cannot make a single choice. One company keeps its accounts in pounds sterling, Dutch guilders, and U.S. dollars.

INTRACOMPANY TRANSACTION EXPOSURE

The problem of exposure within a single company concerns the treasurer at the headquarters of a multisubsidiary corporation. One example will illustrate the issue. The German subsidiary has an inflow of $1 million in 30 days. The Portuguese subsidiary has an outflow of $1 million in 30 days. From the perspective of each subsidiary, there is an exposure. Viewed from headquarters, the amount of the dollar inflow is equal to the amount of the dollar outflow, and the firm as a whole has no exposure. What view should prevail? We explore this issue with the aid of the balls and arrows.

Two lighter shaded balls are subsidiaries, and the dark ball is their parent. The situation facing the subsidiaries is illustrated. Below it is the parent's view of the exposure.

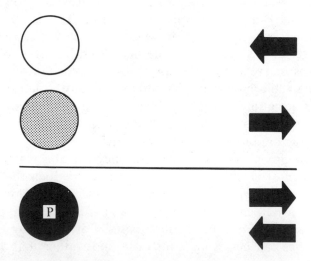

The two subsidiaries view themselves as being exposed, but the parent does not perceive the exposure because it sees an inflow and an outflow of the same currency at the same time. However, if the dollar falls relative to the Deutsche mark, the German company suffers a loss. The fall of the dollar relative to the mark does not means the dollar will fall relative to the escudo and that the Portuguese company will gain. The corporation as a whole can lose money from transaction exposures of its subsidiaries, although it appeared to the parent that there was no exposure.

A different situation occurs if the invoice is in the currency of one of the subsidiaries.

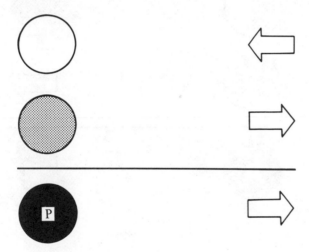

The white subsidiary has exported a rail car load of mufflers to the gray subsidiary, a distributor in another country. The invoice is in the seller's currency. The white subsidiary has no exposure, but the gray subsidiary views itself as having an exposure. The parent, in this case, sees the corporation being exposed because the parent would not aggregate the subsidiary's own currency inflow (the white flow into the white company) for exposure reporting.

In the next situation the subsidiaries sell to one another and the seller uses its currency for billing. There are two transactions. One, a sale by gray to white, invoiced in gray. The second transaction is a sale by white to gray; the billing currency is white. This illustration shows only the payable for each subsidiary; their home currency receivables are not shown. Both the white and the gray subsidiaries recognize an exposure. The parent recognizes an exposure also but may believe that they offset one another.

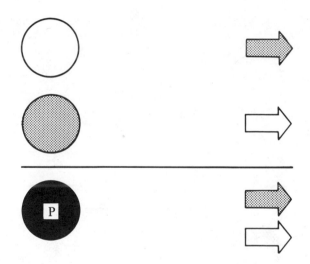

In this situation the parent may have a good case. A rise in the gray currency relative to white produces a loss for the white subsidiary. This is exactly offset by the gain of the gray subsidiary—it pays less to purchase the white currency it needs. All of this holds true if the tax rates in the gray and white countries are the same and if foreign exchange gains are treated the same as foreign exchange losses. If not, the offset is not exact; the global company is exposed.

The last situation looks at the parent as one of the participants in a transaction.

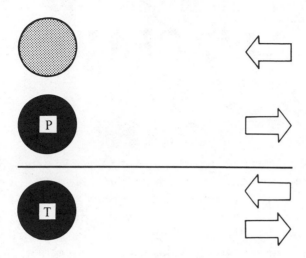

The gray subsidiary sells to the parent and invoices in a third currency. The gray subsidiary has a white inflow and the parent has a white outflow, both are exposed. The consolidation in the treasurer's office shows that the company as a whole is not exposed. The risks are the same as for the parent of the German and Portuguese subsidiaries in the first situation. This case shows most vividly how the centralization of transaction exposures can mask the corporation's real foreign exchange risk.

Intracompany billing in a third currency will always be seen as exposure at the local level while it will rarely be perceived at headquarters. The perceptions of headquarters and the subsidiaries are the same only if one of the parties to the transaction uses its own currency. This analysis of intracompany exposure suggests that subsidiaries may be better equipped to handle their own transaction exposures. They have a more accurate assessment of them.

CHAPTER TWO
ALL OPTIONS

In Chapter 1 we looked at the foreign exchange exposure created by the daily operations of international companies. The purpose of the present chapter is to consider all the options available to these companies for dealing with exposure and how the options work. Some totally eliminate foreign exchange risk, others lessen the potential impact of an exposure, and another group avoids exposure altogether.

An action that eliminates foreign exchange risk is said to *cover* that risk. An option that totally covers an exposure will create a flow of currency in the opposite direction to the exposure, in the same amount, at the same time.

One month

Exposure

Cover

The options are (1) techniques for using the foreign exchange and money markets, (2) invoice, price, and sales and purchasing policies, and (3) trade arrangements. All the options will be defined and related to the effect they have on the basic elements of foreign exchange exposure.

SPOT CONTRACT

A foreign exchange contract to buy (sell) one currency with (for) another at a given exchange rate for delivery two business days from the date the contract is agreed on. The *spot rate* is the exchange rate on the spot date. The word "spot" is often used to refer to both the rate and the date. Saturday and Sunday are not business days for foreign exchange in most parts of the world.

Example. On Wednesday, July 25, Bailie Industries Ltd. calls its bank and agrees to buy £1 million with $2,310,000. The exchange rate is £1 = $2.31. Bailie will get the pounds on Friday, July 27 and will give the bank dollars the same day.

Example. On Thursday, July 26, Bailie calls its bank and agrees to sell to the bank DM 1,800,000 for $1 million. The exchange rate is $1 = DM 1.80. Bailie will give the bank DM 1,800,000 on Monday, July 30 and the same day will get $1 million from the bank.

The spot date, even though it is two business days from today, marks the starting point in the foreign exchange market. Likewise, the spot rate is the starting price for all transactions. All calculations are made with reference to spot. The prices for transactions that fall on any other day are adjusted for the value of time between that day and the spot date.

If a company has an exposure two days from today, it can eliminate that exposure with a spot contract. Say the company is obligated to pay pesos in two days; the company enters into a spot contract with its bank to buy pesos. The pesos delivered by the bank to the company in two days will be used to pay its debt. If the company has an exposure two months from today, it cannot eliminate that exposure with a spot contract. The company must pay pesos in two months, but under the contract it will receive pesos from the bank in two days. The company treasurer will not sit with the pesos in his pocket for two months; there is money to be made by doing something with them. The treasurer will invest the money for two months, and the maturing deposit will be used to pay off the debt. Therefore, a spot contract itself is not sufficient to offset an exposure in the future, and another action is needed to bridge the time gap.

FORWARD CONTRACT

A foreign exchange contract to buy (sell) one currency with (for) another at an exchange rate fixed today for delivery more than two business days from the date the contract is agreed on. There is no exchange of funds until the future day. Usually forward contracts are made for periods of 1, 2, 3, 6, and 12 months, starting from the spot date. The only difference between the spot contract and forward contract is the time of delivery and consequently the rate of exchange.

The following diagram may help to illustrate the difference between the spot and the forward contract; assume a 90-day forward.

	Spot	Forward
Day on which exchange rate is fixed	Today	Today
Day on which monies are paid and received by the company	2 days from today	92 days from today

Example. On Wednesday, July 25, Norris Tools Ltd. calls its bank and agrees to buy £1 million with $2,300,000 for delivery in one month. The exchange rate is £1 = $2.30. Norris will get £1 million on Monday, August 27. (Spot date is July 27; therefore, the one-month date is August 27.) Norris will give the bank dollars the same day. The contracted amounts will be exchanged on August 27 regardless of the exchange rate between pounds and dollars prevailing on that date.

The forward contract itself has the two elements common to most exposure situations—time and currency. A forward contract itself is sufficient to eliminate an exposure in the future. A company knows it must pay pesos in two months; the company executes a forward contract with a bank, and in two months the bank delivers the pesos. The company turns around and pays off its debt. Nothing more is needed, the company has covered its exposure.

BORROWING

Borrowing is an advance of funds by a bank to a company for its temporary use, for which the company pays interest. There is an inflow of funds into the company treasury today as a result of the borrowing and an outflow of the same amount plus interest at some future date. The two most common loan arrangements are (1) advances for a fixed period at an interest rate also fixed for the period and (2) advances for an indefinite, albeit limited, period at an interest rate that will vary with market rates. Eurocurrency advances are typical of the first variety; prime rate borrowing in the United States and overdraft borrowing in Europe are typical of the second type.

Companies borrow money most often to finance their operations. In an exposure situation, borrowing changes the time frame of the foreign exchange risk. Borrowing a foreign currency in which there is a future receivable shifts the risk from the future to the present. The outflow for the loan repayment is offset by the receivable inflow in the future. The net result of the borrowing is an inflow of foreign currency today. Time has been virtually eliminated, but the risk that the foreign currency will change value against the home currency remains. Another action is required to convert foreign currency to home currency.

INVESTING

The placement of funds for a period of time for which interest is earned is an investment. There is an outflow of funds from the company today as a result of the investment, and there is an inflow of the principal amount plus interest at some future date. The type of place-

ments we are most concerned with are short-term money market investments that have a fixed maturity date, such as bank time deposits,
certificates of deposit, banker's acceptances, treasury bills, and commercial paper.

Usually companies invest funds for which they have no current need
in their operations. In an exposure situation investing changes the time
frame of the foreign exchange risk. In this respect it is like borrowing;
however, the two activities differ in the type of exposure they are able
to shift in time. If a company invests a foreign currency in which it has
a future payable, the risk is moved from the future to the present. The
future inflow of the investment offsets the outflow associated with the
payable. The net result of the investment is an outflow of the foreign
currency today. (The question of where the company gets the foreign
currency to invest is addressed shortly.) Again, as in the act of borrowing, although the time has been virtually eliminated, the risk that the
foreign currency will change value against the home currency remains.

MATCHING

A company matches an exposure by creating an opposite flow in the
same currency as the exposure, in the same amount, and at the same
time. A company that has a payable of one million Dutch guilders in
three months will consciously attempt to sell its product in The Netherlands to generate a receivable for one million guilders three months
hence. If this is accomplished, the company has completely covered its
foreign exchange exposure. Both time and currency elements have been
dealt with.

Given the requirements of a perfect match, it is clearly not easy to
accomplish. The product that the company produces must be salable in
every country or currency from which it sources its inputs, or vice versa.
Matching also requires the cooperation of the purchasing and sales
departments with the treasurer. This technique is most applicable to
large, one-time exposure situations where there is time to create the
match.

PAIRING

A company pairs an exposure by creating an opposite flow in a currency allied with the currency of the exposure, in the same amount, at the same time. The difference between pairing and matching is the currency in which the flow is created. A candidate for pairing is a third currency that will move with the currency of the exposure. As it appreciates or depreciates against the home currency, so also will the paired currency. For example, Bailie may have an inflow of Dutch guilders in two months and pair with an outflow of Belgian francs. The two currencies are closely linked in trade and their fluctuation controlled by their central banks.

Although pairing may be easier to accomplish than matching and may give the corporate treasurer greater flexibility, it does not cover the risk as does matching. Pairing is an attempt to lessen the potential impact of a foreign currency risk by creating a situation where a loss in the initial situation will be offset by a gain in the allied currency. Pairing does create a double exposure, and if the allied currency is poorly chosen, a double loss may result. Pairing of two currencies is most applicable when the currencies are bound together by some institutional arrangement. We look at such an arrangement in Chapter 8.

LEADING

Leading is advancing the payment or receipt of money. If a company pays a bill today that is not due for 60 days, it is leading the payment. Most trade invoices reward the debtor for early payment by giving a discount. In this sense leading a payment is very similar to investing. Money is placed today and a return is received. In an investment, it is the interest; in leading, it is the discount. Like investing, leading a foreign currency payable due in the future shifts the time frame of the exposure from the future to the present. Likewise, although time has been altered, the currency risk remains.

An analogy also exists between leading a foreign currency receivable and borrowing. If a company asks one of its customers to pay early, it asks the customer to forego the use of its money for the period of the advance. The customer will receive a discount from the company for moving up the payment. The company is borrowing from its customer. Like borrowing from a bank, the company has an inflow of currency today instead of in the future. In place of giving a bank interest, the company gives its customer a discount. The time element of the risk has been covered, but the currency risk has not been. Leading and lagging (next option) are techniques most often used within multinational companies, rather than between different entities. The subject is fully explored in Chapter 12.

LAGGING

Lagging means delaying the payment or receipt of money. If a company pays a bill 30 days late it is lagging its payment. Most creditors will charge interest for late payment. If a company pays its foreign currency obligation late, it is effectively borrowing that foreign currency from its supplier and paying interest for it. By so doing, the exposed home company is extending in time its foreign currency risk.

If a company requests that its customer hold off paying foreign currency for an additional 45 days, the company extends its exposure in time. There is a similarity between lagging a foreign currency receivable and investing the foreign currency. In an investment funds flow out today, whereas in lagging funds that should have come in, don't. In both there is a future inflow; in both there is a reward for letting someone else use the money.

INVOICE IN HOME CURRENCY/SELL IN THE HOME MARKET

An exporter can often choose the currency to bill the foreign customer. There are three alternatives; (1) currency of the exporter, (2) currency of the customer, and (3) currency in which the product is customarily traded; oil of all origins is invoiced in dollars. Surveys have shown that exporters in industrial countries invoice most frequently in their own currency.* It is easier, however, to sell to customers in their own currency. The customers are more familiar with it, easily relate the price to their current cost structure, easily compare the foreign product to competing home products, and shift the problem of fluctuating exchange rates onto the seller. For these reasons it is natural that the sales force is eager to bill in the customer's currency. It does create foreign exchange exposure for the treasurer's office. If the customer is billed in the seller's currency, there is no foreign exchange risk; the inflow from the sale is in the seller's currency.

The second part of this option accomplishes the same objective as the first. It requires an entire reorientation of the sales effort to sell in the home market.

CHANGE TO LOCAL SUPPLIERS/REQUEST THAT FOREIGN SUPPLIERS BILL IN YOUR HOME CURRENCY

Both of these actions avoid the creation of exposure. All flows are in the company's home currency. The first action may be difficult to execute because the necessary ingredient for the company's productive process may not be available in the local market. If it is available, the price may be higher than the overseas product. The higher home market price can be evaluated against the foreign exchange risk and the cost of eliminating the risk. Persuading the supplier to bill in your currency may be somewhat easier. The cooperation of the purchasing department is needed for this option, it cannot be done by the treasurer alone.

*See Stephen Carre, John Williamson, and Geoffrey Wood, *The Financing Procedures of British Foreign Trade,* London: Cambridge University Press, 1979. See also Marius van Nieuwkerk, "The Covering of Exchange Risks in the Netherlands' Foreign Trade." *Journal of International Economics,* Vol. 9, No. 1, February 1979, pp. 89–93.

DO NOT DO THE DEAL

There are times when the foreign exchange risk created by a prospective transaction is not worth the profit that will be generated. Sales in currencies that constantly depreciate, such as the Brazilian cruezero and the Israeli pound, and for which there is no possibility of protection, should be carefully examined. The large profit on the sale may be totally wiped out by the foreign exchange loss. Such a deal is not worth doing.

BARTER

Barter is the exchange of goods for goods. A Colombian firm wants to buy British steel but has no access to sterling. The British steelmaker has no use for Colombian pesos. An exchange of coffee for steel is proposed. The British firm knows the sterling price of its steel, and there is a world price in sterling for Colombian coffee. The exchange is made and there is no currency exposure for either party. Barter is a more creative alternative to "Do not do the deal" and avoids exchange risk.

ADJUST PRICES FOR RISK

Charge a higher price to the customer who insists paying you in its own currency because by doing so you take on an additional risk. In the many markets where the customer is king, this advice may seem a bit gratuitous. It does work, however, where the seller is the dominant party.

By the same token, if you are on the buying side, attempt to negotiate a lower price as the compensation for accepting billing in the seller's currency. Adjusting prices clearly does not avoid or cover the risk; the risk is still there. The exposure is made somewhat more supportable by the creation of a larger margin in the sales price or a lower price on the buying side.

NESTING

This is a portfolio approach to currency exposure.* A company that exports only or imports only cannot match or pair; it can, however, use this technique. Using the nesting technique, an exporter bills its customers in a variety of currencies. This means the exporter sells in a number of countries or has some flexibility in billing customers in third currencies. These currencies of invoice are chosen such that the shifting values of each currency with respect to the home currency keeps the whole nest of currencies at a constant value with respect to the home currency. Since "constant" is not really feasible, the objective is to minimize the fluctuation of the nest.

PROBLEMS

The problems in this book and their solutions are organized differently than you may be accustomed to. There are four sections—PROBLEMS, RESPONSES, RESPONSE ANALYSIS, and SUMMARY. RESPONSES contains all the elements required to answer the problems. It is up to you to select the most appropriate responses for each problem. Do one problem at a time. Select the responses, note the number, and turn to RESPONSE ANALYSIS. It is keyed to the responses. In this section the author comments on the selections you have made. If the comments indicate that you have not chosen the relevant responses, go back to the PROBLEM and the RESPONSES and try again, using the information gained from the RESPONSE ANALYSIS. If you meet the same result again, go back to the presentation of the material and reread it. Once you select the appropriate response, go to the next problem; it is not necessary to read

*A good article on the construction of a nest has been written. Although it assumes perfect flexibility in the choice of currencies, the method used is applicable to a limited group of currencies. See R. Stafford Johnson and Richard A. Zuber, "A Model for Construction Currency Cocktails," *Business Economics,* May 1979, pp. 9–14.

all the responses. In the SUMMARY the author presents his viewpoint and ties together the different strands of the chapter.*

1. What are the requirements of an option that completely covers an exposure?

2. What is the nature of those options that affect the exposure but do not cover it completely?

3. All the options discussed are similar because they have an impact on exposure. From the point of view of the treasurer of a corporation, certain options would be more attractive than others. Why would a treasurer favor some options over others?

4. The spot contract and the forward contract are the only two options in which one currency is exchanged for another. It would seem that one of these options would be employed either singly, or in conjunction with others, to deal with all exposure situations. This is not so. What is it about some of the other options which make use of these contracts unnecessary?

RESPONSES

1. The home currency is substituted for the foreign currency.

2. An action is taken to avoid creating an exposure.

3. A foreign currency flow is offset by an action that creates a flow in the same foreign currency in the opposite direction.

4. An action is taken that has an effect on the same day the foreign currency will flow.

5. A foreign currency flow is offset by flows in third currencies.

6. Option involves coordination with another department.

7. Option involves prolonged negotiations.

8. Option involves a lot of paperwork.

9. The action compensates for the risk with a supernormal profit.

10. The foreign currency flow is not offset.

11. The effect of the action takes place either before or after the future foreign currency inflow.

RESPONSE ANALYSIS

Problem 1

A. *If you included 1 or 2*: If you have included either of these responses, you have misread the question. The question presupposes that the actions can be exercised after that time.

B. *If you omitted 3 or 4*: These responses are necessary to completely answer the question; they should not be omitted. Covering an exposure requires that the currency flow that has created the exposure be offset at the time it occurs. Options such as matching and the forward contract both completely cover an exposure.

C. *If you included 5*: Flows of third currencies may lessen the risk generated by a single currency flow if the other currencies are carefully chosen. There is, however, no guarantee that they will.

Problem 2

D. *If you included 6 or 7*: It is true that most of the options that do not completely cover exposure must be negotiated, either within the company or with supplier or customer. However, these responses are somewhat peripheral to the question.

E. *If you included 5*: Both nesting and pairing have an effect on a foreign currency exposure. The third currencies are chosen to offset a movement in the exposed currency. Even though it may be possible to offset the exact amount of the exposure at the precise time, there remains the risk that the third currencies will not behave as expected.

F. *If you omitted 10 or 11*: These responses, with response 5, are the key ones for answering this question. Very few of the options that were discussed were complete ones. The spot contract produces an offsetting flow, but not at the right time. Options like leading and borrow-

---

*This setup of problems and responses is adapted from a methodology called *structural communication*. A good example of an entire book using this technique is Keiran Egan, *The Tudor Peace*, London: University of London Press, 1969.

ing affect only the time element of exposure; they do not address the risk that two currencies can change in relative value.

G. *If you omitted 9*: A supernormal profit can be produced by either the exporter or the importer. In the case of the exporter, the greater inflow of foreign currency from the higher prices actually appears to increase the exposure. The exporter's exposure should be thought of in terms of covering the home currency costs of producing the exports. More foreign currency for the same item makes it more probable that the exporter will be able to do so.

Problem 3

H. *If you omitted 6, 7 or 8*: A treasurer faced with an exposure situation is generally anxious to handle it with the tools he or she controls. The treasurer is responsible for the firm's actions in the foreign exchange and money markets. Most can be executed with a single phone call. Options that require coordination or negotiation, such as changes invoicing policies or barter, will be used only if another solution is not available.

I. *If you included 3 and 4*: Certainly the treasurer is more inclined to favor options that will completely cover the foreign exchange exposure.

J. *If you included 1 or 2*: These are types of action that the treasurer would tend to avoid as their implementation requires negotiation both inside the firm and with its customers and suppliers. Invoicing policies and sourcing and sales strategies are not the direct responsibility of the treasurer.

Problem 4

K. *If you omitted 1 or 2*: It is not necessary to purchase or sell foreign currencies if a policy has been established so that all overseas transactions are conducted in your own currency.

L. *If you included 3*: This is not an appropriate response since spot and forward contracts do create an offsetting currency flow.

M. *If you included 5 or 9*: Yes, the actions that produce these effects do deal with exposure, they compensate for the risk, but they do not cover the risk.

SUMMARY

Any action that purports to deal with a foreign exchange exposure can be examined with regard to its effect on the time aspect of the exposure and on the currency aspect of the exposure. These actions can also be distinguished by whether they act after the exposure has been created or before that time. Finally, it should be determined whether the option completely covers the exposure or whether risk remains after the option has been executed.

The schema that follows classifies the options that have been discussed according to their mode of operation.

| | Cover | | | |
| | Time and | | Reduce Impact | Avoid Exposure |
Time	Currency	Currency	of Exposure	Situations
LEAD	FORWARD	SPOT	NESTING	BARTER
LAG	MATCH		PAIRING	DO NOT DO DEAL
BORROW			ADJUSTING	INVOICING IN
INVEST			PRICES	HOME CURRENCY
				HOME SUPPLIERS
				AND CUSTOMERS

Only the forward and matching are self sufficient options for covering. Leading, Lagging, Borrowing, and Investing must be combined with Spot to cover an exposure completely. Chapter 3 shows how this is done. The rest of the book concentrates on the options (except Matching) that cover an exposure and those that utilize the foreign exchange and money markets.

CHAPTER THREE
THE THREE BASIC OPTIONS

The three basic options are those that completely cover foreign exchange exposure. In Chapter 2 any technique that dealt with exposure was considered. The purpose of the present chapter is to learn how the basic options work and the earnings and costs of using them.

TRANSACTION SYMBOLS

The symbols used here to represent different transactions are as follows:

A *spot* contract is represented by two arrows of different shades placed to represent an exchange of currencies two business days from today; this day is designated t_0.

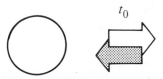

In this example the gray currency is bought with the white currency. Therefore, gray flows in and white flows out.

In the opposite transaction the gray currency is sold for the white currency, gray flows out and white flows into the company.

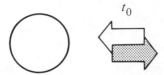

A *forward* contract is represented by two arrows of different colors placed to represent an exchange of currencies in the future. The only difference between it and the spot contract is the placement along the time horizon. t_{90} is 90 days from the spot date t_0.

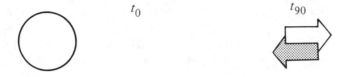

Borrowing is represented by an inflow of money on the spot date and an outflow in the future.

Investing is represented by an outflow of money on the spot date and an inflow in the future.

Lead.   The arrows can also be used to represent an advance of payment. A firm is due to pay its overseas supplier in 30 days; if it decides to pay earlier, in two days, the change can be represented as follows:

The lower arrow on the right cancels out the original payment at 90 days. The arrow on the left represents the payment that the firm has decided to make in two days. The representation of a lead looks very much like an investment, even though the arrow on the right is not properly a flow. You might want to look again at Chapter 2, where the similarity between leading a payment and an investment is discussed.

The symbolism used for advancing a receivable is:

Instead of placing its funds in the money market, a firm may pay off a loan at the bank. There is no less of a return to the company from this than from an actual placement. The same symbolism is used for this type of gain. Opportunity gain can also arise in the event where funds arrive unexpectedly early. The company can use these funds internally for working capital, rather than place them with a bank, thus producing the same benefit as a money market investment.

Opportunity costs are counted as borrowing if a corporation decides to use its funds today to buy foreign currency rather than waiting 60 days until the payment is due. Corporate funds are used for 60 days; they cannot be used for other purposes, including investment in the money market. This use of funds is a cost to the company.

The three basic options are (1) *Forward*, (2) *Borrow–Spot–Invest*, and (3) *Lead*. The mechanical operation of each is described and symbolized for Sloat and Company, Inc. Sloat is a U.S. firm that exports calculators to Belgium and Italy. The company bills its customers on 90-day terms. For the moment, only one inflow will be considered. Sloat has three options to cover the risk that its foreign currency receivables decline in value over the next three months.

FORWARD

The *Forward* covers the exposure by creating a matching outflow in the foreign currency in which Sloat has an inflow. The foreign currency receivable is matched in amount and time. The two foreign currency flows offset one another. The foreign currency the exporter receives from its customer will be delivered to the bank in 90 days to fulfill the forward contract. Sloat is left with an inflow of its own currency.

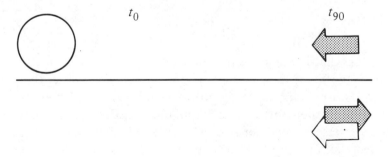

BORROW–SPOT–INVEST

The second option Sloat considers for covering risk is *Borrow–Spot–Invest (BSI)*. Borrowing the foreign currency will shift the time frame of the exposure from 90 days to the spot date. The currency risk is still present, but this is eliminated by a spot contract. Sloat contracts with the bank to sell the foreign currency on the spot date for its home currency. Time is covered and currency is covered, so the exposure is eliminated. Eliminating exposure does not involve only costs; Sloat has its own currency 90 days ahead of schedule. The company has the opportunity of placing its money in a deposit, repaying bank debt, or using the funds for working capital.

The representation of Borrow–Spot–Invest is as follows:

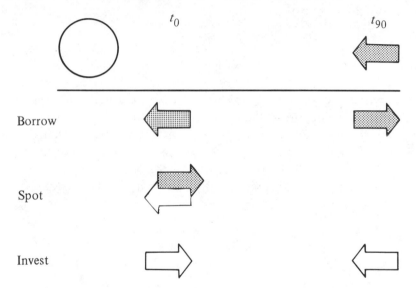

Consider what happens on the spot date, t_0. There is an inflow of gray currency, the loan; that amount of gray is sold for white, that amount of white is invested. All of the inflows and outflows on the spot date cancel one another out. On the future date t_{90} the gray currency due in from the overseas importer is used to pay off the loan from the bank. There rests an inflow of white currency. This is as it should be. Covering an exposure involves the offset of foreign currency flows and a home currency flow in the same direction as the original exposure.

LEAD

Sloat has a third option, the possibility to *Lead* the payment from its customer. If the customer agrees to the discount Sloat offers, the customer will pay in two days rather than in 90 days as originally scheduled. Time exposure is covered. Sloat will then call the bank and agree to sell the foreign currency spot for its home currency. The currency exposure is covered. As in the BSI option, the home currency can be invested in money market instruments or utilized in the firm. The Lead option is symbolized as

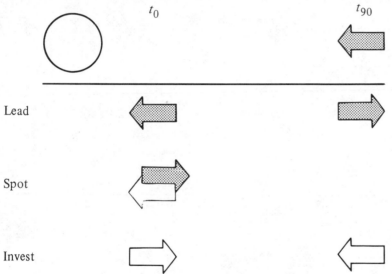

On the spot date t_0 there is an inflow of gray currency from the early payment; that payment is sold for white currency, and that amount of white is invested. All the inflows and outflows on the spot date cancel one another out. On the future date t_{90} there are no actual gray flows, although two are represented. There is an actual inflow of white from the investment.

COMPARING THE OPTIONS

The three basic options are illustrated together.

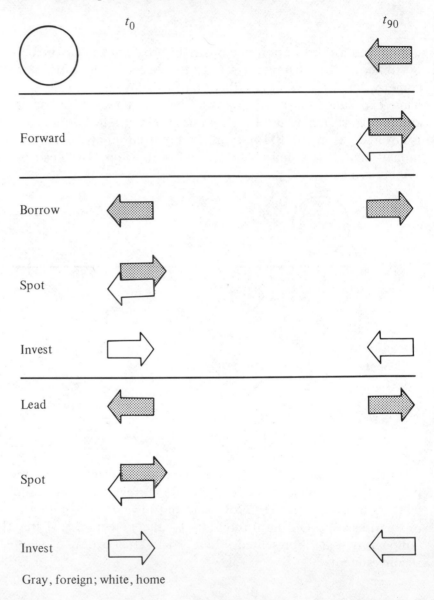

Gray, foreign; white, home

All the basic options completely cover the risk that the foreign currency receivable could decline in value between the present and the future. In all three options the flows of foreign currency flows cancel on the future date, leaving an inflow of the home currency. The similarity among all three options and how they work is more apparent if we note that in the BSI and Lead options all the flows on the spot date cancel, thus leaving all the options looking very much the same on the future date.

The similarity between the Lead and the BSI options is very strong. They differ only in the initial step. In the BSI Sloat borrows from the bank, pays interest, and has an inflow of foreign currency on the spot date. In the Lead, Sloat persuades the customer to pay early (borrows from the customer), pays a discount, and has an inflow of foreign currency on the spot date. The two investment transactions are the same.

COVERING A PAYABLE

The intention of this section is to learn how to cover an exposure situation that consists of a foreign currency payable. Whittemore Trading Ltd. is an importer of chemicals and dyes into Canada. It traditionally imports from Germany and France and has carved a niche in the market by specializing in hard-to-get products. Its suppliers bill on 45-day terms, with discounts given for payment within five days. Whittemore faces the risk that its payables in Deutsche marks and French francs will become more costly in terms of the Canadian dollar in the next month and a half. It has available to it the three basic options for covering an exposure. Whittemore can call the bank and contract to purchase foreign currency 45 days forward. The currency that the bank will deliver to the firm will be used the same day to pay off the European suppliers. In fact, Whittemore simply tells the bank to credit the account of its supplier in Germany. A second way to cover the exposure is to borrow Canadian dollars from the bank, buy Deutsche marks with the borrowed dollars on the spot date, and invest the Deutsche marks for 45 days by depositing them with a bank. Note that in the case of covering a payable it is the home currency that is borrowed and the foreign currency that is invested. This is the reverse, as you would expect, of what happened when the exposure consisted of a foreign currency receivable. Borrowing the home currency is not always necessary. If Whittemore is liquid it may use some of its surplus cash, or sell one of its treasury bills. It would be cheaper than actually borrowing from the bank. The cost is the foregone interest income.

The third alternative for Whittemore Trading is to prepay its supplier and earn the discount. To be able to do this, the firm borrows dollars from the bank and buys marks. Again, BSI and Lead are the same, with the exception of one step. In BSI the marks are invested in the bank for 45 days. In the Lead marks are invested by being paid to the supplier early, and a discount is earned.

PROBLEM

Symbolize the options just discussed for the exposure faced by Whittemore. Colored pens or cut-out arrows (available in most art supply stores), will be useful; one color for each currency. The responses will include all the possibilities that are needed. The response analysis and the summary will provide you the feedback to arrive at the correct answer. Work on one option at a time. Select one or more of the responses to compose a complete option. Then refer to the response analysis and the summary before moving to the next option.

RESPONSES

t_0 t_{45}

1. Buy foreign currency with home currency spot

2. Sell foreign currency for home currency spot

3. Sell foreign currency for home currency 45 days forward

4. Buy foreign currency with home currency 45 days forward

5. Borrow foreign currency for 45 days

6. Borrow home currency for 45 days

7. Invest home currency for 45 days

8. Invest foreign currency for 45 days

9. Lead a payment

RESPONSE ANALYSIS

A. *If you chose for a single option the pairs, 1 and 4, 2 and 3, 1 and 3, 2 and 4*: These combinations produce a double exchange of currencies. In the case of the first two pairs, there is a double purchase or double sale of the foreign currency. In the second two pairs the transaction on the spot date is undone by the one on the forward date.

B. *If you chose 2 or 3 for any option*: In a payable situation it is necessary to purchase the foreign currency, to have currency come in, in order to offset an outflow. These are both foreign currency sales and would result in doubling the exposure.

C. *If you chose 4*: This forward contract will completely cover the foreign exchange exposure. In 45 days the bank will deliver the foreign currency necessary to pay the supplier. The inflow from the forward contract will exactly offset the outflow for the payment, leaving an outflow of home currency.

D. *If you chose 1*: This contract is not sufficient by itself to correct exposure at 45 days. It does not cover the time element, but it is the appropriate spot.

E. *If you chose 5 for any option*: Borrowing the foreign currency where there is a foreign currency payable doubles the exposure. In 45 days there would be two outflows of foreign currency when the objective is to offset.

F. *If you chose 6, 1 and 8*: This combination completely covers the exposure. Home currency is borrowed, sold spot for foreign currency, foreign currency is invested. At maturity the investment is used to pay the debt to the supplier. Whittemore is left with an outflow of its currency, a loan to be repaid in 45 days. It is assumed that Whittemore has an inflow of Canadian dollars at that time. Even if this is not the case, borrowing beyond 45 days is independent of the exposure situation and would be evaluated separately.

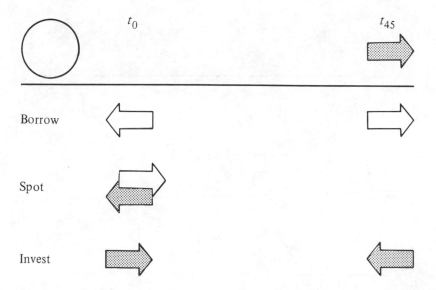

G. *If you chose 7 for any option*: This situation does not generate any home currency to be invested. This transaction is applicable to situations where the sale of foreign currency on the spot date produces the home currency, and in the present instance foreign currency is being purchased, not sold.

H. *If you chose 9, 1 and 8*: This combination completely covers the foreign currency payment risk. The borrowed home currency is used to buy foreign currency on the spot date. The foreign currency is paid to the supplier in Germany. As with the BSI option, Whittemore is left with a loan to be repaid in 45 days.

SUMMARY

The complete solution to the problem is as follows:

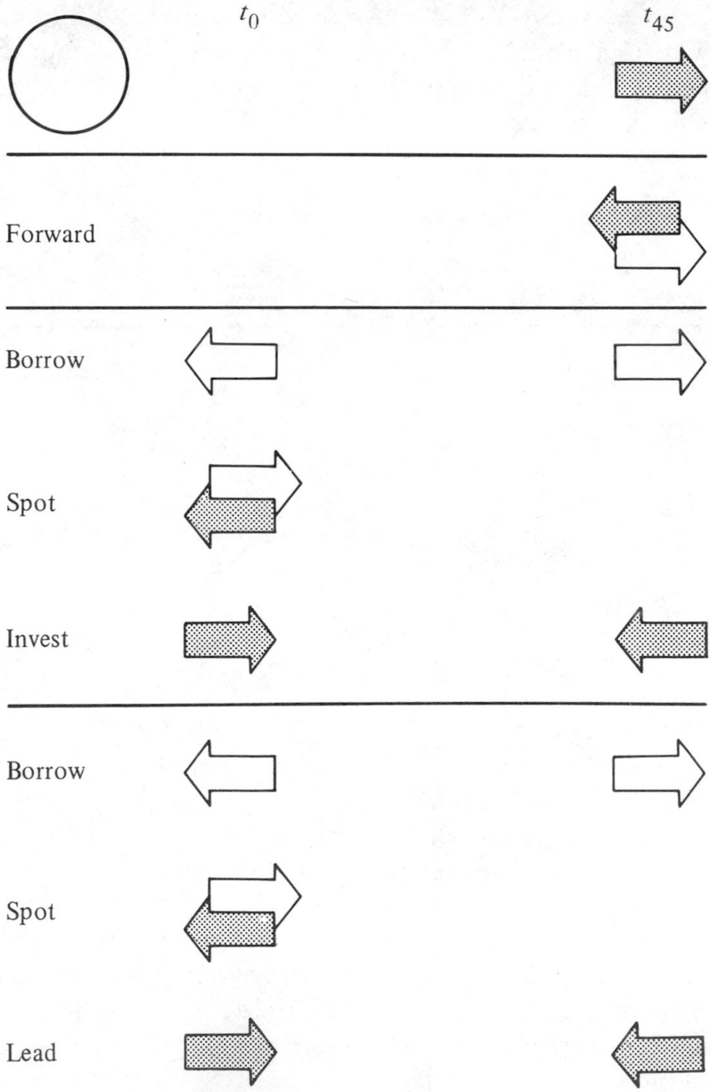

t_0 t_{45}

Forward

Borrow

Spot

Invest

Borrow

Spot

Lead

PRICING THE OPTIONS

It is notable that the BSI and Lead differ in only one respect, the disposition of the foreign currency. In the BSI it is placed in a deposit with the bank to earn interest; in the Lead it is paid to the supplier and a discount is earned. The effect of covering the exposure is to leave the firm with an outflow in its own currency in place of the original outflow of the foreign currency.

Why work at three options when clearly any one of them will eliminate exposure? The reason is that each option has a different cost or earning. (As will become evident shortly, covering an exposure is not synonymous with an expense; in many situations the result of the transactions is positive.) In a given situation we choose the option with the least cost; in another situation we choose the option with the largest earning. The different options produce different earnings and costs because each uses a different combination of money market rates.

Fundamentally there are two different money markets in the world; there is a domestic money market and an external money market for each currency. The external currency market with which most people are familiar is the Eurodollar market. A Eurodollar is a dollar that is deposited in a bank outside the United States. The bank may be a branch of a U.S. bank, as long as it is situated outside of the United States. The dollars may be owned by anyone—U.S. citizens, Germans, Belgians, or others. The essential characteristics are that the deposits are obligations to pay dollars and are obligations of banking offices outside the United States. The dollar deposit of a Frenchman in a New York bank is not a Eurodollar. An American's deposit in a Parisian bank is a Eurodollar. We can substitute most convertible currencies for dollars and have an external money market. There is a Euromark market, a Eurosterling market, a Europeseta market, a Euro-Swiss franc market, and so on. These different currency markets differ vastly in size.

The second market is the domestic market, also termed the resident money market. A domestic dollar is one that is deposited in a bank inside the United States. The bank may be the branch of an English bank in the United States. The dollars may be owned by anyone. The same is true for all currencies. There is a resident sterling money market, a resident Dutch guilder money market, and so forth.

The reason for making such a distinction among the markets is that access to them is not universal. The French do not have access to the Euro-French franc market, but the Canadians do, as do the Dutch. The reason that access is not universal is due to exchange control regulations. The second reason for looking at both markets is that the interest rates for the same currency are not the same in the external and domestic markets. The rate for a resident franc deposit for three months is not the same as the rate for an external franc deposit of the same tenor.

Rates are different between resident and external markets because of government exchange control. Where strict exchange controls exist there is a greater divergence between external and domestic interest rates. The isolation allows rates in each market to be affected by different forces. A second reason why interest rates differ is because reserve requirements are not levied equally on both types of deposit. A reserve requirement means that the value of an individual's deposit to a bank is worth less because a portion of the deposit must be kept interest free with the central bank. Therefore, the bank pays interest in accordance with the level of the reserve kept. The schemata on the facing page give an idea of the forces at work.

Countries that have strict exchange controls put up a double barrier between the domestic rates and external ones, thereby allowing the international factors to play a much greater role. Where there are liberal exchange controls, the difference between domestic and external interest rates is almost entirely the reserve requirement.

There is no established pattern of difference between external and domestic interest rates. Sometimes external rates are higher than domestic, and other times lower; at times the difference is large, and at other times there is no difference. The best published sources of domestic and external interest rates are the *Financial Times* (London), *Agefi* (Paris), and the *World Financial Markets* published by Morgan Guaranty Trust Company; and you can always call your bank. There are a couple of general rules: If a currency is weak on the exchange markets, its external

DOMESTIC AND EXTERNAL INTEREST RATES
Strict Exchange Control Countries

Domestic Economic Factors   International Factors

Inflation rate   Perceptions of
Monetary/fiscal policies   inflation rate
Stage of the business   Perceptions of monetary/
  cycle   fiscal policies
                                             Balance of payments
                                             Size of the external
                                               currency pool

Domestic interest rates

        Reserve requirements
        Exchange controls

        External interest rates

Liberal Exchange Control Countries

Domestic Economic Factors   International Factors

Domestic interest rates

        Reserve requirements

        External interest rates

41

interest rates tend to be higher than the domestic rates. If a currency is strong on the exchange markets, its external interest rates tend to be lower than the domestic rates.

The symbols used for each market are as follows:

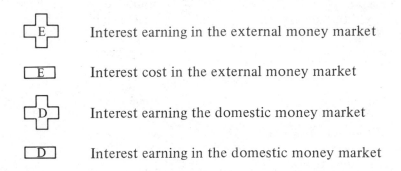

Interest earning in the external money market

Interest cost in the external money market

Interest earning the domestic money market

Interest earning in the domestic money market

Consequently, the following representation means that an investment is made in the Eurocurrency market. The interest earning is at the rate given in the external money market.

The symbol used to represent the spot rate price is △ . The spot rate represents neither a cost nor an earning itself; it is a price. It is the terms of exchange of one currency for another.

The borrowing shown in the above diagram is made in the country of the money in question, and the interest is payable at the rate given in the domestic money market.

We return to the situation of Whittemore Trading Ltd. to examine the differences between the costs and the earnings of each option. Recall that Whittemore is a Canadian company importing chemicals from Germany and France. It has payments due in marks and francs at 45-day intervals. We consider only one currency; the analysis for one applies directly to the other. The first option Whittemore considers is the BSI. The firm can borrow its own currency from a bank in Canada, buy the foreign currency with the home currency on the spot date, and then invest the foreign currency in a time deposit with a Canadian bank to mature in 45 days. The maturing foreign currency deposit would be used to pay off the obligation to the supplier in France or Germany. By this time Whittemore would have sold the chemicals in Canada and have the money to pay off its loan. Because the trading company would be borrowing Canadian dollars from a Canadian bank, it would pay the rate in the domestic money market. Because the trading company would be investing the foreign currency with a Canadian bank, it would earn interest at a rate given by the external money market of the foreign currency. The transaction can be represented symbolically as follows:

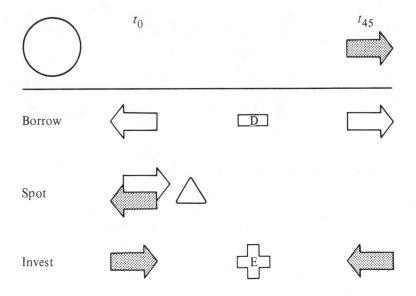

The next option Whittemore examines is the Lead. The company has the possibility of paying its supplier early and earning a discount. To do this, the firm would borrow Canadian dollars from a bank in Canada and would then buy the foreign currency with the borrowed dollars on the spot date. The foreign currency would then be paid to the supplier. As in the previous situation, the cost to Whittemore would be determined by rates in its own domestic money market. The earning to the company is the discount it earns. This is determined largely by the value its supplier places on having money early. Objectively, this value would be determined by what the supplier in the foreign country could do with its own currency. This objective value is given by the domestic money market rates in the foreign country. The Lead option is symbolized as:

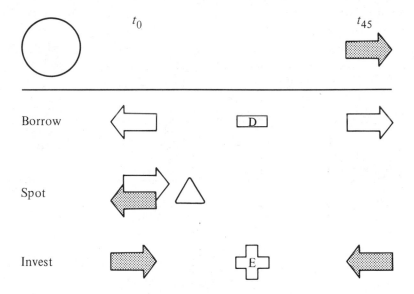

Whittemore also considers the Forward contract as an option. The company can call its bank and arrange for delivery of the foreign currency in 45 days. The foreign currency would be paid for with Canadian dollars, the money Whittemore is receiving from domestic sales of the chemicals. The convention for the pricing of the forward transaction is the external money markets of both the currencies involved. This is represented as:

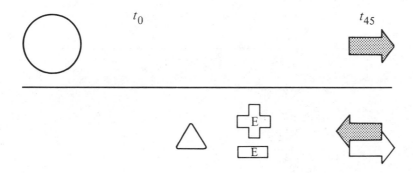

The forward contract is an exchange of currencies in the future; thus it is natural that the pricing of it include both elements of exchange and time, the spot price and interest rates. The fact that external interest rates are used in convention. It is examined in much greater depth in Chapter 9. Compare the placement of the plus and minus signs on the Forward with their placement on the Lead and BSI options. In all cases the minus is associated with the currency flowing out in the future and the plus, with the currency flowing in.

The following illustration shows all the options and the way in which they are priced. The reason for putting in the price symbols is (1) to identify what information is needed for comparing the options and (2) later, when the options become more complex, they provide a means for discriminating among options without using numbers.

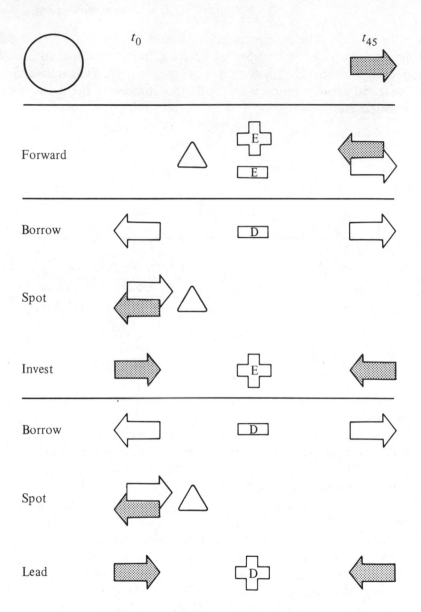

It is evident why it is worthwhile to consider all three options. Because external interest rates differ from domestic interest rates, the cost or earning of each option will be different. Whittemore will choose the option with the lowest cost or highest earning.

To make a decision as to which option is the most preferable, Whittemore needs to know only the domestic and external interest rates of the home and foreign currencies. Plug in some numbers, and you will see. To make a decision on the best option it is not necessary to know the spot rate because it is a common element in all three options. It is necessary to know the spot rate and have an opinion of its evolution in deciding *when* to execute the best option, but not which is the best option. The best option at any point in time is an issue which can be analyzed logically, as we do here. The question of when to execute the best option is a matter of judgment about exchange and interest rates.

PROBLEM

To allow you to become more familiar with the costs and earnings of the options, let's return to the situation of Sloat & Company, Inc., a U.S. electronics firm. Sloat ships electronic calculators to Belgium and Italy and bills its customers in francs and lire on 90-day terms. A discount is given for payment within 10 days. It is necessary to examine only one receivable in one currency. The analysis will apply directly to all others of the same type. Sloat faces the risk that the currency of its receivable will fall in value relative to the dollar in the next month and a half. To cover this risk, Sloat will look at the three possible options and determine the best in this situation. Assume you are the treasurer of Sloat, and lay out the options and the interest rates needed; your assistant will provide the numbers in Chapter 4. The responses will include all the possibilities that are needed. The response analysis and summary comments will provide you the feedback to help you arrive at the best answer. Do one option at a time, and then look at the analysis and summary. Again, colored pencils or arrows are useful in working out this exercise.

RESPONSES

t_0 t_{90}

1. Buy foreign currency with home currency spot
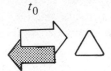

2. Sell foreign currency for home currency spot

3. Sell foreign currency for home currency 90 days forward
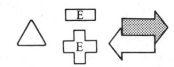

4. Buy foreign currency with home currency 90 days forward
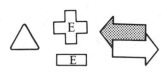

5. Borrow foreign currency for 90 days, domestic money market

6. Borrow home currency for 90 days, domestic money market

7. Invest home currency for 90 days, domestic money market

8. Invest foreign currency for 90 days, domestic money market

9. Lead a receivable, domestic money market

t_0 t_{90}

10. Borrow foreign currency for 90 days, external money market

11. Borrow home currency for 90 days, external money market

12. Invest home currency for 90 days, external money market

13. Invest foreign currency for 90 days, external money market

14. Lead a receivable, external money market

15. Sell foreign currency for home currency 90 days forward

16. Buy foreign currency with home currency 90 days forward

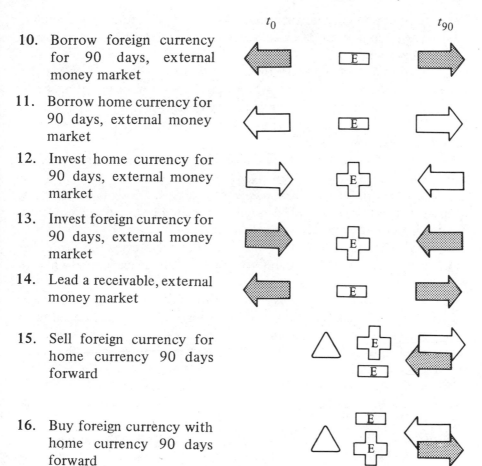

RESPONSE ANALYSIS

A. *If you chose the pairs 1 and 3, 2 and 4, 1 and 15, 2 and 16:* With these pairs you are exchanging currencies twice in the same option. In each pair the transaction that is executed on the spot date is reversed by the one done on the forward date.

B. *If you chose pairs 1 and 4, 2 and 3, 1 and 16, 2 and 15:* With these pairs you exchange currencies two times. The foreign currency is either being bought twice or sold twice. This overcovers the exposure and creates a new one.

C. *If you chose 1, 4, or 16 or any option*: In a receivable situation where the exposure is created by a foreign currency inflow, the covering action must create a foreign currency outflow. This cannot be done by buying the foreign currency, as buying creates an inflow and doubles the exposure.

D. *If you chose 15*: You have chosen an option that covers the exposure, but look again at the pricing. Covering a receivable in the future involves a cost in terms of the receivable currency. This is particularly evident in the BSI option. The pricing indicated here shows an interest earning in terms of the receivable currency.

E. *If you chose only 3*: This option completely covers the exposure. Sloat can arrange with its bank to sell the foreign currency when it comes in at an exchange rate fixed today. The pricing indicates that the rate on the forward contract is a combination of the spot rate, an interest earning, and an interest cost. The interest earning is associated with home currency, and the interest cost is associated with the foreign currency receivable. A comparison with the BSI option will show the validity of this association.

F. *If you chose only 2*: This contract is not sufficient to correct the exposure itself. The spot contract does not cover the 90 days, the time element.

G. *If you chose 8 or 13 for any option*: Investing the foreign currency today when there is a foreign currency receivable doubles the exposure. In 90 days there would be two inflows of foreign currency. The objective is to offset the one inflow.

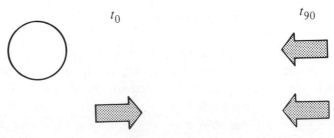

H. *If you chose 10, 2, and 7*: This combination completely covers the exposure. The foreign currency is borrowed and sold on the spot date for home currency, and the home currency is placed in a money market instrument for 90 days. By these transactions Sloat has replaced a foreign currency inflow with an inflow of its own currency in 90 days. Because Sloat will borrow the foreign currency from its local bank, the external interest rate symbol is used. There are few exceptions to the rule that a company that borrows foreign currency must do so in the external money market. National regulations generally prohibit a company from using domestic money market in a foreign country, unless it is situated there. In placing its funds Sloat does have a choice—the domestic money market of its currency, or the external money market of its currency. If Sloat chose the latter, it would be replicating the pricing of the forward transaction. The reason for looking at more than one option is to compare the prices in as many markets as possible. The firm will chose the domestic money market to make the comparison.

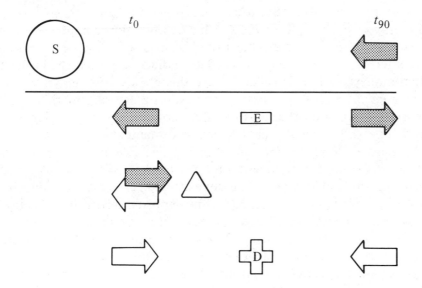

I. *If you chose 5 for any option*: There are few exceptions to the rule that a company that borrows foreign currency must do so in the external money market. National regulations generally prohibit a company from using the domestic money market in a foreign country unless the company has a subsidiary situated there. The exceptions are considered in Chapter 15.

J. *If you chose 6 or 11 for any option*: Borrowing the home currency does not help. Home currency flows in on the spot date; if foreign currency were purchased with it, the result would be a foreign currency inflow on the spot date and on the forward date. Exposure is increased.

K. *If you chose 9, 2, and 7*: This combination completely covers the foreign currency receivable risk. The customer pays early, the early payment is sold on spot date for home currency and the home currency is invested. The customer who is being asked to lead its payment will request a discount related to its cost of borrowing funds in its own market; hence we indicate the domestic money market of the foreign currency. The domestic earning symbol is used to indicate a placement in the local money market. See response analysis **L**.

L. *If you chose 9, 2, and 12*: This combination completely covers the foreign currency receivable risk, but also see response analysis **K**. The external earning symbol is used to indicate a placement in the external money market. Sloat does have this choice, but many European companies do not. Placement in domestic or external market will be chosen depending on the rates in these money markets and depending on the flexibility Sloat wants in its investment. Generally there is a wider range of money market instruments available in local money markets as compared to the external money markets. For example, in the Eurodollar market there are time deposits and certificates of deposit; in the domestic U.S. market there are time deposits, certificates of deposit, commercial paper, banker's acceptances, treasury bills, and so on.

M. *If you chose 14, 2, and 12*: The exposure is completely covered; however, these three transactions are a replica of the cost and earning elements of the forward contract. It is easier to access the external money markets through the forward rather than this combination.

N. *If you chose 14, 2 and 7*: The exposure is completely covered; however, these transactions then duplicate the BSI in cost and earning elements. An advantage to Sloat in this case would occur if the customer could borrow at better rates than Sloat.

SUMMARY

The complete solution to the problem is as follows:

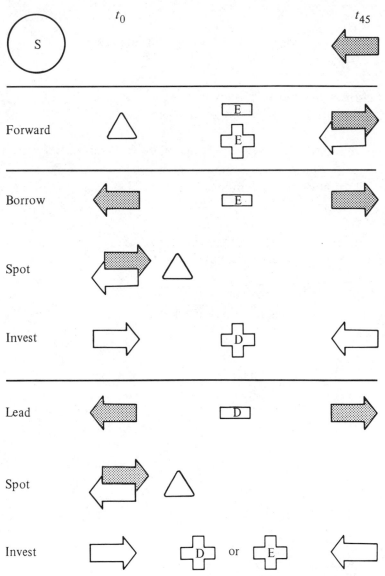

The reason for considering all three options is now more apparent. If the interest rates denoted by D and E are different, each option will have a different cost or earning. The options can easily be compared to one another simply by knowing the interest rates.

Options and Money Markets Used

Forward
Home currency—external money market
Foreign currency—external money market

Borrow (discount receivable, acceptance, bank advance, treasury funds)
Home currency—domestic money market
Foreign currency—external money market

Invest
Home currency—domestic money market
Foreign currency—external money market

Lead, Lag
Home currency—domestic money market
Foreign currency—domestic money market

Some General Guides

For options that cover payables
Cost is associated with the home currency
Earning is associated with the foreign currency

For options that cover receivables
Cost is associated with the foreign currency
Earning is associated with the home currency

It is preferable to be billed in currencies with higher interest rates than your own. It is preferable to bill your customers in currencies that have interest rates lower than your own. Following these two guides will result in an earning when the exposure is covered. More detail on this is provided in Chapter 15.

Options Illustrated

The diagrams on the two following pages show the options and pricing for the two most common exposures: a foreign currency payable and a foreign currency receivable.

FOREIGN CURRENCY PAYABLE EXPOSURE
OPTIONS

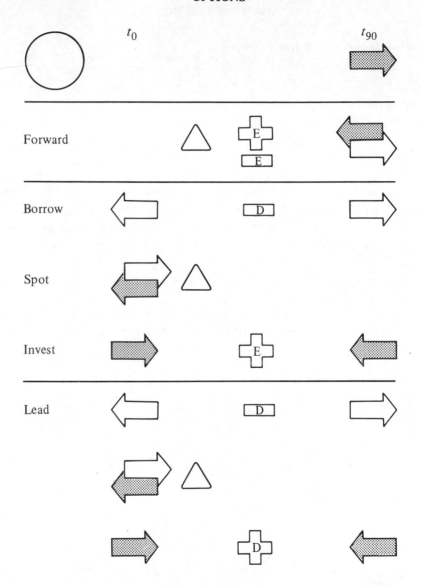

56

FOREIGN CURRENCY RECEIVABLE EXPOSURE
OPTIONS

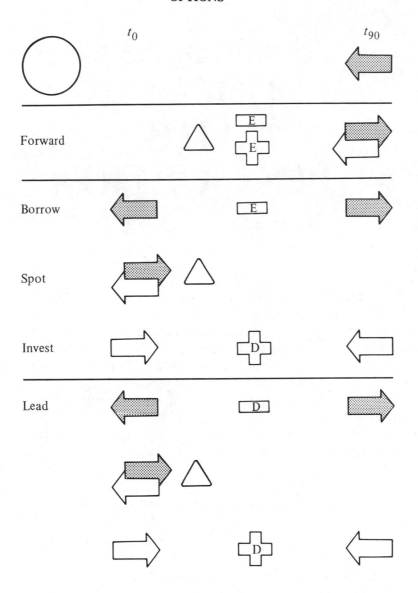

Reprinted with permission from Bank of America NT&SA.

CHAPTER FOUR
CHOOSING THE BEST OPTION

Chapter 3 discussed the three basic options available to the corporate treasurer to cover foreign exchange exposure. The present chapter addresses the problem of choosing among the options. The criterion for choice has been mentioned previously: Choose the option that returns the greatest earnings or the one that has the least cost. Initially, earning and cost are used in a strict financial sense; later in the book other considerations are introduced. The present chapter introduces two additional ways to choose among the options. We saw already that a choice can be made on the basis of interest rates. Some actual numbers are used to show concretely how a decision is made.

NET INTEREST COST AND EARNING

A decision on the best option can be made on the basis of the net interest cost and earning. Each option involves one interest cost and one interest earning element. The difference between these two gives the *Net Interest Cost* or *Earning* for the entire option. To show this in practice we return to the situation of Sloat & Company's Dutch subsidiary, Sloat (Holland) N.V. It exports steam generators to the U.S.

58

and bills its customers on 180-day terms. The exposure it faces on every order and the basic options for covering it are shown in the following diagram. In addition, the relevant spot rate and interest rates are entered.

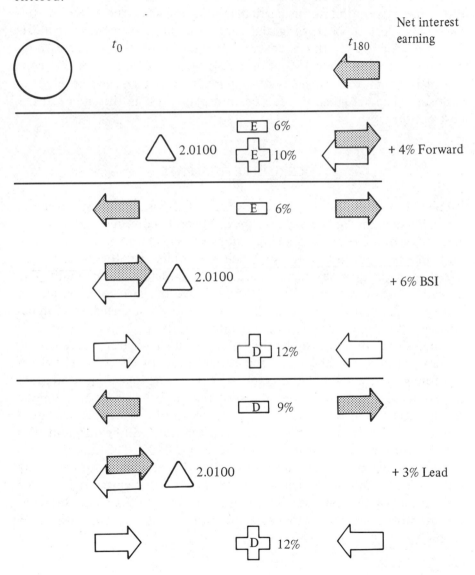

The number 2.0100 is the spot rate; it is the number of white currency units per unit of gray currency. The net interest earning is shown to the right of each option. It is arrived at by subtracting the interest cost of the gray currency from the interest earning of the white. The BSI is the best option in this particular situation since the difference between the cost of borrowing and earning from investment is greatest. The foreign currency risk is covered, and the subsidiary has an earning of 6% per annum over 180 days. It has borrowed money at 6%, converted it to another currency that is invested at 12%, and covered its exposure. The actual spot rate does not play a role in the choice of the best option.

LOCKED-IN FUTURE RATE

The net interest cost/earning is one way of choosing among options. A second way is the *locked-in future rate.* This rate combines all the transactions of one option into a single number. This number is in currency units like the spot rate. If the spot rate is 3 home units to 1 foreign unit, a locked-in future rate might be 3.23 home units to 1 foreign unit. The locked-in future rate says that after you have taken account of all the transactions in an option, you have effectively converted the foreign currency to home currency at this rate. The term "future" is used to distinguish it from the spot rate. It is called "locked-in" because the covering options fix, or lock in, the effective rate of conversion between the foreign currency and the home currency. The locked-in future rate is calculated by starting with the spot rate and then adjusting for the net interest rate difference. Given the same spot rate but two different interest rate differentials, the locked-in future rate will be different. For the BSI option, the locked-in future rate is 2.0685. This number sums up the borrowing of gray currency at 6%, the conversion of each gray unit to 2.01 white units, and the investment of the whites at 12%. The calculation of this number is contained in Chapter 5. At the moment we are most concerned with what the number tells us rather than how to get it.

There is an earning of 6%; this is also indicated by the higher locked-in future rate. It is better to receive 2.0685 whites for each gray than only 2.01. The earnings for the Forward and Lead were less in interest rate terms and so will be less in terms of the locked-in future rate. The following matrix summarizes the information developed on the options so far.

Option	Spot Rate	Net Interest Cost/Earning	Locked-In Future Rate
Forward	2.0100	4%	2.0490
BSI	2.0100	6%	2.0685
Lead	2.0100	3%	2.0389

Whether the best option is chosen according to the net interest earning or the locked-in future rate, the choice and the ranking are the same: BSI, Forward, and Lead.

The most important use of the locked-in future rate is that it provides the basis for judging whether or not to cover. If it is believed that in 180 days the gray to white rate will be 2.08 as opposed to the best option, which is 2.0685, then the company may wait to convert its gray receivable. On the other hand, if the rate in 180 days were forecast to be between 2.02 and 2.00, then the company has much to gain by covering the exposure today. To be more precise concerning the judgment, assume that this is February and the receivable is due August 25. If the Sloat subsidiary forecasts that anytime in the next six months it will be able to cover its exposure on August 25 at a locked-in future rate of 2.08, then it will wait.

POINTS

The third way of choosing among the options is *points*. Points are currency units and are the difference between the spot rate and the locked-in future rate. In our example the corresponding number of points are:

Option	Spot Rate	Net Interest Cost/Earning	Points	Locked-In Future Rate
Forward	2.0100	4%	390	2.0490
BSI	2.0100	6%	585	2.0685
Lead	2.0100	3%	289	2.0389

The size of the points correspond to the net interest cost/earning. Chapter 5 shows how to calculate the points directly from the interest rates. An option may thus be chosen by any of three methods—net interest cost/earning, points, and locked-in future rate.

SLOAT S.A.

To become more familiar with the concepts and their practical application, consider another Sloat subsidiary. The exposure situation, a receivable, the options for covering it and the relevant rates are shown in the diagram on the facing page.

The number 850.00 is the spot rate; it is the number of white currency units per one unit of gray currency. The net interest cost is shown to the right of each option. It is arrived at by subtracting the interest cost of the gray currency from the interest earning of the white. There is a cost in this case because the interest rate of the gray currency in each option exceeds the interest earning from the white. The best option in this situation is the Lead. The Lead covers the foreign currency exposure at a cost of 3% per annum over 90 days.

The locked-in future rate will be lower than the spot rate because Sloat is incurring a cost in covering this receivable. Because the spot rate is expressed as the number of whites per one gray, the company will be worse off by converting a gray receivable to white at a lower rate than at a higher rate. If there is an inflow of 100 grays, the company is worse off if it covers at 840.00 and receives 84,000 whites than if it were able to cover at 850.00 and receive 85,000 whites. The interest

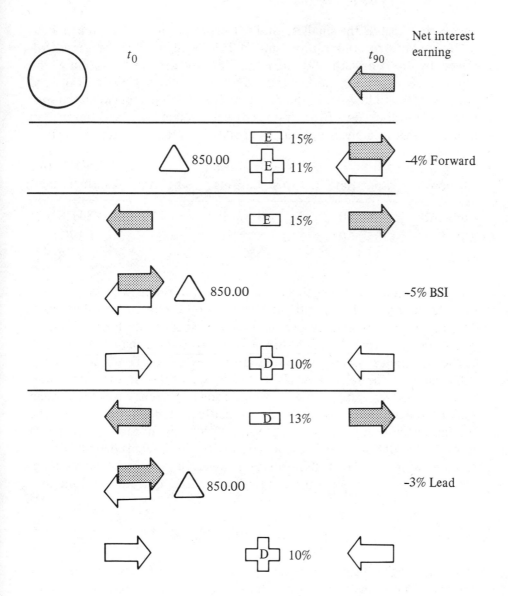

Net interest earning

t_0 t_{90}

E 15%

△ 850.00 E 11% −4% Forward

E 15%

△ 850.00 −5% BSI

D 10%

D 13%

△ 850.00 −3% Lead

D 10%

63

cost of the Lead is the smallest, and it follows from this that the locked-in future rate for this option should be the highest of the three, followed by the Forward and then the BSI. By the same reasoning, the number of points for the Lead are the least, followed by the Forward and BSI. This follows from the fact that the difference between the spot rate and the locked-in future rate is directly related to the difference in interest rates in a given option. The following matrix shows the results.

Option	Spot Rate	Net Interest Cost/Earning	Points	Locked-In Future Rate
Forward	850.00	-4%	819	841.81
BSI	850.00	-5%	1024	839.76
Lead	850.00	-3%	617	843.83

If the company believes that sometime within the next 90 days it will be able to cover this exposure at a rate of 865.00, it will certainly wait. This rate represents an improvement over what it can do today. If a rate of 825.00 were forecast, Sloat S.A. would cover with the Lead option.

The difference in the receivable situations of the Dutch and Italian subsidiaries is the relative levels of the interest rates. In the Dutch situation the interest rate of the incoming foreign currency was lower than that of the home currency; in the Italian case the interest rate of the foreign currency was higher. As the cost element in a foreign currency receivable situation is always associated with the foreign currency, lower foreign interest rates will mean that covering is done at an earning, whereas higher foreign interest rates mean that covering is done at a cost.

QUESTION

A company is faced with an exposure due to a foreign currency receivable. The following spot rate and locked-in future rates are known.

How would you rank the net interest cost/earning from high to low? Is there a cost or an earning?

Option	Spot Rate*	Net Interest Cost/Earning	Locked-In Future Rate
Forward	4.0000		4.1800
BSI	4.0000		4.1000
Lead	4.0000		4.1400

*Spot rate 4 home = 1 foreign.

RESPONSE

The net interest earning is highest in the Forward, followed by the Lead and the BSI. This earning is reflected by the greater difference between the spot rate and the locked-in future rate for the Forward as opposed to the other options. It is an earning since we are dealing with a foreign currency receivable and the rate of exchange is specified as the number of home units to one foreign unit. An inflow of 100,000 foreign units converted at 4.0000 yields 400,000 home units; conversion at 4.18 gives 418,000 home units. The difference is the earning from covering.

CHOOSING OPTIONS FOR PAYABLES

Up to this point only foreign currency inflow situations have been considered. The representation of a foreign currency payable exposure and the three basic options for covering it are shown. This company will be making the final payment on a foreign currency loan and a payment on a large machinery order.

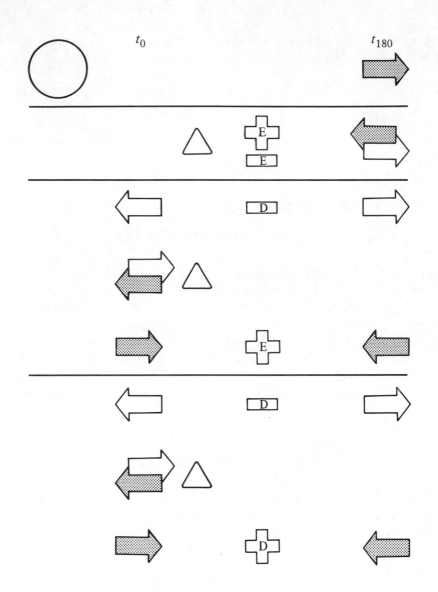

The interest payment is considered first. The interest rates and spot rate that apply to the situation are as follows:

Gray domestic interest rate is 9%.
Gray external interest rate is 13%.
White domestic interest rate is 5%.
White external interest rate is 4%.
Spot rate is 3.0000; that is, there are 3 whites to 1 gray.

Before looking at the following matrix, work out for yourself the net interest cost/earning and decide whether covering this exposure results in a cost or an earning.

| Option | Spot Rate | Net Interest Cost/Earning | | |
		I_w	I_g	Net
Forward	3.0000	4	13	+9%
BSI	3.0000	5	13	+8%
Lead	3.0000	5	9	+4%

There is a net interest earning if the company decides to cover the exposure now. In the payable situation the cost is associated with the home currency, and in this case home (white) interest rates are lower than foreign (gray) interest rates. The Forward is the best option because the earning is the greatest. The locked-in future rate will be lower than the spot rate. In a payable situation a firm earns by paying less for the goods; in this case the goods are another currency. The firm earns by paying out less whites for each gray. Since the spot rate is in terms of the number of whites, the firm's home currency, the locked-in future rate will be less than the spot rate. For the Forward the locked-in future rate is 2.8732. If the loan repayment is 100,000 grays, the company will effectively pay out 287,320 whites in 180 days rather than 300,000 whites if the payment had to be made today. The summary matrix for this situation is as follows:

Option	Spot Rate	Net Interest Cost/Earning	Points	Locked-In Future Rate
Forward	3.0000	+ 9%	1268	2.8732
BSI	3.0000	+ 8%	1127	2.8873
Lead	3.0000	+ 4%	574	2.9426

If the company believed with some certainty that it would be able to cover this exposure at a rate better than 2.8732 (say, 2.8400), it would do nothing now and wait. If a rate higher than 2.8732 were forecast, then the company would lock in its cover now. If the company decides to wait, it has expectations about three different rates—spot rate, gray interest rates, and white interest rates. All can and do change, although the spot rates are less predictable and generally fluctuate more than do interest rates.

This same firm must now consider whether to cover its foreign currency machinery payment. The interest rates and spot rate that apply to this situation are as follows:

Gray domestic interest rate is 3%.
Gray external interest rate is 1%.
White domestic interest rate is 5%.
White external interest rate is 4%.
Spot rate is 5.0000; that is, there are 5 whites to 1 gray.

Before looking at the following matrix, work out for yourself the net interest cost/earning and decide whether covering this exposure results in a cost or an earning; also decide if the locked-in future rate is higher or lower than the spot rate.

Option	Spot Rate	Net Interest Cost/Earning		
		I_w	I_g	Net
Forward	5.0000	4	1	+3%
BSI	5.0000	5	1	+4%
Lead	5.0000	5	3	+2%

There is a net interest cost if the company decides to cover the exposure now. In the payable situation the cost is associated with the home currency, and in this case the home (white) interest rates are higher than the foreign (gray) interest rates. The Lead is the best option. The locked-in future rate will be higher than the spot rate. A net interest cost means the firm pays more in the future than today. The spot rate is in terms of the firm's own currency, white, so it will end up paying out more white units in the future than it would if the payment date were today. The summary matrix for this last situation is:

Option	Spot Rate	Net Interest Cost/Earning	Points	Locked-In Future Rate
Forward	5.0000	–3%	746	5.0746
BSI	5.0000	–4%	995	5.0995
Lead	5.0000	–2%	493	5.0493

The firm would do nothing if it believed it could buy the gray units for less than 5.0493 within the next six months.

SUMMARY

Covering payable and receivable exposures at a cost and at an earning have been discussed. The following table summarizes the relationships among interest rates and the relative level of the spot rate and locked-in future rate in payable and receivable exposures.

Interest Rates	Payable	Receivable
	Cost	Earning
$I_{home} > I_{foreign}$	Future rate > Spot	Future rate > Spot
	Earning	Cost
$I_{home} < I_{foreign}$	Future rate < Spot	Future rate < Spot

The spot rate is expressed as the number of home units per one foreign unit. > means greater than; < means less than.

CHAPTER FIVE
THE FORMULA FOR COMPARING OPTIONS

The relationship between interest rates, points, the spot rate and future rates was discussed in Chapter 4. Points are calculated directly from the spot rate and interest rates. These points, when added to or subtracted from the spot rate, equal the future rate. The present chapter shows the mathematical relation among the rates and points. Two formulas are developed; the first starts with interest rates and the spot rate and calculates points, and the second starts with points and the spot rate and calculates interest. A calculator will enable you to check the calculations as you go along.

POINTS FORMULA

The points formula is used to convert time costs and earnings, which are expressed in percentage terms, to units of currency called *points*. These units are added to or subtracted from exchange rates to show the effect of a combined exchange and money market operation. The resulting number is what we have called the locked-in future rate. This rate is

70

used to choose the best option and to decide if the time is right to execute the best option.

Points are simply amounts of interest that are calculated in much the same way as any interest amount: Principal times Rate times Time. In the points calculation however, there are two rates, that for the foreign currency and that for the home currency. These are combined by using the exchange rate between the two currencies. The following example illustrates how this is done in practice. The exposure situation is an inflow of 1 unit of foreign currency (gray) to a company whose home currency is white. The option used for this example is the BSI. The gray interest rate is 3%, the white interest rate is 10%, and the spot rate is 4.0000. There are 4 white units to 1 gray.

$$t_0 \qquad\qquad\qquad\qquad t_{180}$$

principal $\times$ rate $\times$ time = interest amount

$$1 \times 3\% \times \frac{180}{360} = .0150$$

4.0000

principal $\times$ rate $\times$ time = interest amount

$$4 \times 10\% \times \frac{180}{360} = .2000$$

The company has borrowed 1 unit of gray for which it will pay 3% over 180 days. The amount of interest in gray units is .0150. The 1 borrowed gray unit is converted to white at 4 to 1. The 4 units of white are invested at 10% for 180 days. The interest return is .2000 whites. There is an interest cost of .0150 gray units and an interest earning of .2000 white units. These cannot be combined until the cost and earning are expressed in the same units. The .0150 gray units can be converted to white by using the exchange rate. There are 4 whites to 1 gray, so .0150 grays equal .0600 whites. Now the cost and the earning are expressed in the same terms. The net earning is .1400 white currency units. In addition to the initial investment of 4 white units, the company will have in hand 4.1400 units of its own currency for every 1 unit of the foreign currency receivable at the end of 180 days. The company started out with a principal of 4 white units, invested at a net interest rate of 7% (10% – 3%), for half a year.

$$\text{principal} \times \text{rate} \quad \times \text{time} = \text{interest amount}$$

$$4.000 \quad \times 7\% \quad \times \frac{180}{360} = .1400$$

$$\text{spot} \quad \times I_h - I_f \quad \times \frac{\text{days}}{360} = \text{points}$$

where I_f = Interest rate of foreign currency, external or domestic

I_h = Interest rate of home currency, external or domestic

Spot plus the points equals the locked-in future rate of 4.1400.

  If you look back at the illustration of the option you will note that the interest amount of the gray borrowing is .0150; when this is combined with the principal amount borrowed, 1.0150 units of gray must be repaid. But there is only one unit of gray currency coming in 180 days hence. There is an exposure—a .0150 gray outflow—when the purpose of the option was to cover the exposure completely. If a smaller amount of gray currency is borrowed initially, this problem can be avoided. The amount of gray that the company borrows plus the interest on the loan should equal the amount of the receivable. This involves working backwards to some extent, the interest rate is known and the time period is known, the amount to be borrowed is unknown. The following expression provides the necessary adjustment:

$$\frac{1}{1 + \left(I_f \times \dfrac{\text{days}}{360} \right)} \quad *$$

This expression is multiplied times the amount of the receivable to determine the amount of foreign currency to borrow. The interest rate of the foreign currency is used because it is the foreign currency flows that are being matched. The number on the bottom will be larger than 1, so the whole expression will be less than 1. Therefore, the amount of foreign currency to be borrowed will be less than the amount of the receivable. The same formula is used to determine the amount a customer would pay if paid in advance. It is even more apparent in that situation—the company does not expect to receive the full amount of the invoice if paid early.

*The formula is derived in the Appendix (at the end of the present chapter).

To integrate this adjustment into the previous calculation, the receivable example is used. The white company has an inflow of one gray in 180 days. The BSI option is illustrated. The amount of gray currency to be borrowed is

$$1 \times \frac{1}{1 + \left(I_f \times \dfrac{\text{days}}{360}\right)} \quad \text{or} \quad 1 \times \frac{1}{1 + \left(.03 \times \dfrac{180}{360}\right)} = .9852$$

This number of gray is then converted at the spot rate of 4.0000 into white units—3.9408, and these are invested at 10% for 180 days.

$$\overbrace{1 \times \frac{1}{1 + \left(3\% \times \dfrac{180}{360}\right)}}^{.9852} \times 3\% \times \frac{180}{360} = .0148$$

4.0000

$$\underbrace{4 \times \frac{1}{1 + \left(3\% \times \dfrac{180}{360}\right)}}_{3.9408} \times 10\% \times \frac{180}{360} = .1970$$

The amount borrowed is .9852 gray at 3% for 180 days, and the interest is .0148 gray. The amount borrowed plus the interest equal the receivable .9852 + .0148 = 1. The amount invested is 3.9408 and produces interest of .1970. The amount of money that the company receives from covering its foreign currency receivable is 3.9408 + .1970, which equals 4.1378 units of home currency. This is less than the amount previously found, 4.1400, but that figure didn't account for the fact that there was foreign currency interest which was not covered by the receivable.

The company started out with a principal of 3.9408 white units and invested at a net interest rate of 7% for six months.

$$\text{principal} \quad\quad\quad \times \text{ rate} \quad \times \text{ time} = \text{interest amount}$$

$$4 \times \frac{1}{1 + \left(3\% \times \dfrac{180}{360}\right)} \times 7\% \quad \times \frac{180}{360} = .1378$$

$$\text{spot} \times \frac{1}{1 + \left(I_f \times \dfrac{\text{days}}{360}\right)} \times I_h - I_f \times \frac{\text{days}}{360} = \text{points}$$

The formula can be condensed to

$$\frac{\text{spot} \times (I_h - I_f) \times \dfrac{\text{days}}{360}}{1 + \left(I_f \times \dfrac{\text{days}}{360}\right)} = \text{points}$$

This is now recognizable as the initial formula; only the discount factor has been added to take care of the foreign currency interest. When leading, a discount is paid or earned immediately in lieu of interest being paid on the future date. The same calculation is used when the discount is expressed in terms of percent per annum. The adaptation to a flat discount is made in Chapter 12. This formula is also used for the Forward option in those cases where the points are developed from interest rates.

Before applying the formula to some concrete examples, let's consider the sensitivity of the formula to changes in certain variables. This will help you gain an intuitive feel for the answers.

1. The greater the difference between the interest rates, the greater the number of points, which simply means that a higher interest rate leads to greater interest payment.

2. The more numerous the days, the larger the number of points. The amount of interest paid to the bank is larger if the loan is for one year as opposed to one month.

3. The higher the spot rate, the greater the number of points. Analogously, the larger the amount borrowed, the more will be paid in interest.

4. If the foreign currency interest rate is low and the number of days is small, then the denominator approaches 1 and its effect fades sharply.

THE POINTS FORMULA IN PRACTICE

In the previous chapter we looked at the subsidiaries of Sloat & Company. The Dutch subsidiary exports steam generators to the United States and bills on 180-day terms. The situation for Sloat (Holland) N.V. and the covering options are illustrated in the following diagram.

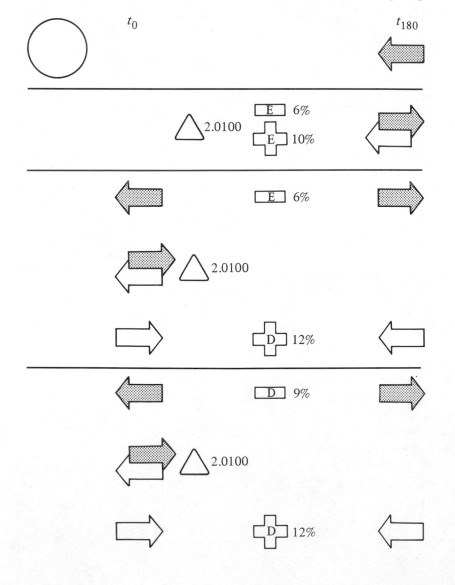

The formula used to calculate the Points is

$$\frac{\text{spot} \times (I_h - I_f) \times \dfrac{\text{days}}{360}}{1 + \left(I_f \times \dfrac{\text{days}}{360}\right)} = \text{Points}$$

Using the numbers from the previous illustration, the calculation for the Forward is

$$\frac{2.0100 \times (.10 - .06) \times \dfrac{180}{360}}{1 + \left(.06 \times \dfrac{180}{360}\right)} = \frac{.0402}{1.03} = .0390 = 390 \text{ points}$$

where 390 is the number of points to be added to the spot rate for the locked-in future rate.

The calculation for the BSI is

$$\frac{2.0100 \times (.12 - .06) \times \dfrac{180}{360}}{1 + \left(.06 \times \dfrac{180}{360}\right)} = \frac{.0603}{1.03} = .0585 = 585 \text{ points}$$

where 585 is the number of points to be added to the spot rate for the locked-in future rate.

The calculation for the Lead is

locked-in future rate. The calculation for the Lead is

$$\frac{2.0100 \times (.12 - .09) \times \dfrac{180}{360}}{1 + \left(.09 \times \dfrac{180}{360}\right)} = \frac{.0301}{1.045} = .0289 = 289 \text{ points}$$

where 289 is the number of points to be added to the spot rate for the locked-in future rate.

In making the calculations, the following conventions should be observed: (1) put the figures expressed in percentage form in decimal form (e.g., 4% = .04); and (2) perform the calculations inside the parentheses first. On the top line subtract the two interest rates before multiplying by spot and time. On the bottom line multiply the interest rate by time before adding 1.

The matrix summarizes the calculations.

Option	Spot Rate	Net Interest Cost/Earning			Points	Locked-In Future Rate
		I_h	I_f	Net		
Forward	2.0100	+10	– 6	= +4%	390	2.0490
BSI	2.0100	+12	– 6	= +6%	585	2.0685
Lead	2.0100	+12	– 9	= +3%	289	2.0389

The matrix conveys the following information:

1. The BSI is the best option by all criteria—net interest, points, and locked-in future rate. The Forward follows, and the Lead is the least attractive option.

2. There is an earning if the exposure is covered now. By executing the BSI Sloat (Holland) N.V. receives an additional .0585 units of its currency for each unit of foreign currency compared with the spot rate.

3. The best locked-in future rate, 2.0685, forms the basis for deciding whether to cover or do nothing now. If Sloat thinks that it can get a better rate anytime within the next six months, it will wait to cover. Either the spot rate could rise, or the interest rate on its currency increase, or the interest rate on the foreign currency decrease, but these latter two factors have less of an effect as time goes on.

The points formula was developed in the framework of a foreign currency receivable. It also works for a foreign currency payable. A payable exposure and the BSI option are shown in the following diagram with some rates.

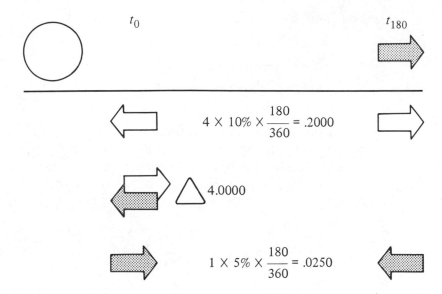

To cover this exposure, 4 units of the home currency are borrowed at 10% for 180 days; the 4 home units are converted at the spot rate to 1 unit of the foreign currency. The foreign currency is invested at 5% for 180 days and earns interest of .0250. Therefore, the total inflow of foreign currency from the investment is the principal of 1 plus the interest of .0250, which equals 1.0250. This is offset by the outflow of only 1 unit of foreign currency. There is a foreign currency exposure. This can be avoided by investing less than 1 unit of foreign currency. The amount to be invested is found the same way as before: multiply the amount of the foreign currency payable by

$$\frac{1}{1 + \left(.05 \times \dfrac{180}{360} \right)}$$

The payable is one unit, so

$$1 \times \frac{1}{1 + \left(.05 \times \dfrac{180}{360}\right)} = .9756$$

If this amount is invested at 5% for 180 days, the interest of .0244 when added to the principal will equal 1, the amount of the payable. This means that less than 4 units of home currency need be borrowed. The amount home currency of be borrwed is

$$4 \times \frac{1}{1 + \left(.05 \times \dfrac{180}{360}\right)}$$

All these considerations are represented in the following diagram.

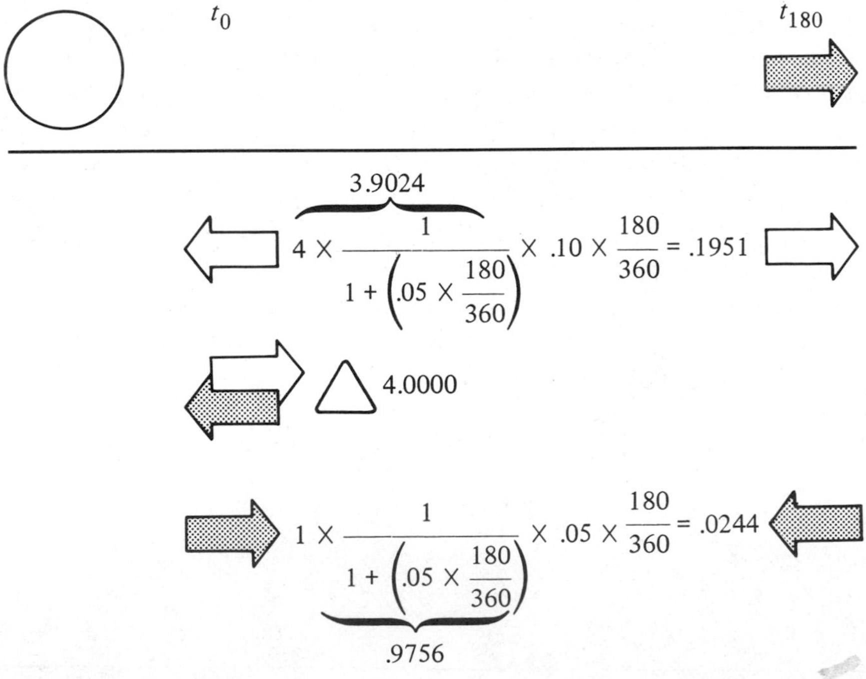

$$t_0 \qquad\qquad\qquad\qquad\qquad\qquad\qquad\qquad t_{180}$$

$$\overbrace{4 \times \frac{1}{1 + \left(.05 \times \dfrac{180}{360}\right)}}^{3.9024} \times .10 \times \frac{180}{360} = .1951$$

$$\triangle \; 4.0000$$

$$\underbrace{1 \times \frac{1}{1 + \left(.05 \times \dfrac{180}{360}\right)}}_{.9756} \times .05 \times \frac{180}{360} = .0244$$

Compare this representation to that of the receivable on page 74. The situations are exactly analogous. The amount of foreign currency borrowed or invested is less than the amount of the receivable or the payable; this is directly reflected in the amount of the home currency. The points formula takes account of these considerations for both the payable and receivable situations. In the example the number of points is 975 [.1951 – (4 × .0244)] and the locked-in future rate is 4.0975. Covering this payable is a cost, meaning that more of the home currency must be paid out compared with the spot rate.

PROBLEM

Before moving to the next section, you may want to practice using the formula. The following situation is designed to do this. Mills Shipyards Ltd. is a Canadian firm that builds container ships. Steel is regularly imported from France on 60-day terms. Mills agrees to be billed in French francs since the French supplier offers a better price in its own currency. Looking at the situations from the point of view of Mills's treasurer, calculate the points and locked-in future rate for the three basic options. The rates are as follows:

Canadian—domestic, 10%; external, 11%.
French—domestic, 12%; external, 14%.
Spot .2750—number of Canadian dollars per 1 French franc.

The problem will be easier to solve if the flows are diagrammed and options are priced before the numbers are entered. Also, the matrix will assist in organizing the answer.

DISCUSSION OF THE SOLUTION

Looking at the cost and earnings elements of the options, it is clear that there is an earning if the exposure is covered. In all instances the cost is in terms of the lower interest rate currency, dollars, and the earnings in terms of the higher interest rate, francs.

This illustration of the BSI option is representative of the other two options.

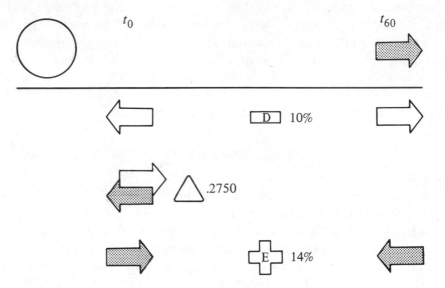

The given information for the matrix is as follows:

Option	Spot	Net Interest Cost/Earning			Points	Locked-In Future Rate
		I_h	I_f	Net		
Forward	.2750	11	14	3%		
BSI	.2750	10	14	4%		
Lead	.2750	10	12	2%		

The calculation of the points for the three options is as follows:

$$\text{Forward} \quad \frac{.2750 \times (.11 - .14) \times \dfrac{60}{360}}{1 + \left(.14 \times \dfrac{60}{360}\right)} = .0013 = 13 \text{ points}$$

$$\text{BSI} \qquad \frac{.2750 \times (.10 - .14) \times \dfrac{60}{360}}{1 + \left(.14 \times \dfrac{60}{360}\right)} = .0018 = 18 \text{ points}$$

$$\text{Lead} \qquad \frac{.2750 \times (.10 - .12) \times \dfrac{60}{360}}{1 + \left(.12 \times \dfrac{60}{360}\right)} = .0009 = 9 \text{ points}$$

In this situation an earnings means that Mills pays out fewer dollars in the future so that the points are subtracted from the spot rate. The complete matrix is:

Option	Spot	Net Interest Cost/Earning	Points	Locked-In Future Rate
Forward	.2750	+3%	13	.2737
BSI	.2750	+4%	18	.2732
Lead	.2750	+2%	9	.2741

A typical Mills order is FF 10,000,000. On an order of this size the difference between the best option and the next best is a savings of C$5,000. (The difference between the Forward and the BSI is .0005 × 10,000,000). Mills expends C$18,000 less for the future delivery compared with the price of French francs today. (Earning of 18 points— .0018 × FF 10,000,000 = C$18,000.)

INTEREST COST/EARNINGS (ICE) FORMULA

Up to now it has been assumed that the information we have to work with for all options is spot rates and interest rates. This was convenient because it served to illustrate the fundamental determinants of future rates. In the foreign exchange market the information about the Forward is conventionally given as a number of points to be added to or subtracted from the spot rate. Points capture in a single number the differential between two external interest rates. Points are this differential in terms of currency units. For the U.S. dollar/Dutch guilder, 329 points less the spot of 2.0180 equals a forward rate of 1.9861. For the Deutsche mark/French franc, 295 points plus the spot of 233.05 equals a forward rate of 236.00. The rules for adding and subtracting points are covered in Chapter 6. It is clear from this example that the points and the spot are lined up on the rightmost number.

Following is an excerpt from the *Financial Times* giving the spot rate and forward points:

THE POUND SPOT AND FORWARD

Aug. 23	Day's spread	Close	One month	% p.a.	Three months	% p.a.
U.S.	2.2225-2.2340	2.2240-2.2250	0.40-0.30c pm	1.88	1.17-1.07 pm	2.01
Canada	2.5905-2.6020	2.5905-2.5925	0.57-0.47c pm	2.41	1.27-1.17 pm	1.88
Nethlnd.	4.45¾-4.49½	4.45¾-4.46¾	2⅛-1⅛c pm	4.37	5½-4½ pm	4.48
Belgium	65.10-65.50	65.13-65.23	15-5c pm	1.84	35-25 pm	1.84
Denmark	11.72-11.79	11.72¼-11.73¼	½-2½ore dis	−1.53	3-5 dis	−1.36
Ireland	1.0785-1.0855	1.0795-1.0805	32-42p dis	−4.11	105-115 dis	−4.07
W. Ger.	4.06-4.09½	4.06¼-4.07¼	2⅝-1⅝pf pm	6.27	7⅜-6⅜ pm	6.78
Portugal	109.35-110.00	109.45-109.75	30-80c dis	−6.02	135-235 dis	−6.75
Spain	146.75-147.50	146.85-147.05	200-250c dis	−18.37	575-675dis	−17.01
Italy	1,816-1,825	1,817½-1,819½	½lire pm-1½ dis	−0.33	4½-6½ dis	−1.21
Norway	11.19½-11.25	11.19½-11.20½	3-1ore pm	2.14	7¼-5¼ pm	2.23
France	9.47-9.52	9.47-9.48	2-1c pm	1.90	4¼-3¼ pm	1.58
Sweden	9.39-9.45	9.39½-9.40½	2⅛-⅛ore pm	1.47	3½-1½ pm	1.06
Japan	483-493	486¾-487¾	3.25-2.95y pm	7.63	9.05-8.75 pm	7.30
Austria	29.70-29.95	29.74-29.79	22-12gro pm	6.85	55-45 pm	6.72
Switz.	3.68-3.71	3.68-3.69	4⅛-3⅛c pm	11.80	11½-10½ pm	11.94

Belgian rate is for convertible francs. Financial franc 67.60-67.70c pm.
Six-month forward dollar 2.09-2.04c pm. 12-month 3.79-3.87c pm.

The following matrix summarizes the basic information available for calculating the cost/earnings of each option and the formula needed for comparing the options.

| Option | Spot | Net Interest Cost/Earning | | | Points | Locked-In Future Rate |
		I_h	I_f	Net		
Forward	.2750	ICE	formula		13	Spot ± points
BSI	.2750	10	14	4%	Points formula	Spot ± points
Lead	.2750	10	12	2%	Points formula	Spot ± points

The ICE formula is used to convert costs and earnings that are expressed in points (interest amounts) to an annualized percentage. This allows the forward contract that is expressed in points to be compared to other options that are expressed in percentages. The formula expresses the percentage difference between buying (selling) an amount of currency on the spot date and buying (selling) that same amount on a forward date. It does that by taking the difference between the spot rate and the forward rate—points—and expressing it as a percentage of the spot rate.

As with the points formula, there is an analogy with the familiar interest calculation. The type of formula wanted is one where the interest amount, the principal, and the time period are known. The unknown is the interest rate. This is found with the expression

$$\text{rate} = \frac{\text{interest amount}}{\text{principal}} \times \frac{1}{\text{time}} \times 100$$

The analogy to this in the foreign exchange market is

$$\begin{matrix} \text{interest percent} \\ \text{(per annum)} \end{matrix} = \frac{\text{points}}{\text{spot}} \times \frac{1}{\text{time}} \times 100$$

For the examples mentioned previously, assuming the time period is 91 days:

$$6.45\% = \frac{.0329*}{2.0190} \times \frac{360}{91} \times 100$$

$$5.01\% = \frac{2.95}{233.05} \times \frac{360}{91} \times 100$$

*The points have as many decimal places as does the spot rate they are associated with.

The percentage found in the first case expresses the difference in terms of guilders—the difference between 2.0190 guilders spot and 1.9861 guilders in 91 days. From the perspective of a Dutch treasurer, this is how he or she would view a spot transaction versus a one month transaction. An American treasurer has another point of view. The American wants to know the difference in dollars between a spot transaction and one in the future. The calculation does not do this. There are two ways of altering the calculation to express the percentage in dollar terms.

1. Turn the exchange rate around so that it is expressed in dollar terms. If DG 2.0190 equal $1 spot, each guilder is worth about 50¢; more precisely, $.4953 (1 ÷ 2.0190). The forward rate is DG 1.9861 equal $1, and each guilder is worth $.5035. The number of points difference is 82. From the point of view of the American, the percentage in dollar terms is

$$6.55\% = \frac{.0082}{.4953} \times \frac{360}{91} \times 100$$

Viewed from New York, the percentage is larger.

2. Change the formula (less difficult than it sounds). The formula that expresses the percentage in dollar terms, even though the exchange rates are expressed in terms of guilders, is

$$\text{interest percent} = \frac{\text{points}}{\text{forward}} \times \frac{1}{\text{time}} \times 100$$

$$6.55\% = \frac{.0329}{1.9861} \times \frac{360}{91} \times 100$$

This method is easier to work with than the first, although the rationale is less intuitive. The derivation of the formula is shown in the Appendix.

The ICE formula used depends on the perspective of the user.

If spot and points are expressed in home currency units, then

$$\text{ICE-1} \ = \ \frac{\text{points}}{\text{spot}} \ \times \ \frac{360}{\text{days}} \times 100$$

Home is the United States and the rates are expressed as the number of dollars per one Swiss franc (SF). Spot SF 1 = $.6135; two-month points are $.0112.

$$10.95\% = \frac{.0112}{.6135} \ \times \ \frac{360}{60} \times 100$$

If spot and points are expressed in foreign currency units, then

$$\text{ICE-2} \ = \ \frac{\text{points}}{\text{forward}} \ \times \ \frac{360}{\text{days}} \times 100$$

Home is the United States and the rates are expressed as the number of Swiss francs per one dollar. Spot $1 = SF 1.6350; two-month points are SF .0292.

$$10.72\% = \frac{.0292}{1.6350} \ \times \ \frac{360}{60} \times 100$$

BRITTAN VALLEY IMPORT CASE

This is an opportunity to apply all the techniques from the previous chapters. Brittan Valley Import Company is located in Laredo, Texas. It is a very large wholesaler of Mexican fruits and vegetables. Orders are paid for within one month of the date received. A new delivery totaling 4 million Mexican pesos (MP) is due in a couple of days. The treasurer of the company believes that the peso will probably weaken relative to the dollar over the next six months on the order of 4%; this is confirmed in conversations with local bankers. Today spot is .04386 dollars for 1 peso. The one-month points are .00033 dollars. They are subtracted from spot. Brittan Valley can borrow dollars at 12% from its local bank. The bank will accept deposits of Mexican pesos at 23%. The exporter on the other side of the border will give a discount equivalent to 19% per annum for payment on delivery. The treasurer will examine the three basic options available, chose the best, and then compare the best option to the forecast about the Mexican peso. Take the role of the treasurer of Brittan Valley, represent the options and do the calculations before reading the discussion that follows.

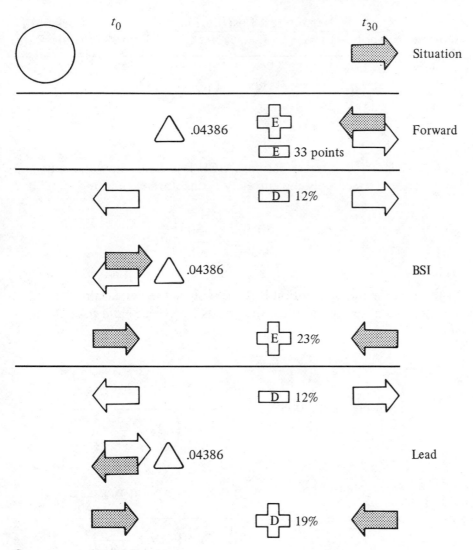

Gray, pesos; white, dollars

Two facts are immediately apparent from this diagram. This exposure can be covered at an earning; the cost of borrowing is less than the earning from investing. The BSI option is more attractive than the Lead. The matrix can be filled in as follows with the information given:

Option	Spot	Net Interest Cost/Earning			Points	Locked-In Future Rate
		I_h	I_f	Net		
Forward	.04386				33	.04353
BSI	.04386	12	23	11%		
Lead	.04386	12	19	7%		

To calculate the interest earnings, ICE-1 is used since the spot and points are expressed in home currency terms. Interest earnings are

$$9.03\% = \frac{.00033}{.04386} \times \frac{360}{30} \times 100$$

Now we know the best option is the BSI since the net earnings are 11%. The next steps are to calculate the points for the BSI and for completeness, the Lead.

$$\text{BSI points} = .00039 = \frac{.04386 \times (.12 - .23) \times \frac{30}{360}}{1 + \left(.23 \times \frac{30}{360}\right)}$$

$$\text{Lead points} = .00025 = \frac{.04386 \times (.12 - .19) \times \frac{30}{360}}{1 + \left(.19 \times \frac{30}{360}\right)}$$

The points will be subtracted from the spot rate because an earnings in a payable situation means that the company pays less of its own currency.

The completed matrix is:

Option	Spot	Net Interest Cost/Earning			Points	Locked-In Future Rate
		I_h	I_f	Net		
Forward	.04386			+9.03%	33	.04353
BSI	.04386	12	23	+11%	39	.04347
Lead	.04386	12	19	+7%	25	.04361

By all the choice criteria, the BSI option is the best. This option is compared to the forecast. The forecast was that the peso would weaken on the order of 4% over the next six months. On a per annum basis this is 8%. This figure can be compared to the per annum earnings of 11% if the exposure is covered. Another way to compare is to calculate the expected rate (assuming a gradual weakening):

$$\underset{\text{Spot}}{.04386} \times \underset{\substack{\text{Percent}\\\text{Change}}}{.08} \times \underset{\text{Period}}{\frac{30}{360}} = .00029$$

This is the reduction from spot expected. The forecast rate is .04357, compared to the BSI of .04347. Given the current forecast, Brittan Valley is better off covering its exposure today rather than waiting for the exchange rate to move.

COMPARABILITY OF NET INTEREST PERCENT

There is a slight inconsistency between the net interest percents of the Forward and the BSI. It does not affect the number of points nor the locked-in future rate nor the choice of option on the basis of interest percentages, except in those infrequent cases where they are very close. Even then an unqualified choice can be made on the basis of the points or the locked-in future rate. The percentage for the Forward represents the difference between the spot rate and a rate in the future. It does not represent the exact difference between two external interest rates because the interest rate of the foreign currency is adjusted as the points are calculated. The adjustment is made to put the future return from the foreign currency in home currency terms. A 23% earnings in pesos is not the same as 23% earnings in dollars because the future return is in pesos, not dollars. The return in dollars is not 23% since pesos in the future, when the interest will be paid, are not worth $.04386 each, but only $.04353. The percentage figure used for the BSI and the Lead are simply interest differentials of two interest rates on two different currencies without adjustment.

There are two ways of making the percentages comparable; the method chosen depends on the desired results:

1. If it is desired to have the percents of the BSI and the Lead express exactly the difference between the spot rate and locked-in future rate simply take the points as calculated from the points formula and use the ICE formula. In the case of Brittan Valley these percentages would be 10.67% for the BSI, compared with the 11% unadjusted; and for the Lead, the percentages would be 6.84% as compared to the unadjusted difference of 7%.

2. If the objective is to show the actual difference between the interest rates, the ICE formula is modified. We simply go back to the points formula and derive the following expression for $(I_h - I_f)$:

$$(I_h - I_f) = \left(\frac{\text{points}}{\text{spot}} \times \frac{360}{\text{days}} \right) \times \left[1 + \left(I_f \times \frac{\text{days}}{360} \right) \right] \times 100$$

The difference in the external rates of the dollar and peso is 9.20%.

This chapter has developed formulas that are used to compare the costs and earnings of options that cover exposure. The discussion of Brittan Valley is an example of a step-by-step procedure for analyzing exposure situations.

APPENDIX

Derivation of the Discount Factor

This factor is used in the points formula to determine the amount of foreign currency to borrow or invest so that future foreign currency flows are exactly matched. The objective is that the principal and the interest from a deposit or a loan match up with a future flow. Setting the future flow equal to 1, the condition is that:

$$\text{principal} + \text{interest amount} = 1.$$

This condition is imposed on the interest formula of principal $\times$ rate $\times$ time = interest amount (rewritten in short form, as $P \times R \times T = A$).

Rewrite the condition $P + A = 1$ as $A = 1 - P$.
Substitute for A in $P \times R \times T = A$.
The result is $P \times R \times T = 1 - P$.
Solve this equation for P.

$$P + P \times R \times T = 1$$

$$P \times (1 + R \times T) = 1$$

$$P = \frac{1}{1 + (R \times T)}$$

where R is equivalent to the interest rate on the foreign currency and the expression for time is days/360. Substitution gives the same expression as shown earlier in the present chapter.

$$\frac{1}{1 + \left(I_f \times \dfrac{\text{days}}{360} \right)}$$

When multiplied by the amount of a future flow, the result is the amount to be borrowed or invested given that the principal plus interest at maturity should equal that flow.

Derivation of ICE-2

The object of ICE-2 is to measure the percentage difference between a spot rate and a future rate in home currency terms when the spot rate and points were expressed in foreign currency terms. Assuming here that spot and points are in foreign currency units, we start with

$$\text{ICE-1} = \frac{\text{points}}{\text{spot}} \times \frac{360}{\text{days}}$$

Just for ease of manipulation, the expression for time is dropped and some symbols are introduced:

$$\text{spot} = S, \text{ points} = P, \text{ and forward (spot} \pm \text{points)} = F$$

The object is to show that

$$\text{ICE-2} = \frac{\text{points}}{\text{forward}} \times \frac{360}{\text{days}}$$

which uses quotes in foreign currency terms, is equivalent to measuring the percentage difference in spot and forward rates expressed in home currency units.

Putting the rates in home currency terms means simply inverting them. Recall also that points can be expressed as $S - F$, or $F - S$.

$$\text{ICE-1 inverted} = \frac{(1/S) - (1/F)}{1/S}$$

The proof that

$$\frac{(1/S) - (1/F)}{1/S} = \frac{P}{F}$$

is as follows:

$$\frac{(1/S) - (1/F)}{1/S} = \left(\frac{1}{S} - \frac{1}{F} \right) \times S = \frac{S}{S} - \frac{S}{F} = 1 - \frac{S}{F} = \frac{F - S}{F} = \frac{P}{F}$$

since $F - S = P$.

Therefore ICE-1 inverted is equal to ICE-2.

CHAPTER SIX
HOW TO READ FOREIGN EXCHANGE RATES

The present chapter unravels the numbers mystery. At what rate do I buy? At what rate do I sell? Why is there a difference between the buying and selling rates, and why does it change from day to day? How do I switch an exchange rate quote from foreign currency terms to home currency terms? How do the forward points relate to the spot rate? When are forward points added and when are they subtracted? What are the conventions for expressing exchange rates?

The *Financial Times* carries the most extensive and accessible daily listing of foreign exchange and money market rates. An excerpt from

THE DOLLAR SPOT AND FORWARD

Aug. 23	Day's spread	Close	One month	% p.a.	Three months	% p.a.
UK†	2.2225-2.2340	2.2240-2.2250	0.40-0.30c pm	1.88	1.17-1.07 pm	2.01
Ireland†	2.0575-2.0630	2.0605-2.0630	1.08-0.98c pm	5.99	3.10-2.95 pm	5.87
Canada	1.1636-1.1660	1.1636-1.1640	0.03-0.06c dis	−0.46	0.06-0.10dis	−0.27
Nethlnd.	2.0075-2.0100	2.0075-2.0095	0.48-0.38c pm	2.57	1.30-1.20 pm	2.49
Belgium	29.30-29.325	29.30-29.315	0.5c pm-1.0 dis	−0.31	1.0 pm-1.0 dis	—
Denmark	5.2710-5.2765	5.2710-5.2725	1.25-1.75ore dis	−3.41	4.25-4.75dis	−3.41
W. Ger.	1.8290-1.8300	1.8290-1.8300	0.75-0.65pf pm	4.59	2.25-2.15 pm	4.81
Portugal	49.13-49.30	49.22-49.30	25-35c dis	−7.31	80-120 dis	−8.12
Spain	66.03-66.10	66.03-66.06	100-120c dis	−19.99	300-320dis	−18.78
Italy	816.85-818.50	818.00-818.50	1.10-1.60lire dis	−1.98	6.0-7.0 dis	−3.18
Norway	5.0335-5.0347	5.0335-5.0345	0.30-0.20ore pm	0.59	0.45-0.05 pm	0.20
France	4.2580-4.2600	4.2580-4.2595	par-0.06 dis	−0.84	0.42-0.52dis	−0.44
Sweden	4.2260-4.2277	4.2265-4.2275	0.05-0.55ore dis	−1.17	0.90-1.10dis	−0.95
Japan	218.90-219.20	219.00-219.20	1.10-0.95y pm	5.6	2.90-2.75 pm	5.16
Austria	13.37-13.381	13.37-13.375	5.80-5.30gro pm	4.98	16.25-14.75pm	4.64
Switz.	1.6557-1.6581	1.6562-1.6570	1.44-1.39c pm	10.25	4.08-4.03 pm	9.79

† UK and Ireland are quoted in U.S. currency. Forward premiums and discounts apply to the U.S. dollar and not to the individual currency.

this newspaper is used as the basis of this chapter—"The Dollar Spot and Forward," August 23, 1979.

Because the clipping is entitled *"Dollar* Spot and Forward," this means that all the rates refer to one U.S. dollar. The country listed in the left of each row identifies the *Currency,* the denomination of all the prices in that row. The two exceptions, as noted, are the United Kingdom (UK) and Ireland. They are expressed as the number of dollars to 1 pound and 1 punt, respectively.

Along the Switzerland row you read:

Aug. 23	Day's Spread	Close
Switz.	1.6557–1.6581	1.6562–1.6570

During the day of August 23 the price of one dollar ranged between 1.6557 and 1.6581 Swiss francs. At the end of the day the spot price was 1.6562 to 1.6570.

Along the Ireland row you read:

Aug. 23	Day's Spread	Close
Ireland	2.0575–2.0630	2.0605–2.0630

During the day of August 23 the price of one Irish punt ranged between U.S. $2.0575 and $2.0630. At the end of the day the spot price was $2.0605–$2.0630.

Why are there two numbers for the spot rate? At the lower rate the customer sells dollars, and at the higher rate the customer buys dollars. The two exceptions are the first two rows; there, the lower rate is the one at which the customer sells pounds, or punt, and the higher rate is the one at which the customer buys. It will be easier to visualize the transaction by using the arrows to represent the currency flows.

Each exchange transaction represents a simultaneous purchase and sale. If dollars are sold, Danish kroner are bought; if dollars are bought, Danish kroner are sold.

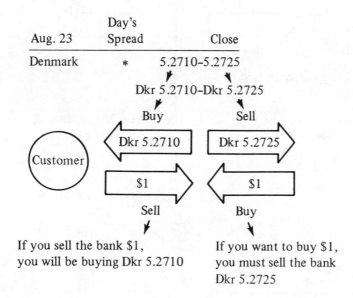

From this point on parts of the present chapter are in the form of a programmed manual; the answers are on the right side of the page. Cover the answers with a blank card until you have answered the question. In the next situations transfer the figures into the arrows to illustrate the transactions to which the figures relate.

	Day's	
Aug. 23	Spread	Close
W. Ger.	*	1.8290–1.8300

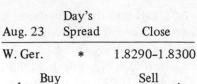

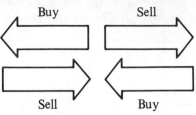

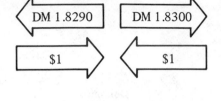

How would you describe each of these transactions?

Left:

Right:

Left: If you sell $1, you will be buying DM 1.8290

Right: If you want to buy $1, you must sell DM 1.8300.

	Day's	
Aug. 23	Spread	Close
Japan	*	219.00–219.20

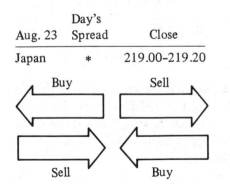

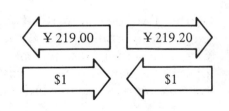

And now for the exception:

Aug. 23	Day's Spread	Close
Ireland	*	2.0605–2.0630

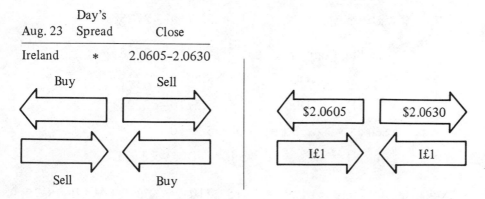

THE CONVENTION FOR QUOTING FX RATES

Aug. 23	Day's Spread	Close
Denmark	*	5.2710–5.2725

The conventional way of expressing this is

$/Dkr 5.2710–25

It is **not** dollars divided by Danish kroner.
It is **not** dollars per Danish kroner.
It **is** the number of Danish kroner per one dollar.

In quoting a rate you would say:
      "THE DOLLAR/DANISH KRONER RATE IS
      FIVE TWENTY-SEVEN TEN TO TWENTY-FIVE."

Aug. 23			Close
Denmark			5.2710–5.2725
Dollar/Denmark			5.2710–5.2725
$/	Dkr		5.2710–5.2725
$1 =	Dkr		5.2710–5.2725
Sell $1 =	buy	Dkr	5.2710
Buy $1 =	sell	Dkr	5.2725

Exchange rates are written $/Dkr 5.2710–25 and £/DM 4.0625–75. The numbers are units of the currency indicated on the right of the slash—Dkr and DM. They are equivalent to one unit of the currency indicated on the left of the slash—$ and £. Here are some exercises in writing exchange rates in the conventional format.

Aug. 23	Day's Spread	Close
Belgium	*	29.30–29.315

How would you quote this rate in words? How would you write it in symbols and numbers?

The dollar/Belgian franc rate is twenty-nine thirty to thirty-one and a half.

$/BF 29.30–315

Aug. 23	Day's Spread	Close
UK	*	2.2240–2.2250

How would you quote this rate in words and write it in symbols and numbers?

The pound/dollar rate is two twenty-two forty to fifty.

£/$2.2240–50

Remember that the pound and the punt are exceptions.

Aug. 23	Day's Spread	Close
Italy	*	?

How would you ask for this rate on the telephone?

What is the dollar/Italian lira spot rate?

In the next situations transfer the figures into the arrows to answer the questions.

The dollar/Swiss franc rate is 1.6562–70. You want to exchange your dollars for Swiss francs. How many Swiss francs will you be able to buy for $100?

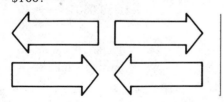

SF 165.62
$/SF 1.6562 ◄──► 70
$1/SF 1.6562 ◄──
$100/SF 165.62

The dollar/Austrian schilling
rate is 13.37–13.375. You
want to purchase Austrian
schillings. At what rate will
you buy them?

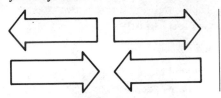

13.37
$/AS 13.37 ◄──► 375
$/AS 13.37 ◄──

The dollar/Spanish peseta rate
is 66.03–06. You want to
sell Spanish pesetas. At what
rate do you sell pesetas?

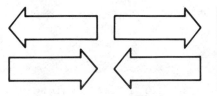

66.06
$/Pts 66.03 ◄──► 66.06
$/Pts   ──► 66.06

Now for the exception:

The Irish punt/dollar rate is
2.0605–30. You want to buy
the punt. At what rate will
you buy the punt?

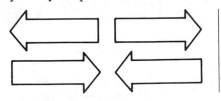

2.0630
I£/$2.0605 ◄──► 30
              ──► 30

To buy the punt, you
must sell dollars.

You can buy U.S. dollars for
2.*XX* Dutch guilders; but if you
sell dollars, you would get 2.*YY*
Dutch guilders for each. How
would you express these rates in
the conventional format?

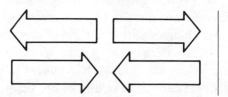

$/DG 2.*YY* - *XX*

The expressions of *bid* and *offer* are often used to describe the two
rates. The *bid* rate is the lower rate, the *offer* rate is the higher one.
These expressions refer to the bank's actions, not the customer's. The
words refer to the currency to the left of the slash. If the spot rate
is $/Skr4.2265–75: The bank *bids* for dollars at 4.2265, and the
customer sells dollars at that rate. The bank *offers* dollars at 4.2275,
the customer buys dollars at that rate.

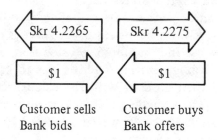

Customer sells   Customer buys
Bank bids   Bank offers

The spread between the bid and the offer rate is typically .05%. The spread exists because of the different views and different interests of the buyers and sellers of a currency. Each will try to make the best deal possible. The sellers offer high, the buyers bid low, and a compromise is reached. Spreads vary during the day and the week and among currencies. The width of the spread is a function of the interest that bank foreign exchange dealers and corporations have in buying or selling a currency at a given time. This interest changes with the time of day—there is greater willingness to deal at 10 a.m. than at 5:30 p.m. There is generally greater interest on Wednesday than on Friday. Willingness to deal is also related to the amount of uncertainty prevailing in the market at a given time concerning what is (1) actually happening (no one knows everything) and (2) expected to happen. Greater uncertainty leads to widening of the spreads.

The spread between the bid and the offer is also influenced by the skill of the dealer who is quoting and his or her interest in the person to whom he or she is speaking. A professional dealer speaking to a good customer will quote a narrow spread.

HOW TO TRANSPOSE RATES

Increasingly in the United States exchange rates are being expressed in terms of European currency units rather than dollars and cents. Not all newspapers express rates both ways, yet there is often a need to see the rate in U.S. terms. In Chapter 5 we saw that one of the ways to deal with a rate in foreign currency terms was to switch it into home currency terms and then proceed with the calculation of ICE. At that point the spot rate was a single number, but now there are two numbers. If we know $/Dkr, how do we find Dkr/$? How do we find the number of dollars per one Danish kroner?

The procedure is simple. Switch the rate on the left over to the right and the one on the right over to the left, and then divide each of them into 1.

$/Dkr 5.2710 – 5.2725

$$5.2725 \quad 5.2710 \qquad \text{Switch positions}$$

$$\frac{1}{5.2725} \quad \frac{1}{5.2710} \qquad \text{Divide into 1}$$

Dkr/$.1896½ – .1897

If you've done it right the number on the left is smaller than the number on the right.

The need to switch the positions of the two rates is more evident when the arrows are used to illustrate the transaction.

$/Dkr 5.2710-5.2725

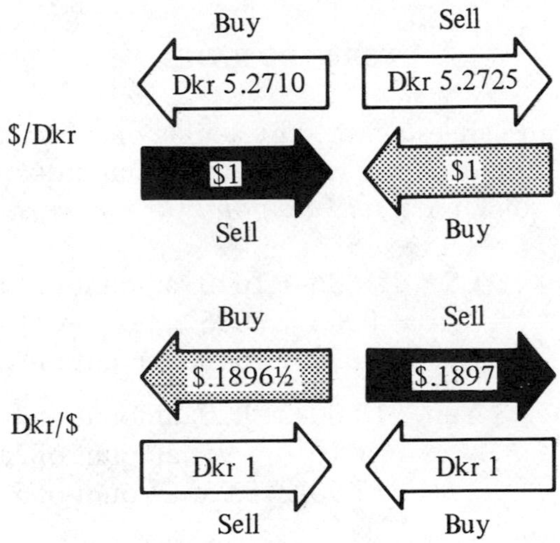

Practice transposing the rates:

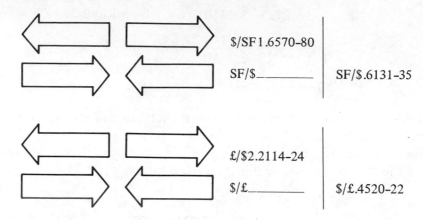

$/SF1.6570–80	
SF/$_____	SF/$.6131–35

£/$2.2114–24	
$/£_____	$/£.4520–22

FORWARD RATES

The forward rates are established by adding or subtracting amounts of currency to or from the spot rate. Those "amounts of currency" are called *points,* or sometimes, *forward points* or *forwards*.

Spot	$/CS	1.1636–1.1640	amount of Canadian dollars
Points		+.0003 +.0006	amount of Canadian dollars
Forward rate		1.1639–1.1646	amount of Canadian dollars
Spot	$/Yen	210.00–219.20	amount of Japanese yen
Points		−1.10 −.95	amount of Japanese yen
Forward rate		217.90–218.25	amount of Japanese yen

The financial newspapers generally report the forward points as units of currency.

THE DOLLAR SPOT AND FORWARD

Aug. 23	Day's spread	Close	One month	% p.a.	Three months	% p.a.
UK†	2.2225-2.2340	2.2240-2.2250	0.40-0.30c pm	1.88	1.17-1.07 pm	2.01
Ireland†	2.0575-2.0630	2.0605-2.0630	1.08-0.98c pm	5.99	3.10-2.95 pm	5.87
Canada	1.1636-1.1660	1.1636-1.1640	0.03-0.06c dis	−0.46	0.06-0.10dis	−0.27
Nethlnd.	2.0075-2.0100	2.0075-2.0095	0.48-0.38c pm	2.57	1.30-1.20 pm	2.49
Belgium	29.30-29.325	29.30-29.315	0.5c pm-1.0 dis	−0.31	1.0 pm-1.0 dis	—
Denmark	5.2710-5.2765	5.2710-5.2725	1.25-1.75ore dis	−3.41	4.25-4.75dis	−3.41
W. Ger.	1.8290-1.8300	1.8290-1.8300	0.75-0.65pf pm	4.59	2.25-2.15 pm	4.81
Portugal	49.13-49.30	49.22-49.30	25-35c dis	−7.31	80-120 dis	−8.12
Spain	66.03-66.10	66.03-66.06	100-120c dis	−19.99	300-320dis	−18.78
Italy	816.85-818.50	818.00-818.50	1.10-1.60lire dis	−1.98	6.0-7.0 dis	−3.18
Norway	5.0335-5.0347	5.0335-5.0345	0.30-0.20ore pm	0.59	0.45-0.05 pm	0.20
France	4.2580-4.2600	4.2580-4.2595	par-0.06 dis	−0.84	0.42-0.52dis	−0.44
Sweden	4.2260-4.2277	4.2265-4.2275	0.05-0.55ore dis	−1.17	0.90-1.10dis	−0.95
Japan	218.90-219.20	219.00-219.20	1.10-0.95y pm	5.6	2.90-2.75 pm	5.16
Austria	13.37-13.381	13.37-13.375	5.80-5.30gro pm	4.98	16.25-14.75pm	4.64
Switz.	1.6557-1.6581	1.6562-1.6570	1.44-1.39c pm	10.25	4.08-4.03 pm	9.79

† UK and Ireland are quoted in U.S. currency. Forward premiums and discounts apply to the U.S. dollar and not to the individual currency.

The abbreviations pm and dis are discussed in Chapter 9. The column % p.a. is calculated by using formula ICE-1 on the midrates. The c stands for cents, centimes, and centavos; pf stands for pfennig; and gro stands for groschen. The common feature is that they are 1/100 of the currency unit—dollars, francs, pesetas, marks, schillings, kroner, and so on. A number that is written as .30c is .0030 dollars or francs; a number written as 1.25 ore is .0125 kroner. The word *par* means zero, no points; the forward rate is the same as the spot rate. Very often banks and currency information services will write points simply as numerals:

Spot	1 mo	2 mo	3 mo	6 mo
£/$2.1015–20	45–40	78–73	107–102	190–185
$/DM 1.8035–40	77–74	162–158	242–238	459–451
$/Lit 815.50	30–60	145–195	300–360•	850–1000
$/BF 29.05–07	2-par	2-par	2½-par	1–3

Then it is not possible to know how many units of the currency the points represent until they are related to the spot rate. There are *three rules for positioning forward points so they can be added to or subtracted from spot*:

1. The sides of the spot and points are lined up, with left side of points with left side of spot, and right side of points with right side of spot.

Spot	Points
$/AS 13.37–39	5–6

The 5 goes with 13.37, the 6 goes with 13.39.

2. Line the points up on the right.

Spot	1 mo		
£/$2.1015–20	45–40	2.1015	2.1020
		45	40

Spot	6 mo		
$/Lit 815.50–80	850–1000	815.50	815.80
		850	1000

3. If there is a fraction involved, line up the numerals as though the fraction were not there, and then tag the fraction on.

Spot	3 mo		
$/BF 20.05–07	$2\frac{1}{2}$–par	29.05	29.07
		$2\frac{1}{2}$	0

Place the following spot rate and points in the proper position for combining. Answers are on the right.

Spot	Points	
A. $/DG 2.0075–95	48–38	A. 2.0075–2.0095
		48 38
B. $/Pts 60.03–06	100–120c	B. 60.03–60.06
		1.00 1.20
C. £/$2.1015–20	$3\frac{1}{4}$–$2\frac{1}{2}$	C. 2.1015–2.1020
		$3\frac{1}{4}$ $2\frac{1}{2}$
D. $/Nkr 5.0335–45	0.30–0.20 ore	D. 5.0335–5.0345
		30 20

There are *two rules for adding and subtracting forward points.* You can determine whether to add or subtract by looking at the pair of points. Do the numbers go up like 5, 6 from right to left, or do the numbers go down like 10, 9 from right to left?

1. If the numbers go up (right side higher than left side), add the points.
2. If the numbers go down (right side lower than left side), subtract the points.

Calculate the forward rates in the following cases:

Currency	Spot	Points	Forward	
$/DM	1.7514–19	10–7	?	1.7504–12
I£/$	2.0114–18	450–440	?	1.9664–78
DG/$	.5104–06	12–14	?	.5116–20

To check your calculation of the forward rates, add the difference between the two sides of the spot to the difference between the two sides of the points. The sum is the difference between the two sides of the forward rate.

	Spot	Points	Forward
	$/Skr4.2265–75	90–110	4.2355–85
	↓	↓	↓
Difference	10 +	20 =	30

If you subtracted rather than added:

	Spot	Points	Forward
	$/Skr4.2265–75	90–110	4.2175–65
	↓	↓	↓
Difference	10 +	20 ≠	10

This result says that someone is willing to pay more for their money than they are selling it for. No market works this way. The interest of people in the market provides another perspective on the wider spread of the forward quotation compared with the spot. It was explained earlier how the spread between the two sides of the spot quote depended on the interest of buyers and sellers. The points represent an operation that covers time. The spread between the points depends on the interest of borrowers and lenders to cover time. A forward transaction is a spot transaction plus a time transaction and should reflect both interests. Therefore, the spread on the forward quotation should incorporate the spread of the spot plus the spread of the points.

Calculate the forward price and check the calculation.

	Spot	Points	Forward	
	$/FF4.2580–95	.042–0.52c		4.2622–47
	↓	↓	↓	
Difference	+	=		

To choose the correct side of the forward rate, the following system will work:

A. At what rate will you contract today to buy dollars and sell escudos in three months? Answer for both quotations.

Spot	Points	
$/Esc 49.22–30	25–35	49.30
		+35
		$/Esc 49.65
Esc/$ .02028–32	14–10	.02028
		−14
		Esc/$ .02014

B. At what rate will you contract today to buy Swiss francs and sell dollars in one month? Answer for both quotations.

Spot	Points	
		1.6030
$/SF 1.6030–40	140–135	−140
		$/SF 1.5890
SF/$ .6234–38	53–35	.6238
		+55
		SF/$ .6293

Earlier, the spot rate was inverted to switch from a rate expressed in foreign terms to one expressed in home currency terms. Very clearly the same procedure can be used to switch the expression of the forward rate. Sometimes, however, there is a need for only switching the expression of the points. The usual method for switching points from foreign currency terms to home currency terms is to (1) switch the spot, (2) switch the forward, and (3) subtract. Points cannot be simply inverted.

In the last two problems the rates are the same, only expressed differently, but there is no evident relationship between these points: $/SF 140–135 and SF/$ 53–55. A relation does exist and can be used to make the switch quickly. If we say that P = points of $/SF and P^* = points of SF/$ and S and F are the spot and forward rates of $/SF, respectively, then $P^* = P/(S \times F)$.[†]

$$\text{SF/\$.0055} = \frac{.0140}{1.6030 \times 1.5890}$$

$$\text{SF/\$.0053} = \frac{.0135}{1.6040 \times 1.5905}$$

INTEREST RATES

Reading money market rates is somewhat easier than exchange rates. Shown is an excerpt of Eurocurrency rates for various currencies:

†Proof of this relation is in the Appendix at the end of the present chapter.

EURO-CURRENCY INTEREST RATES

The folowing nominal rates were quoted for London dollar certificates of deposit — one month 11.45-11.55 per cent; three months 11.65-11.75 per cent; six months 11.65-11.75 per cent; one year 11.20-11.30 per cent.

Aug. 23	Sterling	U.S. Dollar	Canadian Dollar	Dutch Guilder	Swiss Franc	West German Mark	French Franc	Italian Lira	Asian $	Japanese Yen
†Short term	n.a.	$11\frac{1}{8}$-$11\frac{3}{8}$	$10\frac{1}{2}$-$11\frac{1}{2}$	$9\frac{1}{8}$-$9\frac{3}{8}$	$\frac{1}{2}$-$\frac{7}{8}$	$6\frac{5}{8}$-$6\frac{3}{4}$	$10\frac{1}{2}$-$10\frac{3}{4}$	10-13	$12\frac{3}{4}$-$12\frac{7}{8}$	$4\frac{5}{8}$-$9\frac{1}{2}$
7 days' notice	n.a.	$11\frac{1}{4}$-$11\frac{1}{2}$	$10\frac{1}{2}$-$11\frac{1}{2}$	$8\frac{1}{2}$-$8\frac{3}{4}$	$\frac{7}{8}$-1	$6\frac{5}{8}$-$6\frac{7}{8}$	$10\frac{1}{2}$-$10\frac{3}{4}$	$11\frac{1}{2}$-$12\frac{1}{2}$	$12\frac{1}{2}$-$12\frac{1}{2}$	$5\frac{5}{8}$-$6\frac{3}{4}$
Month	14-$14\frac{1}{4}$	$12\frac{1}{8}$-$12\frac{3}{8}$	$11\frac{1}{2}$-$11\frac{7}{8}$	$8\frac{7}{8}$-$9\frac{1}{8}$	$1\frac{5}{8}$-$1\frac{3}{4}$	$6\frac{7}{8}$-7	$11\frac{1}{2}$-$11\frac{3}{4}$	13-14	$10\frac{3}{4}$-$10\frac{7}{8}$	$6\frac{1}{4}$-$6\frac{3}{4}$
three months	14-$14\frac{1}{4}$	$11\frac{3}{4}$-12	$11\frac{1}{8}$-$11\frac{1}{2}$	$9\frac{1}{8}$-$9\frac{3}{8}$	$1\frac{7}{8}$-2	7-$7\frac{1}{8}$	$12\frac{3}{8}$-$12\frac{7}{8}$	$13\frac{3}{4}$-$14\frac{3}{4}$	$11\frac{7}{8}$-$11\frac{7}{8}$	$6\frac{1}{2}$-$6\frac{3}{4}$
six months	14-$14\frac{1}{4}$	$11\frac{7}{8}$-$12\frac{1}{8}$	$11\frac{1}{8}$-$11\frac{1}{2}$	$9\frac{1}{8}$-$9\frac{3}{8}$	$2\frac{1}{2}$-$2\frac{5}{8}$	$7\frac{1}{4}$-$7\frac{3}{8}$	$12\frac{5}{8}$-$12\frac{7}{8}$	$14\frac{3}{4}$-$15\frac{3}{4}$	$11\frac{1}{8}$-$11\frac{1}{8}$	$6\frac{1}{2}$-$6\frac{3}{4}$
one year	$13\frac{1}{2}$-$13\frac{7}{8}$	$11\frac{1}{4}$-12	$11\frac{1}{8}$-$11\frac{1}{2}$	9-$9\frac{1}{4}$	$2\frac{7}{8}$-3	$7\frac{1}{8}$-$7\frac{3}{8}$	$12\frac{5}{8}$-$12\frac{7}{8}$	15-16	$11\frac{1}{4}$-$11\frac{3}{8}$	$6\frac{1}{2}$-$6\frac{1}{2}$

Long-term Eurodollar: two years $10\frac{3}{4}$-$10\frac{7}{8}$ per cent; three years $10\frac{9}{16}$-$10\frac{11}{16}$ per cent; four years $10\frac{7}{16}$-$10\frac{11}{16}$ per cent; five years $10\frac{3}{8}$-$10\frac{1}{2}$ per cent; nominal closing rates. Short-term rates are call for sterling; U.S. dollars and Canadian dollars; two-day call for guilders and Swiss francs. Asian rates are closing rates in Singapore.

Interest rates are also quoted with two sides. A quote of $9-9\frac{1}{4}\%$ for one year guilders means that the customer places money at 9% and borrows guilders for one year at $9\frac{1}{4}\%$ plus the bank lending spread.* In terms of the arrow conventions for borrowing and investing:

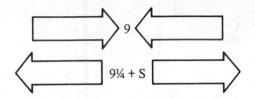

APPENDIX

The object is to show a simple relationship between points expressed in foreign currency and points expressed in home currency.

Define P = points in foreign currency
Define P^* = points in home currency
Define S = spot in foreign currency
Define F = forward in foreign currency

Then $\dfrac{1}{S}$ = spot in home currency

From Chapter 5 we have the relationship that

$$\frac{P}{F} = \frac{P^*}{1/S}$$

where P/F is ICE-2. If both sides are multiplied by $1/S$, then $P^* = P/(S \times F)$.

---

*The bank calculates that it will pay $9\frac{1}{4}\%$ for the money and charges the customer an additional percentage to cover expenses and generate profits.

CHAPTER SEVEN

THE HOOPER COMPANY

You are the assistant treasurer of The Hooper Company in Houston, Texas. It is your job to determine the exposure from the cash flow schedule, decide what options can be used to eliminate the exposure, compare the cost/earning of each option, choose the best option, and decide whether to take action now. The discussion of this case illustrates a way of solving a foreign exchange exposure problem quickly and thoroughly.

The Hooper Company has its headquarters in Houston. Two subsidiaries are located in Ireland and Germany. The company produces electrical switching gears for power plants and oil-field-related electric machines. There is active intercompany trading because each factory is specialized, but the sales units are not. The sales units in each country market all the company's products. Each subsidiary manages its own exposure.

Cash Flow Schedule for The Hooper Company, Houston

| | October | | | | | | | |
	5	6	7	10	11	12	13	14
U.S. $(millions)		5	-5		-3	-1	1	
DM (millions)			3					-3
I£ (millions)			8				-8	

	17	18	19	20	21	24	25	26	27	28
U.S. $	-1	1		-2	-1	3	3	3	-1	
DM	2	2	-2	-3	1				4	-4

| | November | | | | | | | | | |
	31	1	2	3	4	7	8	9	10	11
U.S. $	1	10	2	-1	-1	-4	7	-1	-4	-4
DM	-1	1				-5				
I£			6					-6		

	14	15	16	17	18
U.S. $	4	-2	1	5	6
DM			1	-1	
I£	2	-1	-1		

The numbers without a sign in front of them indicate an inflow of the currency from sales or maturing deposits; those with a minus sign indicate an outflow, payments to be made. Because of the billing cycle and the investment strategy the assistant treasurer can assume that there will be no other foreign currency inflows or outflows during the period shown.

IDENTIFYING THE EXPOSURE

The cash flow schedule is for the U.S. operation of Hooper. For foreign exchange exposure purposes, there is no need to consider the U.S. dollar flows since the dollar is the home currency. The Deutsche mark and Irish punt flows have to be examined.

Deutsche Mark

An inflow on October 7 and an outflow of the same amount on October 14—the flows can be offset by depositing the incoming funds for one week. The maturing deposit will be used to settle the outflow. Small inflows and outflows the weeks of October 17 and 24—these will be offset by short-term deposits and borrowings executed when the time arrives. One day mismatch the week of October 31—this will be offset by borrowing Deutsche marks for one day. This borrowing will normally be executed two business days ahead, October 27. Outflow of DM 5 million the week of November 7—this outflow is unmatched by any inflows of the currency. This outflow constitutes an exposure for The Hooper Company's Houston office; it has a foreign currency payable due in 31 days. The exposure is symbolized as

31 days

Irish Punt

An inflow on October 7 and an outflow of the same amount on October 13—the flows can be matched by depositing the currency for six days. The transaction would normally be executed October 5. An inflow on November 2 and an outflow of the same amount on November 9—On October 31 the assistant treasurer will arrange with his bank to place 6 million punt in an interest bearing deposit starting November 2, for one week. The confirmation that Hooper would receive for this deposit from his bank would look like this*:

138a

BANK OF AMERICA

☆ TIME DEPOSIT CONFIRMATION

☐ SETTLEMENT ADVICE

☐ TRACER

TO

The Hooper Company
100 Travis Street
Houston, Texas   77001

| ACCOUNT | REF. | DATE Oct 31, 1979 |

BROKER   Telephone

WE CONFIRM   [X] YOUR DEPOSIT WITH US   ☐ OUR DEPOSIT WITH YOU

AMOUNT 6,000,000.00	CURRENCY Irish punt			
INTEREST 18,986.00	RATE .165	BASIS 365	FROM Nov 2, 1979	TO Nov 9, 1979	CALL
TOTAL 6,018,986.00				

WE PAY YOU ON Nov 9, 1979

REMITTANCE TO
a/c 17948 Bank of America, Dublin

THROUGH

YOU PAY US ON Nov 2, 1979

REMITTANCE TO
Bank of America, Dublin

THROUGH

SPECIAL INSTRUCTIONS

PLEASE CONFIRM BY SIGNING. DATING AND RETURNING TO US THE ACKNOWLEDGEMENT COPY. UNLESS YOU HAVE ALREADY FORWARDED YOUR CONFIRMATION ADVICE TO US

AUTHORIZED SIGNATURE/TITLE

CUSTOMER CONFIRMATION

CONFIRMED   DATE_____

AUTHORIZED SIGNATURE

Copies:
1. Customer Copy (White)
2. Acknowledgement Copy (Canary)
3. File Copy #3296 (Pink)
BOND-5 3-79- BANK OF AMERICA NT & SA

*Reprinted with permission from Bank of America NT&SA.

Most of the items are self-explanatory, with the exception of *basis*. This indicates the denominator used in the interest calculation. With a 365-day basis the interest amount is calculated as

$$\text{principal} \times \text{rate} \times \frac{\text{days}}{365}$$

This basis is used for the pound sterling and the punt. For most other currencies, the basis is 360, meaning the interest amount is calculated as

$$\text{principal} \times \text{rate} \times \frac{\text{days}}{360}$$

The Appendix shows how to make interest rates on different bases comparable.

An inflow of Irish punt on November 14 and outflows on the two subsequent days—when the time arrives the assistant treasurer would place I£1 million on deposit for one day and I£1 million on deposit for two days.

A thorough examination of the cash flow schedule shows that the only exposure which Hooper Houston is concerned with today is the outflow of DM 5 million in 31 days.

OPTIONS

The three basic options for covering the Deutsche mark payable are (1) Forward contract to buy DM, (2) BSI—borrow dollars for one month, sell the dollars spot to buy DM, and invest the DM for one month, and (3) Lead—borrow dollars for one month, sell the dollars spot to buy Deutsche marks, and lead the payment to the German affiliate.

PRICES

Forward: The price is composed of the spot rate and the external interest rates of dollars and Deutsche marks. The interest rates are expressed in currency units by the forward points.

BSI: Hooper will borrow domestic dollars, exchange them on the spot date for Deutsche marks, and invest the DM in the Euromark market for one month.

Lead: Hooper will generally borrow domestic dollars, although there is nothing hindering the company from borrowing external dollars (the two alternatives will be considered); the dollars are sold spot for Deutsche marks, the Deutsche marks are then paid to the German affiliate, and Hooper Houston will earn domestic German interest for one month.

OPTIONS AND PRICES SYMBOLIZED

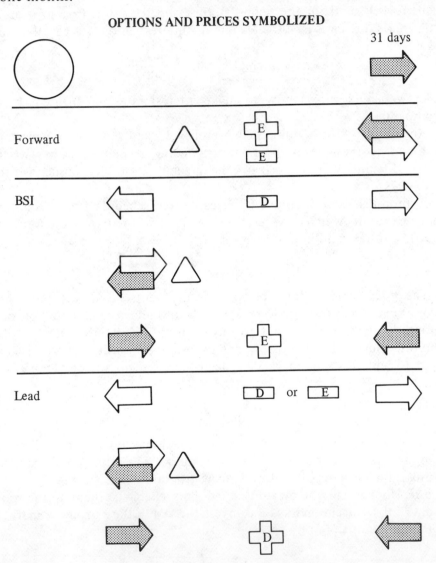

The information now required is: Spot and one-month forward points for dollars/marks; domestic and Eurocurrency interest rates for dollars and marks.

FOREIGN EXCHANGE AND MONEY MARKET RATES

The Hooper Company has arranged with its bank for a facility to borrow money for a fixed period at a fixed rate. The rate for one month is set at $\frac{1}{2}\%$ over the bank's prime rate on the day the advance is made. Hooper's line of credit with its bank also specifies that the company pay $\frac{3}{4}\%$ over the cost of money for external currency borrowings. A bank's cost can be higher than the indicated rate in the newspaper if it is lending external currency to a domestic customer. Central banks often impose reserves on these borrowings. At this time there is no reserve requirement.

The affiliates of Hooper have agreed among one another to pay the market rate in the local country for accelerating payments.

SELECTING THE RATES

The spot rate and forward points for Deutsche marks are found in the section "The Dollar Spot and Forward."

Financial Times Friday October 5 1979

Companies and Markets

CURRENCIES, MONEY and GOLD

EURO-CURRENCY INTEREST RATES

The following nominal rates were quoted for London dollar certificates of deposit; one-month 12.55-12.65 per cent; three months 13.00-13.10 per cent; six months 13.0-13.10 per cent; one year 13.10-13.20 per cent.

Oct. 4	Sterling	U.S. Dollar	Canadian Dollar	Dutch Guilder	Swiss Franc	West German Mark	French Franc	Italian Lira	Asian $	Japanese Yen
†Short term	13 5/8-13 7/8	12 1/8-12 3/8	10 1/2-11 1/2	9 1/4-9 1/2	1/2-3/4	7 3/8-7 1/2	11 1/2-11 3/4	9 1/2-10 1/2	—	11 1/16-4 1/4
7 days' notice	13 1/4-13 3/4	12 1/4-12 1/2	10 1/2-11 1/2	9 1/4-9 1/2	1/2-1 3/4	7 3/16-7 7/16	11 1/2-11 3/4	11 3/4-13 3/4	12 1/4-12 3/8	4 3/8-6
Month	13 3/4-14	13 5/8-13 7/8	11 1/4-11 5/8	9 5/16-9 9/16	1-1 1/8	7 3/16-7 5/16	11 7/8-12 1/4	13 1/2-14 1/2	13 5/8-13 3/4	6 1/8-6 3/4
three months	14 1/16-14 7/16	13 1/8-13 3/8	11 3/4-12 1/8	9 1/2-9 3/4	1 5/16-1 7/16	7 5/8-7 11/16	12 3/4-13 1/8	14 1/2-15 1/2	13 1/16-13 3/16	7 1/4-7 5/8
six months	13 7/8-14 1/8	13 1/8-13 3/8	11 13/16-12 1/16	9 5/8-9 5/8	2-2 1/8	7 5/8-7 11/16	12 3/4-13 1/8	14 3/4-15 3/4	13 1/16-13 3/16	7 3/16-7 1/2
one year	13 1/2-13 3/4	12 7/16-12 11/16	11 3/8-11 3/4	9 1/8-9 5/8	2 5/16-2 7/16	7 1/2-7 5/8	12 3/4-13 1/8	14 3/4-15 3/4	12 7/16-12 9/16	6 5/8-7

Long-term Eurodollar two years 11 3/8-11 1/2 per cent; three years 11 1/8-11 1/4 per cent; four years 11-11 1/8 per cent; five years 10 15/16-11 1/16 per cent; nominal closing rates. Short-term rates are call for sterling, U.S. dollars and Canadian dollars; two-day call for guilders and Swiss francs. Asian rates are closing rates in Singapore.

MONEY RATES

NEW YORK

Prime Rate	13.5
Fed Funds	11.78
Treasury Bills (13-week)	10.27
Treasury Bills (26-week)	10.42

GERMANY

Discount Rate	5
Overnight Rate	8.25
One month	7.85
Three months	8.30
Six months	8.15

FRANCE

Discount Rate	9.5
Overnight Rate	11.375
One month	11.5625
Three months	11.6875
Six months	11.6875

JAPAN

Discount Rate	5.25
Call (Unconditional)	6.6875
Bills Discount (three-month)	7.25

THE DOLLAR SPOT AND FORWARD

Oct. 4	Day's spread	Close	One month	% p.a.	Three months	% p.a.
UK†	2.1775-2.1975	2.1870-2.1880	0.08-0.02c pm	0.27	0.48-0.38 pm	0.79
Ireland†	2.1150-2.1325	2.1150-2.1200	0.90-0.70c pm	4.53	2.50-2.25 pm	4.49
Canada	1.1610-1.1670	1.1636-1.1641	0.01c pm-0.02dis	−0.15	0.19-0.15 pm	0.58
Nethlnd.	1.9465-1.9610	1.9590-1.9610	0.73-0.63c pm	4.16	1.73-1.63 pm	3.43
Belgium	28.35-28.54	28.48-28.50	3-1 1/2c pm	0.95	3-1 pm	0.28
Denmark	5.1315-5.1615	5.1600-5.1615	3.75-4.25ore dis	−9.30	9.50-10.0dis	−7.56
W. Ger.	1.7520-1.7655	1.7627-1.7637	1.0-0.90pf pm	6.46	2.39-2.29 pm	5.31
Portugal	49.20-49.35	49.25-49.35	25-40c dis	−7.91	75-125 dis	−8.11
Spain	66.04-66.07	66.04-66.07	30-40c dis	−6.36	100-115 dis	−6.51
Italy	808.75-815.00	814.50-815.00	par-0.40 dis	−0.29	3.5-4.0 dis	−1.84
Norway	4.8690-4.9100	4.9090-4.9100	2.5-3.5ore dis	−7.33	2.0-3.0 dis	−2.04
France	4.1435-4.1560	4.1435-4.1475	0.70-0.55c pm	1.81	0.50-0.35 pm	0.41
Sweden	4.1380-4.1630	4.1620-4.1630	0.85-0.65ore pm	2.16	0.85-0.65 pm	0.72
Japan	221.80-223.30	223.00-223.20	1.45-1.30y pm	7.39	3.30-3.15 pm	5.78
Austria	12.64-12.71	12.68-12.69	6.40-5.90gro pm	5.82	14.25-12.75pm	4.26
Switz.	1.5750-1.5895	1.5815-1.5830	1.72-1.67c pm	12.85	4.45-4.40 pm	11.19

† UK and Ireland are quoted in U.S. currency. Forward premiums and discounts apply to the U.S. dollar and not to the individual currency.

INTERNATIONAL MONEY MARKET

French rates steady

Interest rates continued to show a stable trend in Paris yesterday, with market conditions described as calm. At the regular tender held by the Bank of France, the Bank bought FFr 2.3bn of first category paper form the market at an unchanged rate of 11¼ per cent. Valuation is today and applies to paper maturing between October 11 and 15.

Interbank rates again showed very little movement, with call money at 11⅜ per cent, a level held since Monday, and one-month money at 11½-11⅝ per cent. The three and six-month rates were static at 11⅝-11¾ per cent and 12-month funds were quoted at 11⅝-11¾ per cent.

FRANKFURT — Call money was quoted firmer at 8.20-8.30 per cent compared with 8.00-8.20 per cent on Wednesday and 4.75-5.25 per cent a week ago. One-month money eased slightly to 7.80-7.90 per cent from 7.85-7.95 per cent, and three-month money was unchanged at 8.25-8.35 per cent. The six-month rate edged slightly firmed to 8.10-8.20 per cent from 8.00-8.10 per cent, with 12-month money at 7.90-8.10 per cent compared with 7.95-8.05 per cent, thus producing a slightly reverse yield curve. At yesterday's meeting of the Bundesbank's central council, credit policies were left unchanged, much in line with market expectations.

AMSTERDAM —Interbank money rates were firmer where changed yesterday, with call money rising to 9⅛-9⅜ per cent from 9¼-9⅜ per cent while the one-month rate remained at 9⅛-9⅜ per cent. Three-month funds rose to 9¾-10⅛ per cent from 9⅝-10 per cent but six-month money was unchanged at 9⅜-9⅝ per cent.

HONG KONG—Conditions in the money market were quite comfortable, with call money at 11¼ per cent and overnight business dealt at 10¾ per cent.

Oct. 4	Day's Spread	Close	One Month
W. Ger.	*	1.7627–1.7637	1.0-0.90 pf

The spot rate is $/DM 1.7627–37. Since a pfennig is $\frac{1}{100}$ of a mark, the points are .0100–.0090 in terms of the spot rate.

Forward

Hooper may arrange a purchase of Deutsche marks forward. At $/DM 1.7627 the company buys Deutsche marks on the spot date by giving dollars. One month hence the company can buy Deutsche marks at 1.7527. The points are subtracted since the numbers go down from .0100 to .0090.

Borrow–Spot–Invest

Hooper would borrow domestic dollars at 14% for one month. In the section "Money Rates" the prime rate is $13\frac{1}{2}$ % and the company pays an additional $\frac{1}{2}$ % for a fixed rate for one month. The borrowed dollars would be exchanged for Deutsche marks at $/DM 1.7627. The Deutsche marks would be invested in the Eurocurrency market at $7\frac{3}{16}$ % (7.1875%). This rate is found in the section titled "Euro-currency Interest Rates," column "West German Mark," line "month." The lower number is chosen since the company is investing.

Lead

The company can borrow either domestically at 14% or in the Euro-dollar market at $13\frac{7}{8}$ % cost of funds plus $\frac{3}{4}$ % lending spread. Borrowing domestically is cheaper. The spot rate is again $/DM 1.7627. To find the rate that the German affiliate will pay, Hooper can consult "International Money Market"—Frankfurt and find 7.80–7.90% for one month. Hooper knows that the German affiliate will pay the lower rate.

The information Hooper has gathered can be summarized in the following matrix.

| Option | Spot, $/DM | Net Interest Cost/Earning | | | Points | Locked-In Future Rate |
		I_h	I_f	Net		
Forward	1.7627				100	1.7527
BSI	1.7627	−14	+ 7.1875	−6.8125%		
Lead	1.7627	−14	+ 7.8	−6.2%		

EVALUATION OF OPTIONS

There is a cost to covering the Deutsche mark exposure because the cost of borrowing dollars is greater than the earnings from investing marks. The cost is also signified by the forward rate—$1 buys fewer marks in the future as compared with today. The Lead is preferable to the BSI because the cost is lower. We don't know about the Forward. To make the comparison convert the forward points to percent by using formula ICE-2.

$$\text{ICE-2} = \frac{\text{points}}{\text{forward}} \times \frac{360}{\text{days}} \times 100$$

Formula ICE-2 is used for the conversion because the exchange rate is expressed in numbers of Deutsche marks, but the home currency is dollars.* The calculation is as follows:

$$\frac{.0100}{1.7527} \times \frac{360}{31} \times 100 = 6.63\%$$

*See Chapter 5.

This cost is greater than the cost of the Lead. The assistant treasurer of Hooper concludes that the best option for covering this exposure is the Lead.

The next step is to calculate the Points and the locked-in future rate for the Lead; it will also be done for the BSI.

$$\text{Lead points} = \frac{1.7627 \times (.14 - .078) \times 31/360}{1 + (.078 \times 31/360)} = \frac{.0094108}{1.006716} = .0093$$

$$\text{Locked-in future rate} = 1.7534$$

$$\text{BSI points} = \frac{1.7627 \times (.14 - .071875) \times 31/360}{1 + (.071875 \times 31/360)} = \frac{.0103405}{1.006189} = 0.103$$

$$\text{Locked-in future rate} = 1.7524$$

The completed matrix for the Hooper Company is as follows:

Option	Spot, $/DM	Net Interest Cost/Earning I_h		I_f	Net	Points	Locked-In Future Rate	Dollar Cost of DM 5 million
Forward	1.7627				−6.63%	100	1.7527	$2,852,741.40
BSI	1.7627	−14	+	7.1875	−6.8125%	103	1.7524	$2,853,229.80
Lead	1.7627	−14	+	7.80	−6.20%	93	1.7534	$2,851,602.60

The additional column shows that the Lead option represents a savings of $1,627.20 over the BSI and $1,138.80 over the Forward.

TO COVER OR NOT TO COVER

Using an analytic approach, Hooper has been able to derive the best solution for covering this exposure. However, having found the best solution, the company must then decide whether to cover the exposure or not. This is a judgment to be made in light of forecasts for the currency and interest rates and the best locked-in future rate. If it were believed that at anytime within the next month the exposure could be covered at a better rate than $/DM 1.7534, nothing would be done immediately. The elements to watch are interest rates, time, and the spot rate. An increase in U.S. dollar interest rates and/or a decrease in mark interest rates would increase the cost of covering. As the payment date approaches, however, the absolute cost of covering is reduced. This is evident from the top portion of the Points formula:

$$\text{Spot} \times (I_h - I_f) \times \frac{\text{days}}{360}$$

A decrease in days reduces the number of points and so narrows the difference between the spot rate and forward rate. The spot rate is the element most likely to change. In the short run the spot rate is subject to unexpected economic and political announcements, central bank intervention in the exchange markets, seasonal influences, and sudden shifts in the underlying sentiment about currency. The cost of 6.20% per annum is equivalent to an absolute cost of only $\frac{1}{2}$ % in a month. During unsettled periods exchange rates have changed that much in one morning.

WALKING THROUGH AN EXPOSURE SITUATION

The process for analyzing an exposure situation can be summarized in the following steps:

1. Identify the exposure.
2. Represent the exposure with symbols.
3. Represent all options that will cover the exposure.
4. Identify the foreign exchange and money markets the options will use.
5. Select the necessary rates from the newspaper or call the bank for the most recent rates.
6. Fill in the matrix with all known interest and exchange rates.
7. Use the formula to convert points to percent and vice versa.
8. Complete the matrix.
9. Choose the best option.
10. Compare the cost/earning of the best option and the locked-in future rate to the currency forecast.

If the decision is made not to cover now, the decision maker is saying that sometime between today and the future date it will be possible to exchange foreign currency for home currency at a price better than the best options available today.

THE HOOPER COMPANY AND ITS FRENCH SUBSIDIARY

This part of the chapter describes briefly a situation similar to the preceding one but involving headquarters in Houston and the French subsidiary. A large shipment has just arrived at the port of Houston. The electrical equipment contained therein has been invoiced at FF 15 million. The money is due to the French affiliate in 90 days. The assistant treasurer must decide how to cover the exposure. This situation is intended as an exercise for those who wish to have more practice with the analytical process and calculations.

The rates are the same as those previously given. The arrangements with the bank and with the affiliates specified there still apply. The completed matrix follows.

SOLUTION

Exposure is an outflow of FF 15,000,000 in 90 days.

Option	Spot	Net Interest/Cost Earning				Points	Locked-In Future Rate	Dollar Cost of FF 15 Million
		I_h		I_f	Net			
Forward	4.1435				$-.48\%$	50	4.1385	$3,624,501.60
BSI	4.1435	-14	$+$	$12\frac{3}{4}$	$-1\frac{1}{4}\%$	125	4.1310	$3,631,082.00
Lead	4.1435	-14	$+$	$11\frac{5}{8}$	$-2\frac{3}{8}\%$	239	4.1196	$3,641,130.20

The Forward is the best option because it costs the least to cover the exposure this way. The BSI and the Lead change rankings as compared with the previous situation because of the relative levels of the external and domestic interest rates. In Germany the domestic rate was higher than the external; therefore, the Lead is better than the BSI. In France the external is higher than the domestic; therefore, the BSI is better.

APPENDIX

Adjusting Interest Rates for Accrual Basis

With the same principal and same interest rate the interest amount calculated on the 365-day basis is less than that figured on a 360-day basis. To compare two rates on different bases, it is necessary to make an adjustment. For example:

10%–360-day basis:

$$1,000,000 \times .10 \times \frac{180}{360} = 50,000$$

10%–365-day basis:

$$1,000,000 \times .10 \times \frac{180}{365} = 49,315.07$$

The 10%–365-day basis is made comparable to the 10%–360-day basis by multiplying 10% by 360/365. This makes the rate 9.8630136%. The calculation is

9.8630136–360-day basis:

$$1,000,000 \times .098630136 \times \frac{180}{360} = 49,315.07$$

To compare pound sterling and punt interest rates to those of other currencies, multiply the pound and punt rates by 360/365.

CHAPTER EIGHT
CROSS RATES AND CROSS-CURRENCY EXPOSURES

"Cross" refers to an exchange rate or an exposure between two currencies, neither of which is your home currency. If you live in The Netherlands, the exchange rate between the Austrian schilling and the French franc would be a cross rate. It is common, however, to say that a cross rate is any rate where the U.S. dollar is not part of the expression. The reason is that in the interbank market for foreign exchange the exchange rate is quoted in terms of the U.S. dollar regardless of the country. The word cross is also descriptive of the procedure for calculating the rate between the Austrian schilling and the French franc when we start with the dollar/Austrian schilling rate and the dollar/French franc rate.

We now look at the uses of cross rates and how they are calculated. The European Monetary System (EMS), a system of limits on currency movement, is examined. The uses of the EMS in exposure situations are explored, and a company exposure situation featuring a cross-currency exposure is considered.

USE OF CROSS RATES

The corporate treasuries that handle foreign exchange for their subsidiaries examine cross-currency exposures daily. If a multinational company makes its home in Canada, then the peso receivable of the Venezuelan subsidiary, the yen payable of the Hong Kong subsidiary and the sterling inflow to the Belgian unit are all cross currency exposures. Although there is some concern with the movement of these currencies against the Canadian dollar, the movement of the peso against the bolivar, the movement of the yen against the Hong Kong dollar, and the movement of the pound against the franc have the most immediate impact on income.

In Chapter 2 pairing was described as one option for reducing the impact of an exposure. The objective of pairing is to offset a foreign currency flow with an opposite flow of another currency. This necessitates finding a cross currency whose rate has historically moved in tandem with it and is expected to do so in the future.

Knowledge of cross rates is valuable for forecasting exchange rates. There exist historical ties among some of the Scandinavian currencies and also between the Dutch guilder and the Deutsche mark and between the Austrian schilling and the Deutsche mark. These ties have developed as a result of extensive trade between the countries or in some instances because their exports compete in the same markets. There are two ways in which knowledge of the relationships are helpful for forecasting: (1) a good forecast of the dollar/Deutsche mark rate will generate good forecasts about the dollar's relations to the guilder and schilling; and (2) independent forecast of the dollar/mark and dollar/guilder can be checked by looking at the resultant mark/guilder rate.

CALCULATION OF CROSS RATES

If you know the rate dollar/Austrian schilling—$/AS 12.97–98—and the rate dollar/Swedish kroner—$/Skr 4.1245–55—how do you find the rate Swedish kroner/Austrian schilling—Skr/AS? The numbers to use for the calculation are not readily identifiable because there are two sides to each rate.

Consider first the situation where there is only one number:

$$\$/AS\,12$$

$$\$/Skr\,4$$

$$Skr/AS\ ?$$

Rewritten, this is

$$\$1\ =\ AS\,12$$

$$\$1\ =\ Skr\,4$$

$$Skr\,1 =\ AS?$$

The equivalence between the schilling and the kroner can be established because both are expressed in terms of $1.

$$Skr\,4 = \$1 = AS\,12$$

and

$$Skr\,4 = AS\,12$$

Thus

$$Skr\,1 = AS\ \frac{12}{4}$$

$$Skr\,1 = AS\,3$$

$$Skr/AS\,3$$

Let's start again with the same rates—$/AS 12 and $/Skr 4, but now you want to know AS/Skr or AS 1 = Skr?. As you know, AS 12 = Skr 4 since both are equal to $1.

$$AS\,1 = Skr\ \frac{4}{12}$$

$$AS\,1 = Skr\,.3333$$

$$AS/Skr\,.3333$$

Do a few cross rates yourself, remembering that you want to express the rate as

$$\text{1 unit currency } X/\text{units of currency } Y$$

Cover up the answers on the right side of the page.

Questions	Answers
A. $/FF4	$1 = DM 2
$/DM 2	$1 = FF 4
DM/FF?	DM 2 = FF 4
	DM 1 = FF$\frac{4}{2}$
	DM/FF 2
B. £/SF 4	£1 = Dkr 12
£/Dkr 12	£1 = SF 4
Dkr/SF?	Dkr 12 = SF 4
	Dkr 1 = SF$\frac{4}{12}$
	Dkr/SF .33
C. $/Yen 200	$1 = ¥ 200
$/HK$5	$1 = HK$5
HK$/Yen?	HK$5 = ¥ 200
	HK$1 = ¥ $\frac{200}{5}$
	HK$/¥ 40

Returning to the problem posed earlier, how do you find Skr/AS when

$$\text{$/AS 12.97–98}$$

$$\text{$/Skr 4.1245–55}$$

Since both currencies are expressed in terms of $1, you can use the same method you have just used with single numbers to establish the equivalence.

$$Skr\,4.1245\text{–}55 = \$1 = AS\,12.97\text{–}98$$

$$Skr\,4.1245\text{–}55 = AS\,12.97\text{–}98$$

To choose the sides of each rate to match up, lay out the rates with the arrows:

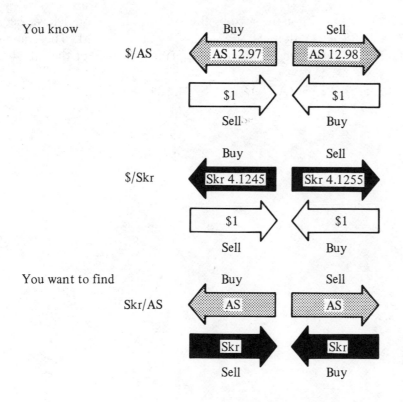

Choosing the numbers to use is as easy as matching the arrows in direction and degree of shading. Remember that this is possible only because both schilling and kroner are expressed in terms of the same unit—$1.

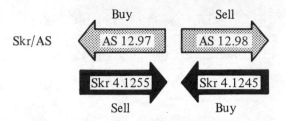

Notice that in matching the arrows the sides of the kroner have been *crossed*—4.1255 is on the left and 4.1245 is on the right. The equivalence has been established between the appropriate sides of the rates

$$Skr 4.1255 = AS 12.97 \qquad Skr 4.1245 = AS 12.98$$

Now we can work just like we did with the single numbers to find

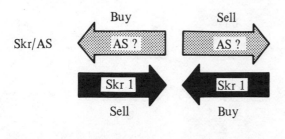

If Skr 4.1255 = AS 12.97   If Skr 4.1245 = AS 12.98

$$Skr\ 1 = AS\ \frac{12.97}{4.1255}$$ $$Skr\ 1 = AS\ \frac{12.98}{4.1245}$$

Skr/AS 3.1439 ⟵⟶ Skr/AS 3.1470

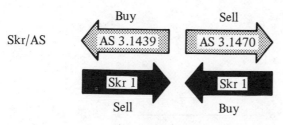

Skr/AS 3.1439-70

We have just found the rate Skr/AS. This is the way a Swedish person would express the rate. But what if you want to express the same rate for an Austrian? Use the quotation AS/Skr.

Thus

You want:

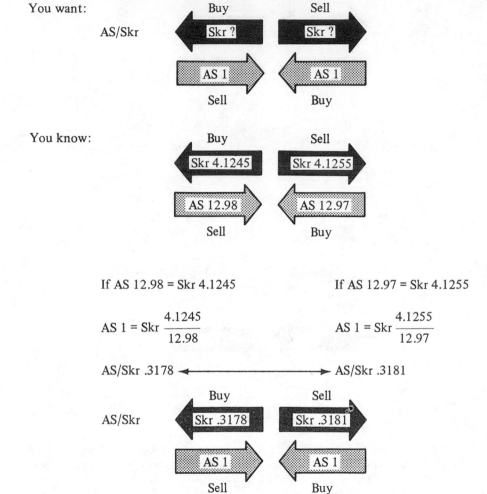

AS/Skr

You know:

If AS 12.98 = Skr 4.1245   If AS 12.97 = Skr 4.1255

$$AS\ 1 = Skr\ \frac{4.1245}{12.98}$$ $$AS\ 1 = Skr\ \frac{4.1255}{12.97}$$

AS/Skr .3178 ⟵⟶ AS/Skr .3181

AS/Skr

AS/Skr .3178–81

Summary of Steps for Calculating a Cross Rate

1. Decide what currency you want to be expressed as 1 unit and place it on the left of the slash. Let's say you want to express 1 unit of currency X as a number of units of currency Y.

2. Set the rates up as follows:

You want   1 unit currency X/units of currency Y

You know $/Y\,4.1925{-}4.1935$

                        $/X\,2.0750{-}2.0760$

3. Cross the sides of $/X$:

$$\$/Y\,4.1925{-}4.1935$$
$$\$/X\,2.9760{-}2.0750$$

4. Divide X into Y:

$$\frac{4.1925}{2.0760} - \frac{4.1935}{2.0750}$$

$$X/Y\ 2.0195{-}2.0210$$

1 unit currency X = currency $Y\,2.0195{-}2.0210$

Try two cross-rate exercises yourself. The answer is on the right-hand side of the page. Cover it up while you are working.

Questions	Answers
A. You know $/DM 1.8050–60 $/FF 4.1545–65	**A.** You want DM 1 = FF?
You want DM/FF	

┌────── DM/FF ──────┐
$/FF 4.1545–4.1565 ◄┘
└► $/DM 1.8050–1.8060
Cross $/DM
$/FF 4.1545–4.1565
$/DM 1.8060–1.8050
Divide
DM/FF 2.3004–2.3028
Usually cross rates among European currencies are written in terms of 100 rather than 1 unit, so for 100 DM–DM/FF 230.04–28

| **B.** You know £/SF 3.4050–65
£/DG 4.0920–40 | **B.** You want SF 1 = DG? |
| You want SF/DG | |

┌────── SF/DG ──────┐
£/DG 4.0920–4.0940 ◄┘
└► £/SF 3.4050–3.4065
Cross £/SF
£/DG 4.0920–4.0940
£/SF 3.4065–3.4050
Divide
SF/DG 1.2012–1.2023
In terms of 100 SF
SF/DG 120.12–23

How do you deal with those cases where the rates are not expressed in terms of a single unit?

You know £/$2.0520–25

$/MP 24.57–59

You want £/MP

First Possibility. Express the rate for pounds and dollars in terms of $1 rather than £1. This would involve transposing the rate, as shown in Chapter 6. Then you proceed as shown above.

Second Possibility. Multiply each side of the rate by the same side of the other rate, and do not switch. That is, to find £/MP, multiply 2.0520 × 24.57 for the left side and 2.0525 × 24.59 for the right side. This works for the following reasons:

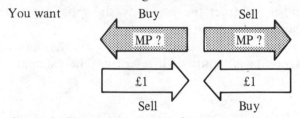

On the Left Side. If you sell £1, how many pesos do you buy? You know from £/$2.0520–25 that if you sell £1, you buy $2.0520. You know from $/MP 24.57–59 that if you sell $1, you buy MP 24.57. If instead of selling $1 you sell $2.0520, you buy MP 24.57 × 2.0520 = MP 50.42. Therefore, if you sell £1, you buy MP 50.42.

On the Right Side. To buy £1, how many pesos must you sell? You know from £/$2.0520–25 that to buy £1 you must sell $2.0525. You know from $/MP 24.57–59 that to buy $1, you must sell MP 24.59. If instead of buying $1 you buy $2.0525, you must sell MP 24.59 × 2.0525 = MP 50.47. Therefore, if you want to buy £1, you must sell MP 50.47.

£/MP 50.42–47

Pound sterling/Mexican peso

Try this one with the Irish punt and the Singapore dollar. The answer is on the right.

You know I£/$2.0110–17   I£/$2.0110–2.0117
        $/S$4.7875–95   X   X

You want I£/S$ $/S$4.7875–4.7895
                                        =   =
                                    I£/S$9.6277–9.6350
                                    Irish punt/Singapore dollar

FORWARD CROSS RATES AND POINTS

The calculation of forward cross rates is the same as the calculation of spot cross rates. Add or subtract the points to the spot rate and then proceed as shown above.

Because points do not express the same thing as exchange rates, the calculation of cross points is handled differently. The calculation for points is:

Spot cross rate *minus* Forward cross rate

You know $/SR spot   3.3550–70

                1 mo   250–240

            $/Nkr spot 5.0515–30

                1 mo   30–20

You want one-month points for Norwegian kroner/Saudi riyals. Calculate

Nkr/SR spot .6640–.6646

            1 mo .6593–.6602

Points   47–44

THE EUROPEAN MONETARY SYSTEM (EMS)

The EMS was launched in March 1979. It is a currency parity system established by European central banks to keep the exchange rates of their currencies within certain limits. A *central rate* is established for each pair of currencies, and *intervention limits* are established $2\frac{1}{4}\%$ to either side of the central rate, (6% for the Italian lira). If the market exchange rate between two currencies reaches an intervention limit, the respective central banks are obliged to act to keep their currencies within the limits. The weak currency is bought and the strong currency is sold. To enable countries with limited reserves to support their currencies, an extensive system of bilateral and multinational credit facilities has been established.

The following chart shows the central rates and the intervention limits for the countries that are participating in the EMS. The descriptions in the chart refer to the numbers in each column. For example, in the column Belgium, row West Germany, the central rate is 16.03 Belgian francs per one Deutsche mark. The upper intervention limit is DM/BF 15.67, and the lower limit is DM/BF 16.40. At the upper limit the Belgian franc is at its strongest point versus the mark. At the lower limit it is at its weakest point.

	Belgium and Luxembourg	Denmark	France
Belgium and Luxembourg	Number of francs per 1 unit of currency, for Italy 1000	18.075 18.486 18.907	14.37 14.69 15.03
Denmark	5.289 5.409 5.533	Number of kroner per 100 units of currency, for Ireland 1, for Italy 1000	77.72 79.49 81.30
France	6.654 6.805 6.960	123.00 125.80 128.70	Number of francs per 100 units of currency, for Ireland 1, for Italy 1000
Ireland	58.22 59.55 60.90	10.763 11.008 11.259	8.555 8.750 8.950
Italy	32.37 34.37 36.49	5.983 6.353 6.746	4.756 5.050 5.362
Netherlands	14.18 14.50 14.83	262.10 268.10 274.20	208.40 213.10 218.00
West Germany	15.67 16.03 16.40	289.80 296.40 303.10	230.30 235.60 240.90

*Limits are $2\frac{1}{4}$% above and below the central rate, except Italy (6%).
The numbers in this chart were correct while the book was being written. They may change in the interim, so the chart should be viewed as being illustrative rather than factual when you read it.

Rates and Upper and Lower Intervention Limits*

Ireland	Italy	Netherlands	West Germany
1.642	27.40	6.742	6.099
1.679	29.10	6.895	6.238
1.718	30.90	7.052	6.380
8.882	148.20	36.47	33.00
9.084	157.40	37.30	33.74
9.291	167.10	38.15	34.51
11.17	186.50	45.88	41.51
11.43	198.00	46.93	42.45
11.69	210.30	47.99	43.42
Number of punt	1631.80	4.014	3.632
per 100 units	1732.70	4.106	3.715
of currency,	1839.80	4.200	3.799
for Italy 1000			
.543	Number of lire	2.232	2.019
.577	per 1 unit	2.370	2.144
.613	of currency	2.516	2.276
23.81	397.40	Number of guilders	88.50
24.35	422.00	per 100 units	90.50
24.91	448.10	of currency,	92.50
		for Ireland 1,	
		for Italy 1000	
26.32	439.30	108.10	Number of marks
26.92	466.50	110.50	per 100 units
27.55	495.30	113.10	of currency,
			for Ireland 1,
			for Italy 1000

"Exchange Cross Rates" is published in the *Financial Times* daily. From this chart a comparison can be made between the market rates of the European currencies and their positions in the EMS.

EXCHANGE CROSS RATES

Nov. 5	PoundSterling	U.S. Dollar	Deutschem'k	Japan'se Yen	FrenchFranc	Swiss Franc	Dutch Guild'r	Italian Lire	Canada Dollar	Belgian Franc
Pound Sterling	1.	2.069	3.705	490.3	8.685	3.403	4.118	1714.	2.454	59.85
U.S. Dollar	0.483	1.	1.791	237.0	4.198	1.645	1.990	828.2	1.186	28.93
Deutschemark	0.270	0.558	1.	132.3	2.344	0.918	1.111	462.5	0.662	16.15
Japanese Yen 1,000	2.040	4.220	7.557	1000.	17.72	6.940	8.399	3495.	5.005	122.1
French Franc 10	1.151	2.382	4.266	564.5	10.	3.918	4.741	1973.	2.825	68.91
Swiss Franc	0.294	0.608	1.089	144.1	2.553	1.	1.210	503.6	0.721	17.59
Dutch Guilder	0.243	0.502	0.900	119.1	2.109	0.826	1.	416.2	0.596	14.54
Italian Lira 1,000	0.584	1.207	2.162	286.1	5.069	1.986	2.403	1000.	1.432	34.93
Canadian Dollar	0.408	0.843	1.510	199.8	3.540	1.387	1.678	698.4	1	24.39
Belgian Franc 100	1.671	3.457	6.190	819.1	14.51	5.685	6.880	2863.	4.099	100.

There is a slight variation in the units in which rates are expressed between the *Financial Times* and the EMS chart.

Look at the Belgian franc column, Deutsche mark row. The market rate on November 5 was DM/BF 16.15, below the central rate of 16.03. Assuming the EMS limits hold, the Belgian franc could further weaken against the mark only 1.55%, (comparing 16.15 to 16.40). On the other hand, the franc could strengthen by 2.97% (comparing 16.15 to 15.67). As a result of rounding, 1.55% plus 2.97% add up to slightly more than $4\frac{1}{2}\%$.

Look at the Italian lira column, Dutch guilder row. The market rate on November 5 was DG/Lit 416.20, above the central rate of 422.00. Within the present EMS limits the lira could further appreciate against the guilder by only 4.52%, (comparing 416.20 to 397.40). It could weaken against the guilder by 7.66%, (comparing 416.20 to 448.10).

Even though the spread between the intervention limits is $4\frac{1}{2}\%$, (lira, 12%), looking at the potential movement of the exchange rate between two currencies at a given time, the possibilities of movement are less. As with the mark and the franc, the largest change upward would be 2.97%, and the most the rate could move downward would be 1.55%. Only if the market rate were at one of the limits would the full movement be possible.

The intervention limits of the EMS are arranged so that the position of one exchange rate in the system affects the position of other rates.

Excerpt—The European Monetary System

	Denmark	France
France	123.00	
	125.80	*
	128.70	
Ireland	10.763	8.555
	11.008	8.750
	11.259	8.950

Assume that the market rate FF/Dkr is at the lower limit 128.70, a strong franc and a weak kroner. Given this situation, the kroner cannot be at its upper limit against any other currency in the EMS. The kroner cannot be at I£/Dkr 10.763 because this means that the rate for French francs and Irish punt is I£/FF 8.3629. Looking in the France column, Ireland row of the EMS chart, the upper limit is I£FF 8.555. The rate 8.3629 would be out of the system altogether. Given the position of the franc/kroner rate then, the kroner cannot be any higher than 11.008 against the Irish punt.

When FF/Dkr is 128.70, I£/Dkr can be between 11.259 and 11.008. As FF/Dkr moves toward the central rate of 125.80, the possible rates for I£/Dkr become 11.008 to 10.763.

Just as the punt/kroner rate is limited, so also is the mark/kroner rate, the lira/kroner rate, and so on. And not only is the kroner restricted with respect to other currencies, the position of the French franc is similarly proscribed.

The system of central rates and limits is one element of the EMS. A second element is the European Currency Unit (ECU). The ECU is a currency basket that contains each of the currencies in the system in proportion to the relative size of their national product and intra-European trade; Germany has the largest weight, France is next, and Luxembourg has the least weight. The ECU acts as the unit of account for credits and debits between members of the system. This value of the ECU is calculated by multiplying the weights of each currency by their exchange rates relative to the other currencies in the EMS. For example:

$$1 \text{ ECU} = BF\,39.8456 \quad = \text{ Belgian weight} \quad \times 1$$
$$\pm \text{ German weight} \quad \times \text{ DM/BF}$$
$$\pm \text{ French weight} \quad \times \text{ FF/BF}$$
$$\pm \text{ Irish weight} \quad \times \text{ I£/BF}$$

The rates DM/BF, FF/BF, and so on change all the time and, therefore, so does the number of Belgian francs per 1 ECU. Just as touching the limits around the central rates is a sign for the central banks to act, touching limits around the ECU also triggers central bank action. The limits around the ECU are called *divergence indicators*. If one of these indicators is hit, one currency has moved too far away from the average of the other currencies. When this occurs, the country that has moved away is responsible for putting its currency back into line. This breaks the symmetry of the grid system of parities that places the responsibility for action on both weak- and strong-currency countries. It is a protection for the small countries against the larger insofar as the spread between the divergence indicators is smaller for Germany and France and larger for Belgium and Ireland. This means that the larger countries will be responsible more often for corrective action.

The *Financial Times* publishes the ECU rates for each currency daily. For example, on November 5 there were FF 5.7999, DM 2.47477, and Lit 1145.06 per 1 ECU. The French franc was close to its upper limit that day.

The European Monetary System: Central Rates for 1 ECU and Divergence Indicators

	Belgium and Luxembourg	Denmark	France	Ireland	Italy	Netherlands	West Germany
DI	39.2360	7.24551	5.77574	.658000	1112.12	2.70586	2.45761
CR	39.8456	7.36594	5.85522	.669141	1159.42	2.74748	2.48557
DI	40.4552	7.48637	5.93470	.680282	1206.72	2.78910	2.51353

The numbers in this chart were correct while the book was being written. They may change in the interim, so the chart should be viewed as being illustrative rather than factual when you read it.

What is the reliability of the parities? Can the countries be counted on to remain in the system? The predecessor to the EMS was the "European Snake," established in April 1972. It, too, had a system of parities among European currencies bounded by intervention limits and central banks were obliged to intervene when the limits were breached. By May 1972 most of Europe was in the Snake. Pressure on sterling forced out Britain and Ireland in June 1972. Italy dropped out in February 1973, but Sweden joined in March. France dropped out in January 1974, rejoined again in July 1975, and left again in March 1976. Sweden dropped out in 1977. At the time of its demise the Snake consisted of Germany, Denmark, Norway, the Netherlands, Belgium, and Luxembourg—five currencies.

In addition to changing membership in the Snake, the central rates were changed over five times during its existence. Parities in the EMS changed within the first six months of its life. This history suggests that the parities and the membership of currency systems are unstable. The EMS is given a somewhat greater chance for stability than the Snake because of the extent of support arrangements among the countries and the system of divergence indicators. Comfort may be drawn from the fact that prior to a parity change or exit from the system there is generally one or two weeks during which it is widely discussed in the press; however, there are more discussions than there are changes.

USES OF THE EMS IN AN EXPOSURE SITUATION

In Chapter 2 *pairing* was discussed as an option that reduces the impact of an exposure situation. The object is to pick a currency that is closely allied with the exposed currency. The currencies of the EMS fit the criteria because their movement against one another is limited. The lira is an exception to this since its possible range is 12%, as opposed to $4\frac{1}{2}$% for the other currencies.

The EMS gives the possibility of cross protection in extended future periods. To see how this works, let us say that a British firm has entered into a transaction where it is obligated to pay Belgian francs in two years. It is difficult to make a transaction two years forward in Belgian francs. The market is nearly nonexistent. Instead, the company buys Deutsche marks two years forward. There is a much larger market for marks in that time period. Because of the existence of the EMS, the British firm can have some assurance that the exchange rate between marks and francs will approximate today's rate two years hence.

The EMS makes it possible to avoid excess costs in covering an exposure. Since the EMS and its limits refer only to spot rates it is possible for the forward rate between two member currencies to fall outside the intervention limits. Likewise, it is possible that a locked-in future rate generated by the BSI and Lead options will fall outside these limits even though the spot rate is within them. At that point the company must make a judgment about the stability of the EMS parities. An example is provided by the French merchant who sells wine to Denmark and expects the proceeds in two months. The spot rate is Dkr/FF 80.90 and the locked-in future rates for the three options, Forward, BSI, and Lead, are 82.01, 81.65, and 81.80, respectively. They are all out of the EMS. The upper and lower limits for France and Denmark are

Dkr/FF 77.72

Dkr/FF 81.30

In the absence of any tension in the currency markets, the exporter may decide not to cover the exposure. The worse off he could be is Dkr/FF 81.30 (lower limit) if the parities in the EMS are unchanged. This represents a savings of 2.6% per annum over the best covering option.

VAN DER ZORN SILVER MANUFACTURERS N.V. CASE

Van der Zorn is a Dutch company dating back to the seventeenth century. It is renowned for its craftsmanship in such items as coffee and mocha services, water pitchers, and personal goods. In January of this year Van der Zorn was visited by the buyer of a major Parisian department store with several branches in the provinces. The buyer had seen his first example of Van der Zorn and had persuaded the store's management to feature Van der Zorn silver the next Christmas season. Half of the available floor space would be devoted to it. The price settled on was excellent from the Dutch point of view, but the Frenchman insisted that the billing be in French francs.

The order was given in January, when the exchange rate was FF/DG 46.90. In the interim the rate had moved in Van der Zorn's favor to the extent of 47.95; yesterday, however, the rate was down to FF/DG 46.30. There are now three months left before the Dutch company is to receive its French francs. You are the assistant treasurer and have been asked by the finance director to see what the cost of covering the exposure would be and recommend a strategy. You have obtained the rates from the newspaper.

Exchange Rates

	Spot	Three months
$/DG	1.9650–65	350–335
$/FF	4.2370–85	70–60

Guilder Interest Rates

Domestic $5\frac{1}{4}$–$5\frac{1}{2}$%
External $5\frac{1}{4}$–6%

Franc Interest Rates

Domestic $10\frac{3}{4}$–11%
External $11\frac{3}{4}$–12%

The Dutch bank charges the silver company a $\frac{3}{4}$% spread on advances. The French bank charges the store a $\frac{3}{4}$% spread on advances.

SOLUTION TO THE CASE

The options are illustrated as follows:

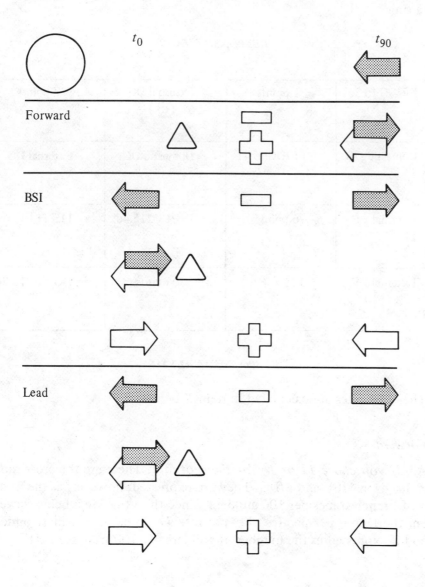

Your next task as assistant treasurer is to select the appropriate rates for each option. The following chart represents all the possibilities. A response analysis follows to explain the proper choices. Do one option at a time.

RESPONSE CHART

FF/DG46.36	71 points	External DG 6% $(+\frac{3}{4})$	337 points
1.	2.	3.	4.
Domestic DG $5\frac{1}{4}\%$	FF/DG46.41	Domestic DG $5\frac{1}{2}\%\,(+\frac{3}{4})$	External DG $5\frac{3}{4}\%$
5.	6.	7.	8.
External FF $11\frac{3}{4}\%$	76 points	DG/FF215.46	11% $(+\frac{3}{4})$
9.	10.	11.	12.
External FF 12% $(+\frac{3}{4})$	$10\frac{3}{4}\%$	360 points	DG/FF215.70
13.	14.	15.	16.

RESPONSE ANALYSIS

The cross rates are calculated in item **X** below.

Forward

A. *If you chose 11 or 16 for the spot rate*: These are the cross rates for the given \$/FF and \$/DG. They are expressed, however, as the number of French francs per 100 guilders. Since the situation is being viewed from the Dutch perspective, the spot rate would be more widely understood if expressed as the number of guilders per 100 francs, FF/DG.

B. *If you chose 6 for the spot rate*: This rate is quoted from the Dutch point of view as it gives the number of guilders per 100 francs. This rate, however, is for a transaction where the customer buys francs and sells guilders. The desired transaction is the other way around.

C. *If you chose 1 for the spot rate*: This is the appropriate rate since the rate chosen for the spot must be in the same direction as the forward transaction, and the forward transaction is a sale of francs and purchase of guilders.

D. *If you chose 4 or 15 as the forward points*: These forward points are the companions to the spot rate expressed as the number of French francs per 100 guilders, the French perspective. Here we are dealing from the Dutch perspective. It is not erroneous to use points this way, but expressing the rate in terms of guilders would be more widely understood.

E. *If you chose 13 or 8 for the forward*: These assuredly are the two markets that go into the formation of the forward rate. As long as the forward exchange market is going to be used, though, it is more accurate to use the points rather than interest rates.

F. *If you chose 2*: This is the wrong side of the market for the forward transaction necessary to cover this exposure. These points, when subtracted from 46.41, give the rate for buying francs, not selling francs.

G. *If you chose 10*: These are the correct number of points for the transaction—sell francs, and buy guilders.

Borrow–Spot–Invest

H. *If you chose 11 or 16 for the spot rate,* See A.

I. *If you chose 13 for the borrowing cost*: This is the right rate to use since 12% plus $\frac{3}{4}$% bank spread is the cost of borrowing external French francs.

J. *If you chose 12 or 14 for the borrowing cost*: These are the rates for the resident money market in France. Only French residents have access to this market. The silver company will access this market, however, through the Lead option.

K. *If you chose 9 for the borrowing cost*: The rates were given as

$11\frac{3}{4}$–12% for the domestic franc money market. The rate of $11\frac{3}{4}$% is for placing funds, not borrowing them.

    L. *If you chose 6 for the spot rate*: See B.

    M. *If you chose 1 for the spot rate*: This is correct since at this rate francs are sold and guilders bought.

    N. *If you chose 3 or 7 as the investing rate*: These are rates for borrowing funds, not placing them. Recall that the rates were given as $5\frac{3}{4}$–6% external and $5\frac{1}{4}$–$5\frac{1}{2}$% domestic. Funds are placed at the lower rate.

    O. *If you chose 8 as the investing rate*: This is not wrong since the Dutch have access to the external market. By choosing the external rate for guilders and combining it with the external rate for francs, you are simply replicating the Forward and at a greater cost since there is a bank spread for the borrowing that is not present in the Forward.

    P. *If you chose 5 as the investing rate*: This is the appropriate rate to use for investing in the BSI option. See also O.

Lead

    Q. *If you chose 11 or 16 for the spot rate*: See A.

    R. *If you chose 6 for the spot rate*: See B.

    S. *If you chose 1 for the spot rate*: See M.

    T. *If you chose 3 or 7 as the investing rate*: See N.

    U. *If you chose 8 or 5 as the investing rate*: Both are correct since the Dutch have access to both their domestic and external money markets. You would choose the best return, namely, $5\frac{3}{4}$%, the external interest rate.

    V. *If you chose 9 or 13 as the rate the store charged the silver company to lead the receivable*: These rates are not appropriate since French residents do not have access to the external franc market. Additionally, 9 would represent undercharging since it is the rate for placing funds.

    W. *If you chose 12 as the rate the store charged the silver company to lead the receivable*: This is the rate the department store would have to pay its bank to borrow money for three months.

X. *The calculation of the cross rates*:

You want   1 unit French francs/units of Dutch guilders

You know $/DG 1.9650–1.9665
                         $/FF 4.2370–4.2385

Cross the sides of $/FF $/DG 1.9650–1.9665
                             $/FF 4.2385–4.2370

Divide the second line into the first and the result is:
                         FF/DG .4636–.4641

For 100 French francs spot: FF/DG 46.36–41

The forward rates are: $/DG 1.9300–1.9330
                            $/FF 4.2300–4.2325

They are handled the same as previously to produce the cross forward rate: FF/DG 45.60–70
To find the three-month points, the forward rates are subtracted from the spot rates, 76 – 71.

RECAP

The options and the appropriate prices are illustrated as follows:

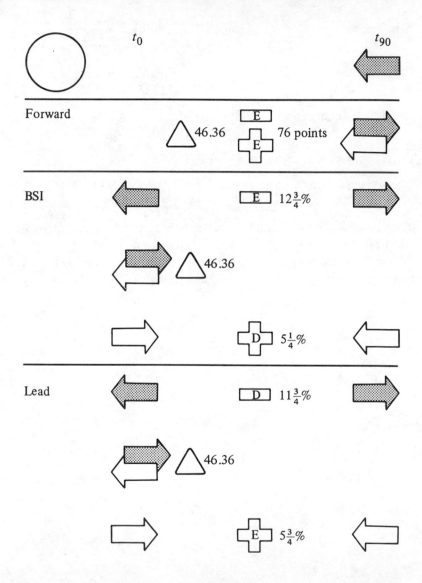

Comparing the Options

The next task of the assistant treasurer is to make the calculations necessary to compare the options. Do this before looking at the completed matrix.

| Option | Spot | Net Interest Cost/Earning | | | Points | Locked-In Future Rate |
		I_h	I_f	Net		
Forward	46.36			−6.56%	76	45.60
BSI	46.36	$5\frac{1}{4}$	$12\frac{3}{4}$	$-7\frac{1}{2}\%$	84	45.52
Lead	46.36	$5\frac{3}{4}$	$11\frac{3}{4}$	−6%	$67\frac{1}{2}$	$45.68\frac{1}{2}$

For the calculations, the points formula was used to find the points for the BSI and Lead, and ICE-1 was used to calculate the percentage for the Forward.

The least expensive option is the Lead. The cost is 6% per annum to cover, compared to the next-best Forward, which costs more than $6\frac{1}{2}\%$ to cover the exposure. The same fact is shown by the LIFR—Van der Zorn would receive $45.68\frac{1}{2}$ guilders per every 100 francs, as opposed to 45.60 if the Forward were executed.

The Decision to Cover

The cost to Van der Zorn Silver if it covered its exposure would be 6% per annum. This means that the company must deduct about $1\frac{1}{2}\%$ off the proceeds that it could receive if payment were made today. Is this necessary? Not if there is confidence that the EMS parities will remain unchanged for the next three months. Consulting the chart shown earlier in the chapter, the upper limit FF/DG is 45.88. This is a more favorable rate than $45.68\frac{1}{2}$. The fourth option then is to place confidence in the EMS. With this fourth option the greatest cost would be 4.14% per annum, or a deduction of about 1% off today's possible proceeds.* On an order of FF 10,000,000 the margin of saving offered by the EMS would be about FF 42,000. The decision to place confidence in the EMS rests upon a number of factors—current degree of stability in the exchange markets, not only among the European currencies, but also the U.S. dollar; degree of imbalance in the EMS as shown by the divergence indicators, or currencies remaining at or near their intervention limits for extended periods; length of time since the last parity change; and inflation rates and monetary policy in the countries of the major trading currencies.

If option four is taken, it is not irreversible. It is always possible to execute one of the other options if there is pressure on the parities, or if there is a favorable movement of the spot and interest rates.

*The difference between spot 46.36 and the upper limit 45.88 is 48 points: $.48/46.36 \times 360/90 \times 100 = 4.14\%$

CHAPTER NINE
THE FORWARD MARKET

The first thing to learn about the forward market is some of its terminology, then the techniques, and finally some theory. The excerpt from the *Financial Times* is "The Dollar Spot and Forward."

THE DOLLAR SPOT AND FORWARD

Nov. 5	Day's spread	Close	One month	% p.a.	Three months	% p.a.
UK†	2.0560-2.0720	2.0685-2.0695	0.23-0.33c dis	−1.62	0.30-0.40dis	−0.68
Ireland†	2.0685-2.0735	2.0685-2.0715	0.30-0.10c pm	1.16	1.0-0.70 pm	1.64
Canada	1.1857-1.1867	1.1859-1.1862	0.19-0.15c pm	1.72	0.34-0.30 pm	1.08
NethInd.	1.9850-1.9900	1.9870-1.9885	1.05-0.95c pm	6.03	2.75-2.65 pm	5.43
Belgium	28.81-28.945	28.92-28.935	6-4½c pm	1.97	12-10 pm	1.52
Denmark	5.2665-5.2955	5.2940-5.2955	1.10-1.60ore dis	−3.06	3.5-4.0 dis	−2.83
W. Ger.	1.7860-1.7910	1.7895-1.7905	1.18-1.08pf pm	7.57	3.02-2 92 pm	6.64
Portugal	50.45-50.70	50.45-50.55	10-20c dis	−3.55	30-65 dis	−3.75
Spain	66.23-66.34	66.23-66.27	45-65c dis	−9.96	115-140 dis	−7.70
Italy	828.20-831.90	828.30-828.70	par-0.50 lire dis	−0.36	2.25-2.75dis	−1.21
Norway	5.0130-5.0295	5.0140-5.0150	par-1.0ore dis	−1.20	0.50-1.50dis	−0.80
France	4.1900-4.1975	4.1960-4.1975	0.85-0.75c pm	2.29	1.20-1.0 pm	1.05
Sweden	4.2370-4.2398	4.2370-4.2380	1.50-1.30ore pm	3.96	3.50-3.30 pm	3.21
Japan	236.70-237.40	236.85-236.95	2.0-1.85y pm	9.75	4.65-4 50 pm	7.72
Austria	12.85¼-12.86½	12.85½-12.86½	8.5-8.0gro pm	7.70	22.75-21.25pm	6.84
Switz.	1.6345-1.6450	1.6435-1.6445	1.85-1.80c pm	13.32	4.83-4.78 pm	11.69

† UK and Ireland are quoted in U.S. currency. Forward premiums and discounts apply to the U.S. dollar and not to the individual currency.

159

We have discussed everything here except the words *one month, three months, dis,* and *pm.* One month means the same date next month, and three months means the same date three months hence. If the spot date is June 13, the one-month transaction or value date is July 13. There are a couple of conventions governing the forward value dates.

1. If on the same date next month one or both of the countries are on holiday, the value date is the next business day they are both open.

Date	Paris	New York
July 13	Holiday	Holiday
July 14	Holiday	Open
July 15	Open	Open

July 15 is the value date for a one-month forward, transaction $/FF.

2. If the spot date is the last possible spot date in the month, June 30, the forward value dates are the last days in the month both centers are open.

Date	Paris	New York
July 29	Open	Open
July 30	Open	Holiday
July 31	Open	Holiday

July 29 is the value date for the one-month forward. If both centers were open all three days, the value date for the one-month forward would be July 31, not July 30.

The term dis stands for discount. A currency that is at a **discount** has less value in the forward market than in the spot market. The term pm stands for premium. A currency that is at a **premium** has more value in the forward market than in the spot market. In the excerpt, dis and pm refer to the currency in which the rate is denominated. Look at the three-month quotes.

UK	£/$0.30–0.40dis—the U.S. dollar is at a discount with respect to the pound.
Canada	$/C$0.34–0.30pm—the Canadian dollar is at a premium with respect to the U.S. dollar.
Italy	$/Lit 2.25–2.75dis—the lira is at a discount with respect to the U.S. dollar.

The lira at a discount with respect to the dollar also means that the dollar is at a premium with respect to the lira. Some publications follow the latter convention and speak of premium and discount with respect to the currency on the left of the slash. If you are not sure, refer to the external interest rates of two currencies. The currency with the higher rate will be at a discount to the currency with the lower rate. The reason for this is demonstrated shortly.

There is a relationship between premium and discount and the way the forward points are written. These are the three-month quotes:

UK	£/$—the dollar is at a discount: points are 30–40.
Canada	$/C$—the Canadian dollar is at a premium: points are 34–30.
Italy	$/Lit—the lira is at a discount: points are 225–275.
Switzerland	$/SF—the franc is at a premium: points are 483–478.

When the points go up, from left to right, the currency to the right of the slash is at a discount. When the points go down, from left to right, the currency to the right of the slash is at a premium.

The word *par* means zero points; the forward rate is the same as the spot rate. See the one month quote for Italy. The word *flat* is used synonymously with par. Another expression used in quoting forward points is *around*. Literally, it means around par. A rate quoted "5–10 around" means that the first number is subtracted from the left side of the spot rate and the second number is added to the right side of the spot rate. For example,

£/Nkr spot 10.37–38

1 mo   5–10 around

1 mo forward 10.32–48

A quote for two months of 15–5 around would result in a two-month forward of 10.22–10.43.

To understand why a currency is at a discount or a premium with respect to another currency, we take a look at the BSI option. It provides insight into what happens in the bank when a forward transaction is executed and, as such, is appropriate for understanding how the forward market works and why some currencies are at a premium and others at a discount. The initial situation is a foreign currency payable due in three months. A Canadian company will pay out U.S. dollars.

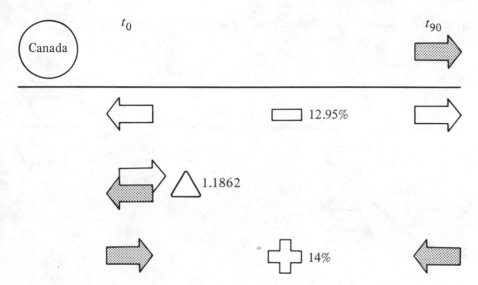

Canada is the home country, its currency is white; the
U.S. dollar is the foreign currency, gray

The number of points resulting from this interest rate differential is
30, and the locked-in future rate is 1.1832. The reason for subtracting
the points is that this operation results in an earnings of 1.05% for the
Canadian company. This means that the company pays out only 1.18*32*
Canadian dollars per one U.S. dollar to cover the exposure in 90 days
compared to today's cost of C$1.18*62*. A contract established today
to buy U.S. dollars 90 days hence costs fewer Canadian dollars than a
contract to buy for delivery today does. The Canadian dollar is at a premium with respect to the U.S. dollar. This is because Canadian interest
rates are lower than U.S. interest rates—12.95%, compared to 14%.
Therefore, a currency at a premium with respect to another currency
has a lower interest rate.

Another example is an Italian firm with a U.S. dollar payable.

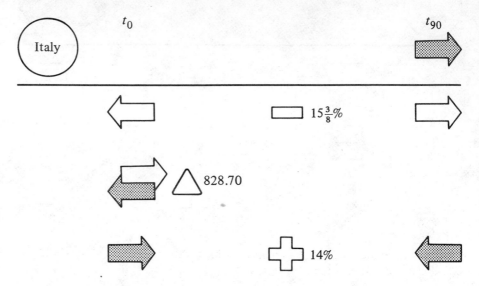

Italy is the home country, its currency is white; the
U.S. dollar is the foreign currency, gray.

The number of points resulting from this interest rate differential is 275 and the locked-in future rate is 831.45. The reason for adding the points is that this operation results in a cost of $1\frac{3}{8}\%$ for the Italian company. This means that the company pays out 831.45 lire per one U.S. dollar to cover the exposure in 90 days compared to today's cost of 828.70. A contract established today to buy dollars 90 days hence costs more lire than a contract to buy for delivery today does. The lira is at a discount with respect to the U.S. dollar. This is because lira interest rates are higher than dollar interest rates—$15\frac{3}{8}\%$, compared to 14%. Therefore, a currency that is at a discount with respect to another currency has a higher interest rate.

By reversing the exposure situation and showing an Italian company with a dollar receivable, it is possible to show how the other half of the forward points is developed.

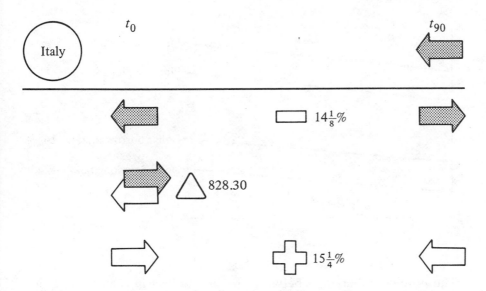

Notice that the dollar interest rate is higher in this situation than in the previous one. This is because it costs the company more to borrow money than it receives from investing funds; the lira rate is lower for the same reason. The number of points resulting from this interest rate differential is 225 and the locked-in future rate is 830.55. The points were added because this operation results in an earning for the Italian company. The company receives 2.25 lire more with a cover forward than it would receive today.

Notice that the points correspond to those shown in the excerpt as the three-month quotation. The Eurocurrency interest rates, without bank spreads, have been used to illustrate the interrelation between interest rates and forward points and the similarity between the Forward and BSI options.

Another way to look at the same relationship is through the following graph, which shows the yield curves of lire and U.S. dollars. This is simply a plot of today's interest rates for different periods.

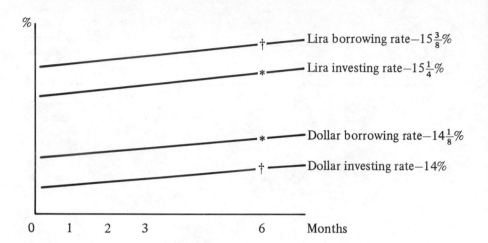

The interest differential between lira and dollars in the first situation compared the "dollar investing rate" of 14% with the "lira borrowing rate" of $15\frac{3}{8}$%. This is because in the payable situation lire were borrowed and dollars placed in the money markets. This is represented on the graph by the two daggers. In the second situation the difference was between the "dollar borrowing rate" of $14\frac{1}{8}$% and the "lira investing rate" of $15\frac{1}{4}$%. In the receivable situation dollars were borrowed and lire placed in the money markets. This is represented on the graph by the two asterisk's. The graph illustrates why the points for an operation of borrowing dollars and investing lire (225) are less than for an operation of borrowing lire and investing dollars (275). Where the interest rates are external interest rates, as in this case, this is the way in which the set of forward points is generated. It follows that the points themselves signify a particular operation.

At 225 dollars are borrowed and lire are invested.
At 275 dollars are invested and lire are borrowed.

A forward rate is composed of a spot rate and points. The points bridge the time gap between spot and the future date. In a sense, the operation implicit in the points carries the spot from the present to the future date. This representation is a 90-day receivable and a sale of dollars and purchase of lira spot.

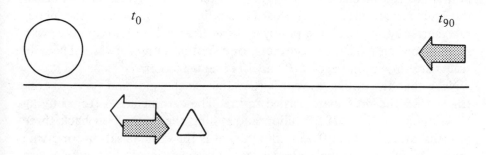

Since the exposure is in the future another operation is needed, an operation whereby dollars are borrowed and lire are simultaneously invested is required.

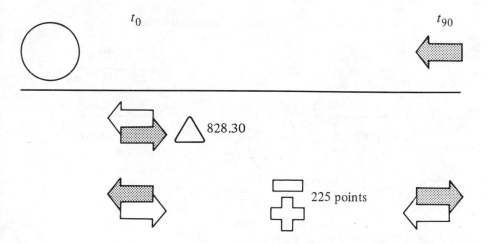

The result is that the flows on the spot day cancel out, leaving a sale of dollars and purchase of lire on a forward date.

The operation where one currency is borrowed for a period of time and another currency is invested simultaneously in one transaction is called a *swap*. Forward points are also referred to as *swap points*. The swap is an operation that has all the characteristics of a money market operation but that is executed in the foreign exchange market. The points are the mechanism of paying and receiving interest. If you invest the higher rate currency, you earn the points. If you borrow the higher rate currency, you pay the points. This is arranged by booking the swap as two foreign exchange contracts, one spot and one forward. The contracts are shown on pages 170 and 171; refer to them.

Note that the dollar amount is the same on the spot and forward contracts, and the points are earned in lire. The earning arises from buying $1 million for Lit 828.3 million and selling the $1 million back three months later for Lit 830.55 million. That is the compensation for giving up lire which earn a high interest rate and accepting dollars, which earn a lower interest rate, for three months. If the foreign currency amount, the currency on the left of the slash ($/Lit), is held constant as it is in this case, then the formula ICE-1 is used to calculate the cost/earning of the swap.

Dollar amount the same, lira amount changes:

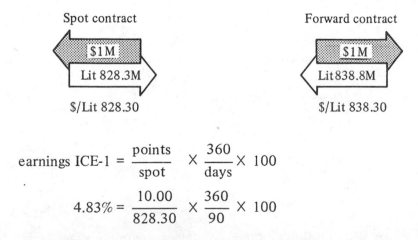

Spot contract

$1M

Lit 828.3M

$/Lit 828.30

Forward contract

$1M

Lit 838.8M

$/Lit 838.30

$$\text{earnings ICE-1} = \frac{\text{points}}{\text{spot}} \times \frac{360}{\text{days}} \times 100$$

$$4.83\% = \frac{10.00}{828.30} \times \frac{360}{90} \times 100$$

There are reasons why the lira amount may be the same on the spot and forward contracts. In that case to calculate the cost/earning of the swap, formula ICE-2 is used. The reason is that the points are earned in dollars, but the spot rate and the points are in lire. ICE-2 shows that the calculation using the points and the forward is the same as if the actual dollar amounts were used to calculate the swap earnings.

Dollar amount changes, lira amount the same:

Spot contract

$1M

Lit 828.3M

$/Lit 828.30

Forward contract

$988.071M

Lit 828.3M

$/Lit 838.30

$$\text{earnings ICE-2} = \frac{\text{points}}{\text{forward}} \times \frac{360}{90} \times 100$$

$$4.77\% = \frac{10.00}{838.30} \times \frac{360}{90} \times 100 = \frac{\$11,929}{\$1,000,000} \times \frac{360}{90} \times 100$$

BANK OF AMERICA
NATIONAL TRUST AND SAVINGS ASSOCIATION

SAN FRANCISCO

CUSTOMER	
THE HOOPER COMPANY 100 TRAVIS STREET HOUSTON, TEXAS 77001	**CONTRACT DATE** November 3, 1981 **ACCOUNT NO.** **CONTRACT NO.**

WE CONFIRM

HAVING PURCHASED FROM YOU	RATE	HAVING SOLD TO YOU
LIT 828,300,000.00	828.30	USDOL 1,000,000.00

MATURITY DATE	OPTION DATE	BROKER
Nov 5, 1981		

CURRENCY
Italian lire

PLEASE PAY TO ___ BANCO DI ROMA, MILAN ___

FOR ACCOUNT OF ___ OURSELVES ___ ACCOUNT NO. ___

CURRENCY
U S DOLLARS

WE WILL PAY TO ___ BANKAMERICA INTERNATIONAL-HOUSTON ___

FOR ACCOUNT OF ___ YOURSELVES ___ ACCOUNT NO. ___ 5943-4 ___

THROUGH ___ ACCOUNT NO. ___

SPECIAL INSTRUCTIONS ___

PLEASE CONFIRM BY SIGNING, DATING AND RE-
TURNING TO US THE ACKNOWLEDGMENT COPY.

PLUS ADDITIONAL CHARGES

TYPE	AMOUNT
TYPE	AMOUNT

AUTHORIZED SIGNATURE

CUSTOMER CONFIRMATION

CONFIRMED THIS DATE ___

AUTHORIZED SIGNATURE

FX-280 5-79

Copies:
1. Customer Copy (White)   3. File Copy #3296 (Pink)
2. Acknowledgment Copy (Canary)

Reprinted with permission from Bank of America NT&SA.

BA **BANK** OF **AMERICA**
NATIONAL TRUST AND SAVINGS ASSOCIATION

SAN FRANCISCO

CUSTOMER

THE HOOPER COMPANY

100 TRAVIS STREET

HOUSTON, TEXAS 77001

CONTRACT DATE
November 3, 1981

ACCOUNT NO.   CONTRACT NO.

WE CONFIRM

HAVING PURCHASED FROM YOU	RATE	HAVING SOLD TO YOU
USDOL 1,000,000.00	830.55	LIT 830,550,000.00

MATURITY DATE	OPTION DATE	BROKER
Feb. 5, 1982		

CURRENCY
U S DOLLARS

PLEASE PAY TO BANKAMERICA INTERNATIONAL-NEW YORK

FOR ACCOUNT OF   OURSELVES   ACCOUNT NO.

CURRENCY
Italian lire

WE WILL PAY TO BANCO COMMERCIALE ITALIANA, MILAN

FOR ACCOUNT OF   YOURSELVES   ACCOUNT NO. 779-114

THROUGH   ACCOUNT NO.

SPECIAL INSTRUCTIONS

PLEASE CONFIRM BY SIGNING, DATING AND RE-
TURNING TO US THE ACKNOWLEDGMENT COPY.

PLUS ADDITIONAL CHARGES

TYPE	AMOUNT
TYPE	AMOUNT

AUTHORIZED SIGNATURE
CUSTOMER CONFIRMATION

CONFIRMED THIS DATE

AUTHORIZED SIGNATURE

FX-280 5-79

Copies:
1. Customer Copy (White)   3. File Copy #3296 (Pink)
2. Acknowledgment Copy (Canary)

Reprinted with permission from Bank of America NT&SA.

171

The bank uses the swap, together with the spot to effect forward operations for its customers. The following illustrations show how.

1. The bank's customer has an exposure, a foreign currency payable—gray.

2. The customer buys the foreign currency forward from the bank with its own currency—white.

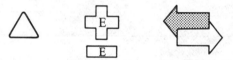

3. The bank has contracted to sell foreign currency and buy the home currency.

Look at the customer's original exposure and the bank's position now. The customer has shifted its exposure to the bank.

4. Banks separate their operations in the spot market and in the forward market. The bank will do a spot to cover the currency element and a swap to cover the time element of its exposure.

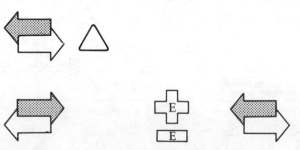

Compare the pricing of the customer's forward (2) with the bank's coverage of its exposure. The bank passes on to the customer its cost and earnings.

There is a convention as to how the swap points are written, which is related to the way spot is expressed. If we consider that spot is expressed as foreign currency/home currency, then for the points:

Number on the left signifies— borrowing foreign currency and investing home currency

Number on the right signifies— investing foreign currency and borrowing home currency

This means that the rates should be written as

$$\text{\$/Lit } 828.30\text{--}828.70$$

$$\text{Points } 225\text{--}275$$

Placing an arrow at each end of the dash can help you remember.

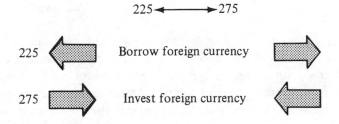

The complete operation:

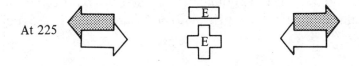

Dollars are borrowed, lire are invested.

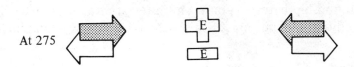

Dollars are invested, lire are borrowed.

Now to explain more fully *par* and *around*. A par quotation occurs when the rate for investing one currency is the same as the rate for borrowing another. An around quotation occurs when the investing and borrowing rates of two currencies fall inside one another. The illustration is a fragment of the yield curve for pounds sterling and Norwegian kroner at six months. The six-month points are 10–5 around, and spot is £/Nkr 10.37–38.

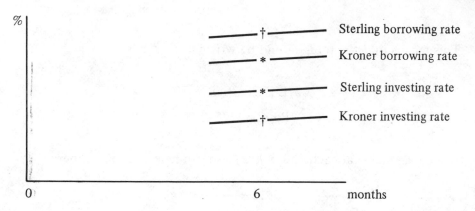

The swap of borrowing sterling, investing kroner is done at 10. This is noted on the graph at the daggers. The kroner interest rate is lower than sterling's; therefore, the kroner is at a premium with respect to the pound. An indication of the kroner premium is a fewer number of kroner per £1 at a future date. To confirm the rule stated before, the 10 points are subtracted from 10.37. The swap of borrowing kroner, investing sterling is done at 5. It is noted on the graph at the asterisks. The kroner interest rate is higher than sterling's; therefore, the kroner is at a discount against the pound. The kroner discount is indicated by a greater number of kroner per £1 at a future date. The 5 points are added to 10.38.

THE DETERMINATION OF FORWARD POINTS

The relationship between points and interest rates is formalized in the points formula. The purpose of this section is to draw a relation specifically between forward points and external interest rates. It was due to convenience, and subsequently by convention external currency interest rates have become allied to forward points. External currency markets have a single short term instrument with standard maturities, the time deposit. Money is placed in a deposit, or a deposit is taken (money borrowed), at fixed rates, for fixed periods of time. The standard maturities in the external currency markets are the same as those in the forward market—1, 2, 3, 6, and 12 months. As in the foreign exchange market, time starts on the spot day; a time deposit changes hands two days from the date of transaction. External currency deposits have the same degree of risk. The uniformity of the external currency time deposit and its conformity to the conventions of the foreign exchange market make it a convenient standard.

Points and interest rates are both prices of the operations of borrowing and investing. Points refer to a money market operation executed in the foreign exchange market. Interest rates refer to direct acts of borrowing and investing in the money market. *Arbitrage* is the mechanism that ensures that the points reflect external interest rates; and, in turn, external interest rates reflect the points. Assume it is possible to borrow a currency at 5%, swap it for a second currency at a cost of 4%, and then place the second currency on deposit at 10%. The total cost is 9%; the earnings are 10%. Those with access to the money and exchange markets will engage in this activity until either the cost of borrowing rises, the cost of the swap rises, or deposit rates fall. Depending on the depth of the markets, all three will occur to varying degrees. The following illustration shows how the operation is executed without any exposure for those doing it.

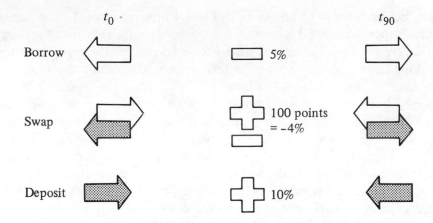

If the cost of the borrowing rises to $5\frac{1}{2}\%$ and the cost of the swap rises to 106 points or $4\frac{1}{4}\%$, and if the rate paid for deposits drops to $9\frac{3}{4}\%$, there is no further incentive to undertake the arbitrage. The cost of the operation is now equal to the earnings from it. The profit motive ensures that the forward points reflect precisely the difference between two Eurocurrency interest rates. The equality between the interest rate differential and the forward points is termed *interest rate parity*. Another way of expressing this is that in the Eurocurrency markets all interest rates are equal through the forward foreign exchange market.

The line of causation flows both ways; changes in interest rates cause changes in points, and changes in points cause changes in interest rates. The relative importance of the money market and foreign exchange market is different for each currency. The influence of each market also differs according to the nature of outside events. The depth of a market is a crucial ingredient in its influence. A deep market is marked by a large number of bank and other financial and commercial participants with a nearly constant interest in dealing. Large transactions can be undertaken without moving rates or prices substantially. Outside events are absorbed without major price fluctuations or changes in trading patterns. The best example is the Eurodollar market. In the space of one year it adjusted to the recycling of Organization of Petroleum Exporting Countries (OPEC) country surpluses and a major bank failure. The depth of a market can also depend on the time of day and day of the week. There is more interest at 10 a.m. on Wednesday than at 4 p.m. on Friday.

People are interested in the forward markets to cover exposures due to exports, imports, borrowing, and lending; to speculate on the future spot rate of a currency (sell a currency forward with the aim of buying back later at a lower price); to arbitrage with the deposit markets; and to speculate on changes in interest rate differentials.

The external money markets represent a readily available unregulated pool of funds. Funds are easily borrowed by governments and corporations for working capital, investment, and other projects. The money markets accept excess funds for as short as a day and for as long as five years from governments, corporations, and individuals. Banks and individuals use the market to speculate on the future course of interest rates. For example, place a deposit for six months at 10% and borrow to cover this a month at a time at 8%. Such speculation gives depth to the market and enables banks to give their customers a ready quotation. Banks also use the external currency markets to earn on the currencies they have purchased and are holding temporarily with the hope of selling at a profit later. Central banks have used the Eurocurrency markets to earn interest on money they purchased in supporting an exchange rate. External money market rates are heavily influenced by their domestic counterparts, particularly where there is little exchange control.

The dominant market, money or foreign exchange, for a given currency depends on the actors in each market. A few examples will illustrate the interaction of the two markets. In late 1976 the pound sterling came under heavy pressure in the exchange markets. Any commercial enterprise having sterling receivables, or even expecting to generate sterling receivables, sold them forward. Forward sterling was at a discount against most European currencies for the whole year. To the extent possible companies in the United Kingdom purchased foreign currencies by selling pounds forward. Anyone who had sterling payables held off covering them in anticipation of buying cheaper. Speculators saw an opportunity for profit by selling pounds forward to buy back later cheaper.

The sale of sterling forward consists of two operations, a spot sale and a swap. This is illustrated here:

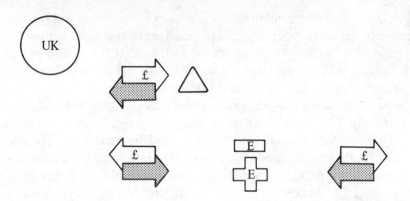

As pounds were borrowed and other currencies lent through the swap, the forward points increased. The Bank of England also executed swaps like this one as a part of her intervention tactics. By increasing the discount on forward sterling, the bank hoped to discourage people from selling future receivables and to make it attractive to buy for those who had obligations in sterling. It also decreases the reward to speculation by moving the break even rate further away. As the forward points increased, the Eurosterling rate rose in tandem. Arbitrage ensured that this would occur.

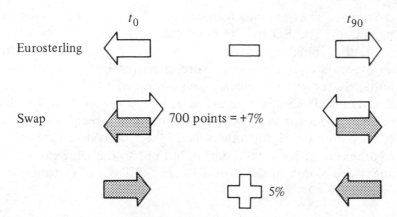

Sterling was borrowed in the Eurosterling market until the rate rose to parity (12%) with the points and other currencies. The rise was given an assist by a withdrawal of some traditional suppliers. Countries that had been holders of sterling for reserve purposes sold it.

The story of sterling in 1976 is an instance where pressure against sterling in the exchange market moved the forward points and, in consequence, the Eurosterling rates. The external rates of other currencies were not so affected as the move out of sterling was spread among many currencies.

Forward sales or purchases of a currency affect the spot rate as well as the swap points. Usually the spot rate is affected more than the swap. The reasons are that spot rates are more volatile than swaps and there are more ways to offset a swap exposure than a spot risk. Consider the position of a bank covering the exposure caused by forward sales. The spot exposure can be covered only by another spot transaction. A swap risk of two months can be offset by another swap for two months, or partially by swaps of one or three months, or by a loan and investment of one, two, or three months, in either external or domestic markets. The effect of many two-month swap transactions can be well spread out, but not so with many spot transactions.

On October 5, 1979 the U.S. Federal Reserve imposed new reserve requirements on certain classes of funds borrowed by banks in the

United States. The effect was to raise the marginal cost of funds to the banking system. The Federal Reserve also announced that the key day-to-day rate that it had managed was to be set free, with the understanding that it would rise. The moves were in response to high inflation in the United States and the precarious position of the dollar on the exchange markets. Domestic interest rates in the United States rose and with them, Eurodollar rates. On October 4 the three-month rate was $13\frac{1}{4}\%$; on November 5 the rate was $15\frac{3}{4}\%$. Interest rates rose somewhat in other countries in the interim, but not to the same extent. Compare the three-month points for \$/¥ and \$/DG on October 4 and November 5.

Currency	Oct. 4	Nov. 5
Yen	330–315	465–450
Guilder	173–163	275–265

The increase in external dollar interest rates directly affected the points in the foreign exchange market.

Where there is a viable external money market, its influence will generally dominate the exchange market. Such money markets are few—U.S. dollar, Canadian dollar, Deutsche mark, Dutch guilder, Swiss franc. Smaller markets exist for French francs, sterling, Belgian francs, lire, and yen. Even without a large external market, domestic money rates in a country will set the general parameters for the forward points. In these cases, however, events and expectations in the foreign exchange market can become the dominant forces for change.

PROBLEMS

1. The following chart describes the relation between interest rates, forward points, discounts, and premiums. When filled in, it will give you a handy way of remembering these relations. Consider two cases: (a) foreign interest rates are lower than home interest rates ($I_f < I_h$); and (b) foreign interest rates are higher than home interest rates ($I_f > I_h$).

	Home Currency Is at a Discount or Premium Against Foreign Currency	Points Are Added to or Subtracted from Spot	Forward Points Are Written High to Low or Low to High
$I_f < I_h$			
$I_f > I_h$			

Spot is written as foreign currency/home currency.

2. Is there any possibility for profitable arbitrage in the following situation?

	Spot	Three months
£/Yen	489.75–490.75	890–860

Eurosterling, 3 months	$15\frac{1}{8} - 15\frac{3}{8}\%$
External yen, 3 months	$6 - 6\frac{1}{4}\%$

Assume that you do not pay a lending spread.

RESPONSES

1. Perhaps the easiest way to reason out the responses for this chart is to set up the schema for the spot and swap, that is, a forward, with a foreign currency receivable exposure.

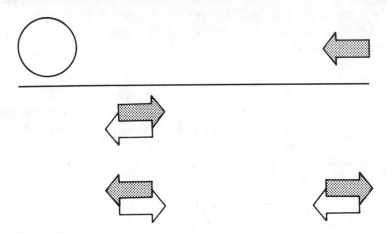

Spot is written as 1 unit of foreign currency = units of home currency. In the first instance the foreign interest rate is less than the home interest rate, so there is an earning to the spot/swap covering operation. An earning means the customer receives more units of home currency per foreign unit in the future. This is a sign that the home currency is at a discount to the foreign currency. A currency is less valuable if it takes more units to equal another currency. Because it is an earning, the points are added to spot. Recalling Chapter 5, points added to spot were written low to high. The first line of the box reads

$$I_f < I_h \quad \text{discount} \quad \text{add} \quad \text{low–high}$$

On the second line the foreign interest rate is greater than the home interest rate, so there is a cost to the spot/swap covering operation. A cost means the customer receives fewer units of home currency per foreign unit in the future. This is a sign that the home currency is at a premium to the foreign currency. A currency is more valuable if it takes fewer units to equal another currency. Because it is a cost, the points are subtracted from spot. Points subtracted from spot are written high to low. The second line of the box reads

$$I_f < I_h \qquad \text{premium} \qquad \text{subtract} \qquad \text{high–low}$$

2. The first thing to do is to calculate the swap cost/earnings associated with the points. Formula ICE-1 is used.

$$890 \text{ points is } 7.27\%$$

$$860 \text{ points is } 7.01\%$$

Lay out the general arbitrage schema.

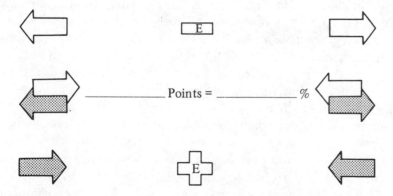

Try different combinations: (a) borrow sterling at $15\frac{3}{8}\%$, swap sterling for yen and earn 860 points, 7.01%, invest yen at 6%—with this operation there is a cost of $15\frac{3}{8}\%$ and an earning of 13.01%; this is not profitable; or (b) borrow yen at $6\frac{1}{4}\%$, swap yen for sterling at a cost of 890 points, 7.27%, invest sterling at $15\frac{1}{8}\%$—with this operation there is a cost of 13.52% and an earning of $15\frac{1}{8}\%$; this is profitable.

CHAPTER TEN
FOREIGN CURRENCY LOANS

The principal reason many companies borrow foreign currency is that it is cheaper than their own. Another reason is that foreign currency may be available when theirs is not. Credit restrictions imposed by central banks often have the effect of drying up the supply of domestic credit, especially for medium-sized enterprises. For those firms and governments who want to borrow very large sums, there are only a few money markets in the world large enough to accommodate them— U.S. dollars, Canadian dollars, Deutsche marks, Swiss francs, and sterling. The sophistication of some money markets allows the borrower greater flexibility in loan pricing and conditions than he would have in his own currency. Another good reason to borrow foreign currency is to cover a specific foreign currency receivable. As an extension of this idea, a British firm investing in a plant in Austria for sales in that market would borrow schillings to match the continuing flow of its receivables with its interest expenses.

These last two types of foreign currency loan do not involve any risk on the part of the borrower; they cover existing risk. But borrowing foreign currency because it is cheaper or more available or because the terms are more flexible does involve a risk. Foreign currency is con-

184

verted to home currency today. The risk is that the foreign currency appreciates against the home currency. The borrower has to spend more home currency to buy back the foreign currency at the maturity of the loan than was received when foreign currency was converted to home currency initially.

Why take the risk? The interest saving can be large. In December 1979 there was a 6% saving if Swiss francs were borrowed for five years as opposed to U.S. dollars, and there was an 11% difference between borrowing Swiss francs for one year instead of pounds sterling. On the equivalent of a $1 million loan, this represents a *saving* of $300,000 in the first case and $110,000 in the second. It would seem worth while to take a gamble on the exchange rate. In the first instance the company is betting that the Swiss franc will not appreciate against the dollar by more than 30% in five years and in the second, that the franc will not appreciate against the pound by more than 11% in one year.

It pays to look more closely at this gamble; the margin for change is not as wide as it appears. Over time, as the Swiss franc appreciates against the dollar, the cost of buying the periodic interest payments increases, in dollar terms. The following formula takes this into account. It calculates the percent change in the value of a foreign currency loan equivalent to a home currency loan.*

*See the derivation of this formula in the Appendix.

$$\text{percent change} = \frac{(I_h - I_f) \times \text{time}}{1 + \left(I_f \times \sum_{k=1}^{N} \frac{k}{N}\right)}$$

$$\text{example: } 26.1\% = \frac{(.11 - .05) \times 5}{1 + \left(.05 \times \sum_{k=1}^{5} \frac{k}{5}\right)}$$

The top half of the equation is the difference in interest rates over the time period of the loan. The bottom half represents the increasing cost of periodic interest payments in terms of the home currency. As a result, the appreciation of the franc that makes borrowing francs equivalent to borrowing dollars is 26.1% rather than 30%.

The example assumes that interest is paid annually and the appreciation of the franc proceeds uniformly over five years. The sign Σ indicates a summation over the number of years involved;

$$\sum_{k=1}^{5} \frac{k}{5} \text{ is equivalent to } \frac{1}{5} + \frac{2}{5} + \frac{3}{5} + \frac{4}{5} + \frac{5}{5}$$

This is the way the effect of increasing yearly interest payments is counted. For quarterly interest payments, substitute 20 quarters for five years in the summation of interest payments, $N = 20$.

$$\text{percent change} = \frac{(I_h - I_f) \times 5}{1 + \left(I_f \times \sum_{k=1}^{20} \frac{k}{20}\right)}$$

The more frequent interest payments allow for an even smaller appreciation before borrowing francs becomes equivalent to borrowing dollars; the change is 19.7%, compared to 26.1%.

Borrowing foreign currency is risky if there are no proceeds of that currency for the repayment. The formula allows an evaluation of that risk and specifies the judgment that must be made about the exchange rate. If spot $/SF is 1.5665, a 26.1% appreciation of the franc would result in a rate of $/SF 1.1576 in five years. At this rate the Swiss franc loan at 5% borrowed by a U.S. firm for use in the United States would be the equivalent of a U.S. dollar loan at 11%, for five years. If the company expects $/SF to be 1.25, it would borrow francs; if it forecasts $/SF 1.05, the company would borrow dollars.

Foreign currencies with high interest rates are sometimes borrowed in the expectation that the currencies will depreciate against the home currency before the loan must be repaid. The belief is that the depreciation of the foreign currency will more than offset its higher interest rate. Sterling loans during 1976 and dollar loans in 1978 fulfilled these expectations. The same formula can be used to determine the amount of depreciation necessary for a high interest foreign currency loan to be equivalent to borrowing the home currency.

COVERING A FOREIGN CURRENCY LOAN

If a company has borrowed foreign currency but subsequent events indicate that the currency is appreciating more rapidly than forecast, the company can cover the principal and interest exposure.

A firm whose primary motive for borrowing is availability or flexibility of terms may not wish to be open to the exchange risk from the very beginning. When the loan is drawn down (received), the foreign currency is converted spot to the home currency. The repayment of the loan plus interest is covered by a Forward. (The BSI and Lead options are not applicable since they involve a home currency loan.) The spot and forward transactions together have the same representation as the swap. It is cheaper for the company to approach the initial conversion and forward cover as a single transaction rather than two separate ones. It avoids entering the spot market on both sides. This illustration of the spot and forward (a spot and a swap) makes that clear.

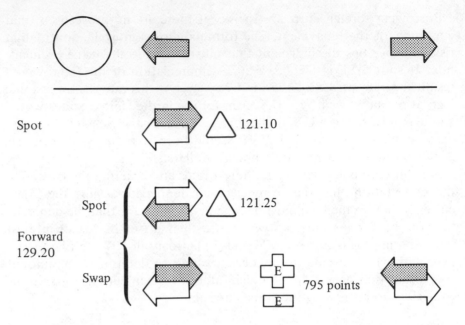

Spot   121.10

Spot   121.25

Forward
129.20

Swap   795 points

The swap is the only transaction needed. The two spot transactions are superfluous and cost the company money.

The effect of covering the foreign currency loan is to borrow the home currency in the external market. The foreign currency is borrowed in the money market but is then immediately invested in the foreign exchange market through the swap.

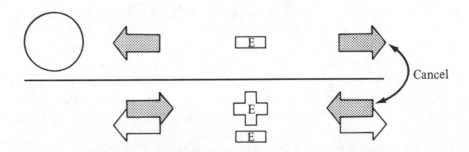

Cancel

To totally cover the exposure of a foreign currency loan, the interest on the loan is purchased forward also. A Swiss franc loan of 5 million at 5% has an interest payment of SF253,472.22 at the end of a year. A Dutch company goes to its bank and says that it would like to swap SF5 million spot against one year for guilders and at the same time buy SF253,472.22 one year forward with guilders. The company sells SF5 million spot at SF/DG121.25 and buys SF5,253,472.22 forward at SF/DG129.20, a cost of 795 points. The bank combines the future portion of the swap with the forward contract for the interest.

To calculate the cost of the operation of raising home currency by (1) borrowing foreign currency, (2) swapping it for home currency, and (3) buying foreign currency interest forward, three elements must be considered:

1. I_f, the interest rate of the foreign currency
2. The cost/earning of the swap as calculated by ICE-1

$$\text{ICE-1} = \frac{\text{points}}{\text{spot}} \times \frac{360}{\text{days}}$$

3. The cost/earning of buying the foreign currency interest forward as calculated in the following formula:

$$\text{interest amount exposed} \times \frac{\text{points}}{\text{spot}} \times \frac{360}{\text{days}}$$

$$= I_f \times \frac{\text{days}}{360} \times \frac{\text{points}}{\text{spot}} \times \frac{360}{\text{days}}$$

$$= I_f \times \frac{\text{points}}{\text{spot}}$$

Adding 1, 2, and 3 together gives an expression for I_h, interest rate of the home currency.

$$I_h = I_f \pm \frac{\text{points}}{\text{spot}} \times \frac{360}{\text{days}} \pm I_f \times \frac{\text{points}}{\text{spot}}$$

Combining some terms gives the formula for calculating the Total Covered Cost (TCC) of a foreign currency loan; equivalently, the cost of borrowing home currency through the money market and the swap.*

$$I_h = \left(I_f \times \frac{\text{forward}}{\text{spot}} \pm \frac{\text{points}}{\text{spot}} \times \frac{360}{\text{days}} \right) \times 100$$

Reading from the left, this equation says that the interest rate on home currency raised by a combination money market and exchange transaction is equal to the interest rate on the foreign currency times a factor to account for covering the foreign currency interest forward, plus/minus the cost/earning of the swap.

Example. A Dutch company borrows Swiss francs at 5% for one year. It will convert the francs to guilders for use in Holland. The cost of borrowing the francs and totally covering the exposure gives the effective cost of borrowing guilders.

SF/DG spot 121.10–25

one year 775–795

Interest cost of Dutch guilders is 11.79%.

$$11.79\% = \left(.05 \times \frac{129.20}{121.25} + \frac{7.95}{121.25} \times \frac{360}{365} \right) \times 100$$

*The Appendix contains an alternative derivation of TCC.

The cost of covering the Swiss franc interest payment adds .32% to the cost of borrowing the guilders.

In the Appendix are sections containing modifications of the TCC formula. These modifications deal with (1) currencies with different interest accrual bases, (2) the exchange rate in foreign terms, and (3) interim interest payments.

PROBLEMS

The four problems illustrate different uses of foreign currency loans and the swap. Each situation is described and all of the elements of the answer are given under the heading RESPONSES. The problem, response, and response analysis sections are a bit different from the ones in previous chapters. The responses are less specific, with emphasis on describing the options rather than calculation. The RESPONSE ANALYSIS for each problem does not include every response. Do one problem at a time and read the response analysis before going on to the next one. It will be helpful if you symbolize the options for yourself; colored pencils or arrows are useful.

1. The Gold Mountain Trading Company in Hong Kong is a subsidiary of a U.S. company by the same name. The trading company imports chemicals from the United States and Japan for sale in Hong Kong, Singapore, and Taiwan. The Hong Kong operation needs financing between purchase and sale of its merchandise. It has access to local and external money markets. In addition, the parent company has offered a two-month loan in U.S. dollars at $1\frac{1}{2}\%$ below the rate Gold Mountain can obtain from its bank. The attractiveness of this offer is tempered by the volatility of the Hong Kong dollar in the exchange markets. Assume that external and domestic Hong Kong dollar interest rates are the same. What are the alternatives Gold Mountain has to finance its operation?

2. Snediker Gmbh is a German establishment that specializes in trade with Spain and Portugal. As a result of its activities, the

company has a temporary surplus of external Spanish pesetas. Snediker will be in this position for about three months. The company is finding it somewhat difficult to locate a temporary investment for its pesetas; nothing is available in Spain. The company's objective is to maximize the number of pesetas it will have at the end of three months without undue risk. What can it do?

3. Higgins Ltd. is a multinational pharmaceutical concern. Its headquarters are in London; its production units are in Mexico, Ireland, Italy, Turkey, and Singapore; the primary markets are continental Europe, Canada, and Japan. The Mexican plant is the principal supplier to Canada, who pays at quarterly intervals in Canadian dollars. You have just taken over as treasurer of the Mexican subsidiary and are charged with finding a way of obtaining working capital at the lowest possible cost, without creating any exposure for the company. The prospects appear gloomy. Local peso financing is not available for the subsidiaries of foreign companies. The Mexican federal and state governments impose a 26.75% withholding tax on foreign borrowings. The tax is based on the interest rate. For example, an external loan at 10% has an effect cost of

$$13.65\% = \frac{10\%}{1 - .2675}$$

The interest rates for three months' external money are:

Mexican pesos	25%
Canadian dollars	$13\frac{1}{4}\%$
U.S. dollars	$14\frac{1}{2}\%$
Sterling	17%
Swiss francs	4%

What alternatives does the treasurer of Higgins (Mexico) have to raise working capital? What is the best alternative?

4. Perrine & Company Ltd. is a Canadian corporation with head-quarters in Quebec. It sells sporting goods in North America and Europe. The company has decided to expand its European operation and wants to build a new plant in Belgium. It needs financing for one year. The company can borrow locally, or it can use the surplus funds of other subsidiaries. The Belgian government, however, imposes a 10% withholding tax on intracompany loans. The finance subsidiary of Perrine & Company in Nassau has recently generated a surplus of U.S. $2 million that could be used for the project. The company is not anxious to pay the withholding tax since it would add about $1\frac{1}{2}\%$ to the cost. Equally, the company is not anxious to create a foreign exchange exposure for any of its subsidiaries. Prevailing interest rates for one year are:

Belgian francs, external and domestic	13%
U.S. dollars	$13\frac{1}{2}\%$
Deutsche marks	8%
Swiss francs	2%

What are the alternatives for financing the new plant in Belgium, and what is the best alternative?

RESPONSES

The interest rates in the problems apply to both interest cost and earning, and the spread between borrowing and investing rates is ignored. *A loan from a bank has an additional cost of 1%.*

1. Hong Kong dollar loan.
2. External U.S. dollar loan.
3. Sterling loan.
4. Deutsche mark loan.
5. Swiss franc loan.
6. Belgian franc loan.
7. External peso loan.
8. Parent/affiliate U.S. dollar loan.
9. Canadian dollar loan.
10. U.S. dollar investment.
11. Deutsche mark investment.
12. Swiss franc investment.
13. Swap.
14. Spot.
15. Forward.
16. Lead receivables.

Problem 1

Gold Mountain's options are:

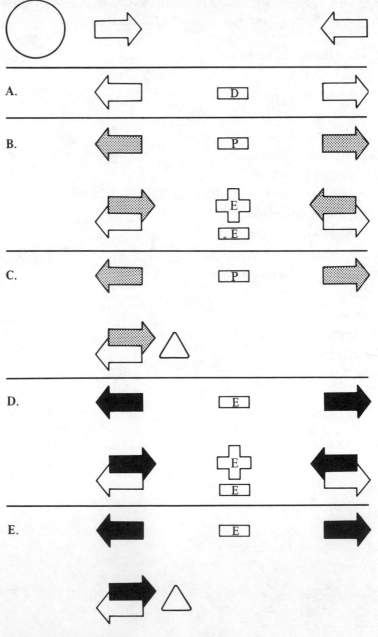

White, Hong Kong dollar; gray, U.S. dollar;
black, Swiss franc

Gold Mountain has an outflow of Hong Kong dollars today. This represents the need for financing until customers pay for their orders, the inflow.

A. *Response 1*: Hong Kong dollar loan from a local bank. The cost is the domestic Hong Kong dollar interest rate plus 1% bank spread. There is no foreign exchange exposure.

B. *Responses 8, 13 and 15*: Parent U.S. dollar loan, swap of the U.S. dollars for Hong Kong dollars, and forward purchase of interest on the dollars. The future portion of the swap and the forward contract are shown as the same flow. The cost of the parent loan is $1\frac{1}{2}\%$ below the cost of a bank loan and, therefore, $\frac{1}{2}\%$ below the rate for external U.S. dollars. (A bank would add 1% to the external U.S. rate.) Through the swap the company earns the external Hong Kong dollar rate (equal to the domestic rate). The company has a net earning of $\frac{1}{2}\%$ on the U.S. dollar elements of this option. Therefore, the net cost to Gold Mountain is the domestic Hong Kong dollar interest rate less $\frac{1}{2}\%$. There is no foreign exchange exposure.

C. *Responses 8 and 14*: Parent U.S. dollar loan and a spot, sell U.S. dollars, buy Hong Kong dollars. The known cost of this option is the external U.S. dollar rate less $\frac{1}{2}\%$. The cost in terms of Hong Kong dollars is not known because this option creates an exposure; in two months there is an inflow of Hong Kong dollars and an outflow of U.S. dollars. If interest rates in the United States are higher than those in Hong Kong, the company would be expecting a depreciation of the U.S. dollar during the next two months to make up for its higher interest rates. The formula for percent change would be used to determine the amount of depreciation that would make two situations equivalent. Rather than comparing the rate on the parent loan to the domestic Hong Kong dollar rate, option A, it should be compared to option B since it is the best covered option Gold Mountain can execute.

D. *Responses 4, 13 and 15*: Swiss franc loan, swap of Swiss francs for Hong Kong dollars, and forward purchase of interest on the Swiss francs. The future portion of the swap and the forward contract for the interest are shown as the same flow. The cost of borrowing is the external franc rate plus 1% bank spread. Through the swap the company earns back the franc rate, leaving it with a cost of 1% on the Swiss franc portion of this option. Through the swap the company incurrs the cost of Hong Kong dollar interest rates (domestic = external). The net result is that Gold Mountain borrows Hong Kong dollars at the domestic Hong Kong dollar interest rate plus 1%. There is no exposure. This result is essentially the same as option A. There is no benefit from borrowing a low interest rate currency if it is to be covered. The company ends up paying the cost of its own currency in the external market. The benefit in option B was the below-market rate of the parent loan.

E. *Responses 4 and 14*: Swiss franc loan and sale of francs, for Hong Kong dollars spot. The known cost is the external interest rate for Swiss francs. The cost in terms of Hong Kong dollars is not known. This option creates an exposure. As in option C, the appropriate comparison is between the interest rate on Swiss francs and the best covered option, option B. The expectation is that the Swiss franc does not appreciate by more than the difference between the cost of borrowing francs and the cost of option B.

Summary of the Costs and Risks of the Options

Option	Interest Cost	Risk
A	Domestic HK$ plus 1%	None
B	Domestic HK$ less $\frac{1}{2}$%	None
C	External US$ less $\frac{1}{2}$%	U.S.$ appreciation
D	Domestic HK$ plus 1%	None
E	External SF plus 1%	SF appreciation

Problem 2

Since Snediker has difficulty locating a direct investment for the pesetas, the company considers investment in other currencies, on a covered and on an uncovered basis. The temporary surplus is illustrated by an inflow of funds today and an outflow in three months. The basic options are:

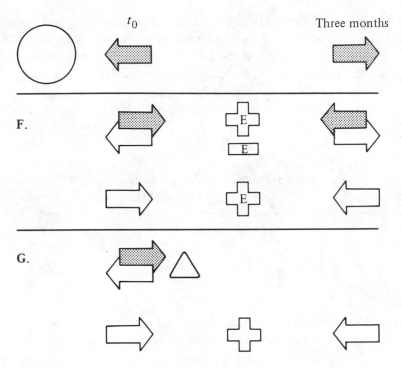

t_0 Three months

F. *Responses 13, 11 and 15:* Swap the pesetas for Deutsche marks, invest the marks, and convert the mark interest to pesetas with a forward contract. The three-month end of the swap and the forward are shown as the same flow. Through the swap Snediker earns the external peseta interest rate and incurs the cost of external mark rates. The investment earns the external or the domestic mark interest rate, whichever is higher. Assume the external rate is the higher. It is clear that the Deutsche mark elements of this option effectively cancel out, with the exception of the small spread between borrowing and investing rates; the cost in the swap against the earning of the investment. The net gain from this option is the external interest rate of the peseta. Pesetas are invested, albeit indirectly. A swap of pesetas for any other currency would produce the same net result.

G.   *Responses 14 and 11*: Sell pesetas, buy marks spot, and invest the marks. The marks can be invested in either the domestic or the external mark money market. The earning in terms of pesetas is not known since there is the possibility of a change in the mark/peseta rate in three months. The pesetas could also be sold spot for any other currency and that currency invested. Snediker would evaluate these possibilities in the following manner:

Currency	Interest Rate	Appreciation or Depreciation	Probability of Compensating Movement
Lira	27%	D 1%	30%
Sterling	17%	A $2\frac{1}{3}$%	10%
Deutsche mark	8%	A $5\frac{1}{3}$%	80%
Option F	24%	0	Not required

The numbers are for illustration only. For each currency the chart lists the earning for a three-month deposit, the percentage appreciation or depreciation of the currency necessary to make it equivalent to option F, and the probability of a movement. The number in the third column is calculated with the formula for percent change, assuming all interest is paid at the end of the period. The probabilities are determined by Snediker after analyzing the foreign exchange market and consulting with its bankers. This determination is the judgmental aspect of the decision. The framework for the decision is set up, so it is easy to plug in different numbers for the probability if it is hard to decide on one.

A lira investment, although it involves some risk, appears to be the most likely alternative to option F. The interest rate is 3% higher, and there is only a 30% chance the lira will depreciate enough to wipe out the extra earning. Sterling interest rates are high, although lower than option F. There is little probability, however, that the 7% gap will be compensated for by the appreciation of sterling. The interest rate on marks is low, and although the chance of a compensating movement in the currency is high, it must be large to make up the difference in interest rates.

As an exercise in the use of the TCC formula find the earning of option F given:

DM/Pts spot 35.95–98

3 mo points   141–151

DM deposit $8-8\frac{1}{4}\%$

The calculation is given in the section of the Appendix entitled "Calculation of the Earning of Option F, Problem 2."

Problem 3

Options for Higgins Mexico are illustrated. The situation: financing in pesos is needed today and Canadian dollars will flow in in three months.

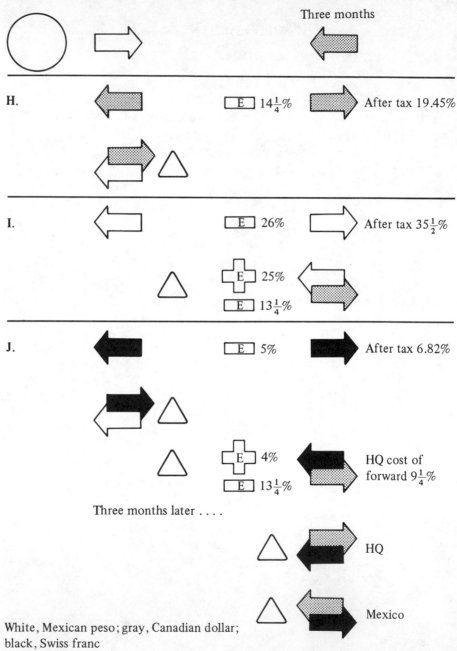

Three months

H.   E $14\frac{1}{4}$%   After tax 19.45%

I.   E 26%   After tax $35\frac{1}{2}$%

E 25%
E $13\frac{1}{4}$%

J.   E 5%   After tax 6.82%

E 4%   HQ cost of forward $9\frac{1}{4}$%
E $13\frac{1}{4}$%

Three months later . . . .

HQ

Mexico

White, Mexican peso; gray, Canadian dollar; black, Swiss franc

H. *Responses 9 and 14, or 16 and 14*: Canadian dollar loan and sell Canadian dollars for pesos spot; or lead the Canadian dollar receivable and sell it spot for pesos. In both cases the withholding tax is applied to the transaction, leading a foreign receivable is considered equivalent to borrowing the foreign currency. The effective cost is 19.45%. It is assumed for this example that the cost of leading and an external loan are the same. It will be seen shortly that a difference of 1 or 2% is not important to the decision.

I. *Responses 7 and 15*: External peso loan and a forward contract to buy pesos and sell the incoming Canadian dollars. The withholding tax is levied, even on external peso loans; this raises the effective cost of borrowing to $35\frac{1}{2}\%$. Even with the earning through the swap of $11\frac{3}{4}\%$, this is an expensive option.

J. *Responses 5, 14 and 15*: Swiss franc loan, sell francs spot for pesos, buy francs forward with Canadian dollars. The idea is to borrow the currency with the lowest interest rate to minimize the impact of the withholding tax. The total cost of the loan plus the forward is 16.07%, 3.38% less than option H. The forward contract is made at Higgins headquarters in London so that the subsidiary does not appear to be avoiding tax by borrowing a low interest rate currency and then immediately covering its exposure.

Three months later the subsidiary will sell its Canadian dollar receivable to repay its Swiss franc loan. At the same time Higgins in London will buy Canadian dollars and sell Swiss francs to offset its original forward contract. Banks are able to arrange offsetting contracts at the same rate for two parts of the same corporation. Only transactions costs are charged.

Regardless of the spot rate of Swiss francs, and Canadian dollars in three months the option will cost only 16.07%. Any cost above this which is incurred by the Mexican company in buying the Swiss francs is compensated for by earnings in London from offsetting its contract.

Problem 4

The options of Perrine & Company for financing the Belgian plant are:

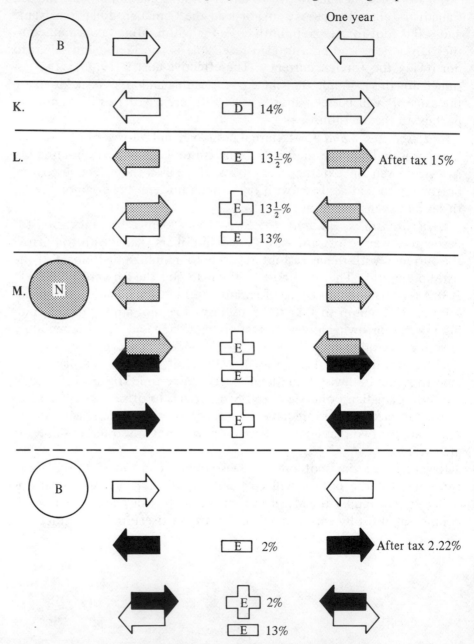

White, Belgian francs; gray, U.S. dollars; black, Swiss francs

K. *Response 6*: A Belgian franc loan completely takes care of the situation at a cost of 14%; 13% cost of money plus 1% bank lending spread. It is the simplest option, but not the least costly.

L. *Responses 8, 13 and 15*: A U.S. dollar loan from the Nassau affiliate, swap of the dollars for Belgian francs and purchase forward of the dollar interest. Again, swap and forward are shown as the same flow. The withholding tax makes the effective cost of the intercompany loan 15%. There is an earning of $\frac{1}{2}$% in the swap, so the total cost is $14\frac{1}{2}$%. There is no exposure.

M. *Responses 13, 15, 12, 5, 13 and 15*: This option looks at both the Nassau finance subsidiary and the Belgian manufacturing subsidiary. The temporary surplus of the Nassau unit is symbolized by the inflow of dollars today and the outflow in a year. Nassau swaps those dollars for Swiss francs, lends the Swiss francs at the market rate to Belgium, and sells the franc interest forward. The investment by Nassau and borrowing by Belgium are both shown. Belgium has an after-tax cost of 2.22% on the Swiss franc loan. The Swiss francs are then swapped at a cost of 11% for one year for the Belgian francs needed to construct the plant. Interest on the Swiss francs is bought forward. The total cost to the Belgian unit is 13.22%, a saving of .78% over the simplest option. If the plant costs BF 60 million, the savings from option M is BF 468,000, and there is no exposure for the company. In all of the options the Nassau finance unit earns the same rate.

APPENDIX

Derivation of the Formula for Equating a Home Currency with a Foreign Currency Loan

$$C = \frac{(I_h - I_f) \times t}{1 + I_f \times \sum_{k=1}^{N} \frac{k}{N}}$$

The assumption is that the foreign currency principal and interest payments are purchased with home currency. The starting point is to equate the principal plus interest payments on the home currency to the principal plus interest payments on the foreign currency and include a factor to account for the appreciation of the foreign currency. The symbols used are:

P principal
I_h interest rate, home currency
I_f interest rate, foreign currency
C appreciation/depreciation rate of the foreign currency over the period of the loan
t time period of the loan in years
N also the time period of the loan, but specified as to how interest is paid, for instance, if annually for five years $N = 5$; if quarterly for five years, $N = 20$

$$P + (P \times I_h \times t) = P + (P \times I_f \times t) + (P \times C) + \left(P \times I_f \times \sum_{k=1}^{N} \frac{k}{N} \times C \right)$$

The first P on the left is the principal of the home currency loan, and the term $(P \times I_h \times t)$ is the total amount of interest over the term of the loan; together the two terms represent the total amount of money paid back to the bank. The first two terms on the right side of the equality sign represent the same thing for a foreign currency loan. It is assumed the amount borrowed P is the same whether borrowed in home currency or foreign currency. The term $(P \times C)$ is the additional amount of money that must be paid out for the principal amount if the foreign currency appreciates against the home currency. The last term accounts for the increased cost of foreign currency interest payments due to an appreciation.

Solving the long equation for C is done by first recognizing that P is a common term and eliminating it from the equation, moving the term $(I_f \times t)$ to the left of the equal sign and then collecting the C terms remaining on the right.

Modification of TCC for Currencies with Different Interest Bases

Interest on loans and investments in some currencies is calculated on the basis of a 365-day year; on many others, it is calculated on a 360-day basis. Chapter 7 shows the difference five days makes. Using the TCC formula involves mixing the two bases at times, so a modification must be made to ensure that the resulting rate is appropriate to the currency:

$$\text{TCC: } I_h = \left[\left(I_f \times \frac{\text{forward}}{\text{spot}}\right) \pm \left(\frac{\text{points}}{\text{spot}} \times \frac{360}{\text{days}}\right)\right] \times 100$$

If I_h is on a 365-day basis and I_f on a 360 day basis:

$$I_h = \frac{365}{360} \times \left[\left(I_f \times \frac{\text{forward}}{\text{spot}}\right) \pm \left(\frac{\text{points}}{\text{spot}} \times \frac{360}{\text{days}}\right)\right] \times 100$$

If I_h is on a 360-day basis and I_f on a 365-day basis:

$$I_h = \frac{360}{365} \times \left[\left(I_f \times \frac{\text{forward}}{\text{spot}}\right) \pm \left(\frac{\text{points}}{\text{spot}} \times \frac{360}{\text{days}}\right)\right] \times 100$$

If both I_h and I_f are on a 365-day basis:

$$I_h = \left[\left(I_f \times \frac{\text{forward}}{\text{spot}}\right) \pm \left(\frac{\text{points}}{\text{spot}} \times \frac{365}{\text{days}}\right)\right] \times 100$$

Modification of TCC When the Exchange Rate is Expressed in Foreign Terms

The home currency is the one the spot rate is denominated in. It generally coincides with the country the company is in. England, Ireland,

Australia, and New Zealand are the only consistent exceptions. Companies native to those countries would use this modified formula.

The object is to express a percentage difference in terms of one currency when the numbers being used are in terms of another currency. This is the rationale behind ICE-2. The total covered cost formula is modified by substituting ICE-2 for ICE-1 in the two places where that formula is used: (1) cost/earning of the swap and (2) cost/earning of buying the foreign currency interest forward. These substitutions result in the following formula:

$$I_h = \left[\left(I_f \times \frac{\text{spot}}{\text{forward}}\right) \pm \left(\frac{\text{points}}{\text{forward}} \times \frac{360}{\text{days}}\right)\right] \times 100$$

If, in addition, I_h is sterling or another currency where interest is calculated on a 365-day basis, and if I_f is on a 360-day basis, the formula would be

$$I_h = \frac{365}{360} \times \left[\left(I_f \times \frac{\text{spot}}{\text{forward}}\right) + \left(\frac{\text{points}}{\text{forward}} \times \frac{360}{\text{days}}\right)\right] \times 100$$

Adaptation of TCC to Interim Interest Payments

On loans of six months and longer interest is often paid at quarterly intervals rather than at the maturity of the loan. We want to incorporate that consideration into the cost formula for totally covering the exposure of a foreign currency loan. It is done by adjusting the last element of the formula—cost/earning of buying interest forward; that is:

$$\text{interest amount} \times \frac{\text{points}}{\text{spot}} \times \frac{360}{\text{days}}$$

which is equal to

$$I_f \times \frac{\text{points}}{\text{spot}}$$

If interest is paid quarterly, simply divide I_f by 4, since effectively one-quarter of the interest rate is paid each time. Then add as many terms

$$\frac{I_f}{4} \times \frac{\text{points}}{\text{spot}}$$

as there are quarters in the loan period. If interest payments are monthly, use 12 instead of 4. Putting this back into TCC yields

$$I_h = \left[I_f + \left(\frac{\text{points}}{\text{spot}} \times \frac{360}{\text{days}} \right) \pm \frac{I_f}{4 \times \text{spot}} \times (\text{points}_1 \right.$$
$$\left. + \text{points}_2 + \text{points}_3 + \cdots + \text{points}) \right] \times 100$$

Points$_1$, points$_2$, and so forth refer to the points to the first interest payment, the second interest payment, and so on. Points without any subscript are those to the end of the loan period.

As an example of how this formula works, let's consider the Swiss franc loan of the Dutch company. The loan is for one year and interest is payable quarterly. The rates are

$$\begin{array}{ll}
\text{SF/DG spot} & 121.10\text{--}25 \\
3 \text{ mo} & 255\text{--}265 \\
6 \text{ mo} & 450\text{--}465 \\
9 \text{ mo} & 610\text{--}630 \\
1 \text{ year} & 775\text{--}795
\end{array}$$

The effective interest cost of borrowing guilders by borrowing Swiss francs and swapping them for guilders is 11.69%:

$$11.69\% = \left[.05 + \left(\frac{7.95}{121.25} \times \frac{360}{365} \right) + \frac{.05}{4 \times 121.25} \times (2.65 \right.$$
$$\left. + 4.65 + 6.30 + 7.95) \right] \times 100$$

Buying interest quarterly is cheaper by .10% than paying everything at the maturity of the loan because it costs fewer guilders to buy the Swiss francs in the earlier periods. On the other hand, paying interest on a quarterly basis rather than annually means that you forego the use of that money during the year. This is an added cost of .52%, assuming that the money could be reinvested at the guilder interest rate.

Alternative Derivation of TCC

Assume that a company borrows $1 for a certain number of days. At the end of the period the company must repay the principal plus interest:

$$\$1 + \$1 \times I_\$ \times \frac{days}{360}$$

where $I_\$$ is the interest rate on dollars. The company wants to make an investment in Malaysia for the same period and wants to earn at least the equivalent number of dollars through a ringitt investment and a foreign exchange transaction. The number of ringitts available at the end of the period will be the number bought on the spot date plus the interest earned on this number of ringitts:

$$S + S \times I_R \times \frac{days}{360}$$

where I_R is the interest rate on ringitts and S is the spot rate $/MR. The number of dollars this equates to today is given by the forward rate, $S \pm P$, where P stands for points. The dollar equivalent of the Malaysian investment is given by the expression:

$$\frac{S + S \times I_R \times \frac{days}{360}}{S \pm P}$$

The equation that gives the break-even point between the dollar borrowing and the ringitt investment is

$$\$1 + \$1 \times I_\$ \times \frac{\text{days}}{360} = \frac{S + S \times I_R \times \dfrac{\text{days}}{360}}{S \pm P}$$

To make the equation more general, call dollars the foreign currency and ringitts the home currency since the exchange rate is written \$/MR or FC/HC. The equation is then rewritten as

$$1 + 1 \times I_f \times \frac{\text{days}}{360} = \frac{S + S \times I_h \times \dfrac{\text{days}}{360}}{S \pm P}$$

Solving the equation for I_h yields the TCC formula; solving the equation for P yields the points formula; solving the equation for $(I_h - I_f)$ yields the modified ICE formula shown in Chapter 5.

Calculation of the Earning of Option F, Problem 2

The problem is to find the earning resulting from a swap of pesetas for marks and an investment of marks for three months. The rates are:

$$\text{DM/Pts spot } 35.95\text{--}98$$

$$3 \text{ mo points } \quad 141\text{--}151$$

$$\text{DM deposit} \quad 8\text{--}8\tfrac{1}{4}\%$$

The formula to use is TCC:

$$I_{\text{Pts}} = \left[\left(I_{\text{DM}} \times \frac{\text{forward}}{\text{spot}} \right) + \left(\frac{\text{points}}{\text{spot}} \times \frac{360}{\text{days}} \right) \right] \times 100$$

The calculation is

$$24\% = \left[\left(.08 \times \frac{37.36}{35.95} \right) + \left(\frac{1.41}{35.95} \times \frac{360}{90} \right) \right] \times 100$$

CHAPTER ELEVEN
LOCKING IN FUTURE INTEREST RATES

The treasurer of Antigone Shipping knows that in one month the company will receive its quarterly charter fees. This money has been designated for the down payment on a new vessel three months later. During the interim period the company wants to earn as much as possible on the surplus funds. The problem the treasurer faces is that she sees interest rates falling and thinks that in one month the three-month investment rate may be at least 1% lower than today.

Indian Key Sugar has just received a fixed price contract from the government of Honduras to build a sugar refinery in that country. The contract is in Deutsche marks. Financing for the project will begin in six months; outstandings will average DM 10 million for the following two years. With inflationary pressures building in West Germany and the consequent effect on interest rates, the management of Indian Key would like to fix the cost of their financing today.

In July Lowden Breweries, Inc. plans to issue $4 million of three-month commercial paper in September for working capital purposes.

Commercial paper is a certificate of indebtedness for specific maturities issued by corporations to raise money. The paper is bought by investors in short-term money market instruments. The treasurer is quite convinced that in September he will pay at least $\frac{3}{4}\%$ more than if he could issue the paper today.

The treasurer of Wie Textiles Ltd. notes that the yield curve for fixed period deposits in the UK has a positive slope, such as:

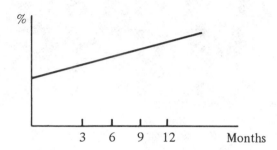

He expects present rates to hold for the next three to four months; therefore, he should be able to place the money coming in in two months at the same rate as today. Company operations will require the funds four months later for the annual wool purchases. The treasurer feels, however, that he could be better off by arranging the investment of the incoming funds today.

Common to all these companies is the desire to borrow or invest starting at some point in the future. The treasurers are trying to lock in rates today for a future period because they believe that when the future becomes present the rate they receive may be less attractive. The treasurer of Wie sees an opportunity in the current rate structure. The desire of the treasurers is not immediately accommodated by the market because deposits and advances conventionally start within two days from today, not one month from today.

Antigone wants to make a three-month investment one month from today. The treasurer could invest money today, for four months, to take advantage of higher rates. Since the company does not have the money today, the treasurer could borrow from the bank for one month and pay the bank off when the charter fees come in. The net effect would be to invest money for three months starting one month from today, at a rate fixed today. In symbols, Antigone has:

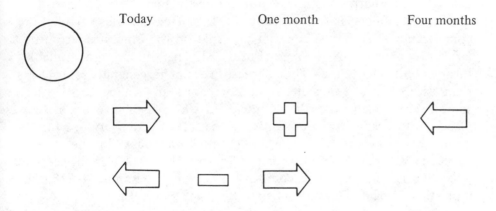

If the investment rate for four months is 10% and the borrowing rate for one month is $9\frac{1}{2}\%$, including 1% bank lending spread. Antigone has fixed a rate of 10.17% for the three-month investment. The calculation is

$$10.17\% = \frac{10\% \times 4 \text{ months} - 9\frac{1}{2}\% \times 1 \text{ month}}{3 \text{ months}}$$

$$\text{rate} = \frac{\text{earning} - \text{cost}}{\text{period of investment}}$$

There is a better way to do the same thing. Antigone can ask its bank to arrange a *forward–forward* deposit. The bank will do the same as Antigone—place money for four months, borrow money for one month, and accept Antigone's charter fees on deposit for the last three months. This is better because the bank does not charge a lending spread of 1% to Antigone, since it has not extended credit to the company. The one-month borrowing rate used in the calculation is $8\frac{1}{2}\%$ rather than $9\frac{1}{2}\%$. As a result, Antigone can earn $10\frac{1}{2}\%$ rather than 10.17% for three months. The reason the rate for three months is higher than the rate for four months is that there is a positive spread (earning) between the borrowing and lending rates in the first month.

A third alternative for a U.S. dollar investment is the purchase of a three-month financial futures contract, U.S. Treasury bills (T bills) or commercial paper. These contracts are sold on the Chicago Mercantile Exchange and the New York Futures Exchange and are available through brokerage houses. Though these investments generally return less than external dollar deposits some companies are willing to sacrifice some return to diversify the countries in which their investments are placed. A futures contract bought today calls for the delivery of a three-month T bill at a certain price one month from today. In one month Antigone will pay $975,000 for the Treasury bill. Three months later when the bill matures, the company will receive $1 million–$25,000 more than it paid. Treasury bills are discount paper; they do not carry an interest rate. An investor earns by buying a bill at discount, for example $97.50 per $100, and receiving $100 at the maturity of the bill.

Indian Key wants to fix a borrowing rate for a two-year loan starting in six months. The company could borrow Deutsche marks for two and one-half years and then invest the money for six months. The result would be a loan for two years at a fixed rate. In symbols, Indian Key would do the following:

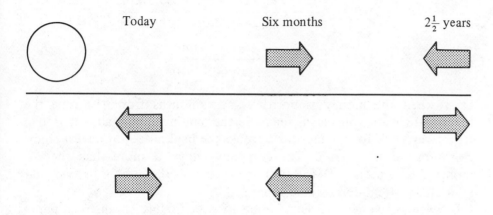

The loan and investment match the flows required for construction of the sugar refinery.

If the $2\frac{1}{2}\%$-year loan rate is $8\frac{1}{2}\%$, including $1\frac{1}{2}\%$ bank lending spread, and the investment rate for six months is 6%, Indian Key has fixed a rate of $9\frac{1}{8}\%$ for two years. The rate is higher than the $2\frac{1}{2}$-year rate because in the first six months the company incurs a cost of $2\frac{1}{2}\%$ (difference between $8\frac{1}{2}\%$ loan and 6% investment). Another way of thinking about this arrangement is that the company pays $2\frac{1}{2}\%$ for the six months before the loan starts and then pays $8\frac{1}{2}\%$ for two years.

However, like Antigone, Indian Key can go to its bank and request a *forward–forward* loan and be better off. The bank borrows for two and one-half years at 7% and places a deposit at 6% for six months. The money from the maturing deposit is given to Indian Key at $8\frac{3}{4}\%$, including bank spread. The bank calculates its cost of money to be $7\frac{1}{4}\%$.

$$7\frac{1}{4}\% = \frac{7\% \times 30 \text{ months} - 6\% \times 6 \text{ months}}{24 \text{ months}}$$

$$\text{rate} = \frac{\text{cost} - \text{earning}}{\text{period of loan}}$$

Only when the money is borrowed, six months from the time the forward–forward contract is made, is the lending spread added. Indian Key saves $1\frac{1}{2}\%$ for six months because the bank does not have a credit exposure for this period. The company pays $\frac{1}{4}\%$ more than the 30-month rate, a total of DM 50,000 to ensure that the rate on its two-year loan of DM 10 million is fixed today.

Lowden Breweries Inc. is planning to issue 90-day commercial paper in September, two months from today. The treasurer believes that the rate the company will pay in the future will be higher than today's rate. Lowden could issue commercial paper for 150 days and invest the proceeds until the money is needed. Or the treasurer can sell 90-day September commercial paper futures contracts. If interest rates rise as expected, there will be a profit on the contracts. This profit can be realized by offsetting the September sales contracts with September purchase contracts. The profit is then set against the higher cost of issuing the company's paper. If interest rates fall, there will be a loss on the contracts, but Lowden will be able to issue its commercial paper at lower rates. Either way the company knows today its costs of raising money in September.

Commercial paper is issued on both a discount basis, like T bills, and with a coupon. Today the rate for 90-day paper is 10%, and the September future is 10.20%. At 10.20% Lowden sells commercial paper futures. The company contracts to receive $974,500 for each $1 million and deliver commercial paper. The calculation of $974,500 is

$$1,000,000 \quad \times .1020 \quad \times \frac{90}{360} = 25,500$$

$$\underset{\substack{\text{face amount} \\ \text{of contracts}}}{} \times \underset{\substack{\text{discount} \\ \text{rate}}}{} \times \text{time} = \text{discount}$$

$$1,000,000 \quad - 25,000 \quad = 974,500$$

$$\text{face amount} - \text{discount} = \underset{\text{contracts}}{\text{value of}}$$

In September, as expected, rates rise to 10.80% for 90-day commercial paper. Lowden makes money by offsetting its future contracts; it sold at 97.45, and it buys back at 97.30. The profit is .15. The company will issue commercial paper at 10.80%, that is, receive 97.30 per 100 issued. The profit on the futures contract raises the receipt to 97.45 (97.30 + .15). This means that the effective rate of issue is 10.20%. This is calculated as follows:

$$\underset{\text{rate}}{\text{discount}} = \frac{\text{face amount} - \text{value of contract}}{\text{face amount}} \times \frac{360}{\text{days}} \times 100$$

$$10.20\% = \frac{100 - 97.45}{100} \times \frac{360}{90} \times 100$$

Had interest rates fallen to 9.80%, Lowden would have lost money on its futures contracts. It would have to offset its sales at 97.45 with purchases at 97.55, a loss of .10. It would have the advantage however, of issuing its own commercial paper at 9.80%, receiving 97.55 per 100. The loss of .10 leaves the company with net receipts of 97.45, equal to a rate of 10.20%. If Lowden takes out the futures contracts, it effectively locks itself into the rate on those contracts.

The treasurer of Wie Textiles believes that even though rates will remain the same for three to four months, he can achieve a better yield for his future inflow by arranging his deposit now. The rates for a fixed period resident sterling investment are

One month	$12\frac{3}{4}$–13%
Two months	$13\frac{1}{4}$–$13\frac{1}{2}$
Three months	$13\frac{1}{2}$–$13\frac{3}{4}$
Four months	14–$14\frac{1}{4}$
Five months	$14\frac{1}{2}$–$14\frac{3}{4}$
Six months	15–$15\frac{1}{4}$

Wie wants to place money for four months starting two months from today. The treasurer calculates that the bank will pay $15\frac{3}{4}$%, appreciably better than the four-month rate today, and what he expects it will be in the future. The bank would invest money for six months at 15%, borrow for two months at $13\frac{1}{2}$%, then take Wie's sterling for four months. The rate is higher than the current four month rate because the bank passes on to Wie the positive spread of $1\frac{1}{2}$% ($15 - 13\frac{1}{2}$) it would earn in the first two months. Wie is able to benefit from a forward–forward investment because the borrowing rate for two months is lower than the investment rate for six months. Were the borrowing rate higher, the company could be worse off. The calculation that Wie makes is

$$15\frac{3}{4}\% = \frac{15\% \times 6 \text{ months} - 13\frac{1}{2}\% \times 2 \text{ months}}{4 \text{ months}}$$

Wie calls the bank and learns that the bank will pay only 15.40% for the deposit and that the interest rates are the same ones Wie used. The bank explains that it must pay interest on the loan at the end of two months, but it does not receive any interest income for another four months. When banks borrow from one another, they conventionally pay interest at maturity when it is less than one year. The cost of borrowing the interest for that period reduces the rate from $15\frac{3}{4}\%$ to 15.40%.

Bank's Interest Flows on £1 Million

	Two months	Six months
Cost of 2-month loan, $13\frac{1}{2}\%$	−22,500	
Cost of borrowing £22,500, 15.40%		−1,155
Earning from investment, 15%		+75,000

The amount available to pay to Wie Textiles is £51,345. This amount, paid on £1 million for four months, is equivalent to an interest rate of 15.40%.

The same rate can be calculated as follows:

$$15.40\% = \frac{15\% \times 6 \text{ months} - 13\frac{1}{2}\% \times 2 \text{ months}}{4 \text{ months} \times \left[1 + \left(\frac{13\frac{1}{2}\%}{100} \times \frac{2 \text{ months}}{12 \text{ months}} \right) \right]}$$

The additional expression on the bottom of the equation accounts for the extra interest cost.* The general formula for calculating the rate on a forward–forward investment is given in terms of days since this is more accurate. There are some six-month periods that have 179 days, and others, because of holidays and weekends, have 185 days. The forward–forward investment rate is

$$\frac{(\text{investment rate} \times \text{days}) - (\text{borrowing rate} \times \text{days})}{(\text{days in forward period}) \times \left[1 + \left(\text{borrowing rate} \times \frac{\text{days}}{36,000} \right) \right]}$$

*This equation is derived in the Appendix.

Earlier in the chapter we saw that Antigone calculated it would be paid $10\frac{1}{2}\%$ for its deposit, but that did not take account of the cost of borrowing the interest on the loan. As a short exercise find how much the bank would be willing to pay Antigone for a three-month deposit, one month from today. The investment rate for four months is 10%, and the borrowing rate for one month is $8\frac{1}{2}\%$. The one-month period has 31 days and the four-month period, 122 days. The answer is 10.43%; try to find it before referring to the details in the Appendix.

The calculation of the forward–forward borrowing rate is also adjusted to account for the interest flows. Hall-Laird & Company wants to borrow for six months, three months from today and wants to fix the cost of its loan even though it expects no change in interest rates. The rates are

Three months	$7-7\frac{1}{4}\%$
Six months	$6-6\frac{3}{4}\%$
Nine months	$5\frac{3}{4}-6\%$

The forward–forward loan would be produced by borrowing money for 271 days and investing it for 92 days. The cash flow of interest at the bank would be:

Bank's Interest Flows on C$1 Million

	Three Months	Nine Months
Earning on investment, 7%	+17,888.89	
Earning on $17,888.89, 5.39%		+479.43
Cost of borrowing, 6%		−45,166.67

Taking account of the earning on the interest from the three-month investment, the borrowing rate is 5.39%; were this not taken into account, the rate would be 5.49%. Incorporating the interim interest flow reduces the borrowing rate and, as we have seen, reduces the investment rate. With the declining rate structure (negative yield curve), Hall-Laird is able to obtain six-month money in three months cheaper than it would be able to obtain six-month money today.

The general formula for calculating the forward–forward borrowing rate is*

$$\frac{(\text{borrowing rate} \times \text{days}) - (\text{investment rate} \times \text{days})}{(\text{days in forward period}) \times \left[1 + \left(\text{investment rate} \times \dfrac{\text{days}}{36,000} \right) \right]}$$

$$5.39\% = \frac{(6\% \times 271) - (7\% \times 92)}{(271 - 92) \times \left[1 + \left(7\% \times \dfrac{92}{36,000} \right) \right]}$$

A forward–forward money transaction is characterized by fixing an interest rate today for a period that begins in the future. The effect is to lock in the cost of a loan or the return from an investment. A company can execute the transaction for itself; however, it costs less (earns more) if it asks its bank to arrange the transaction. The company saves the lending spread during the period its operations do not actually require credit. The primary reason for the forward–forward is that the company thinks interest rates will shift and adversely affect a planned operation. A secondary reason is that a company may take advantage of the shape of the interest rate yield curve, even when there is no expectation of a change in interest rates. Wie Textiles is able to earn an additional 1.40% over the current four-month rate by its forward–forward investment. Hall-Laird is able to save 1.36% over the current six-month rate with its forward–forward loan.

FINANCIAL FUTURES CONTRACTS

In addition to commercial paper and T bill futures contracts, there are contracts for Treasury notes and bonds, and Ginnie Mae (Govern-

*This is derived in the Appendix.

ment National Mortgage Association) securities. All of the markets can be used by the investor, depending on the length of the investment. The commercial paper futures contract is most appropriate for the corporate borrower. The use of T bill futures contracts to guard against a rise in the cost of future borrowing protects a company from a general rise in interest rates but does not lock in a borrowing rate. The interest rates on all money market instruments do not move together. Therefore, the profit of a T bill futures contract will not necessarily offset completely the increased cost of borrowing.

There are two additional features of financial futures that have not been mentioned: (1) security deposit and (2) timing of profits and losses. For each $1 million contract, a security deposit of $1500 is required. Of this $1000 must remain on deposit with the broker at all times, $500 is the variation margin that covers fluctuations in the value of the futures contracts. If the variation is less than $500, there is no call for an additional deposit from the company. If the variation is greater than $500, the company must place that amount on deposit, in addition to the $1500 previously placed. The deposit may be kept in cash or U.S. government securities. Use of the latter means that the company does not lose interest while holding its security deposit.

At the end of each day all the futures contracts are revalued according to the closing price for that specific contract. Lowden sold September commercial paper futures at 97.45 (10.20%) with the expectation that interest rates would rise. If, on the other hand, interest rates dropped and that contract went to 9.80% one week after the contract were entered into, the value of September contracts would be 97.55. Lowden sold at 97.45 and so is showing a loss of 0.10 or $1000 per $1 million. Lowden would be required to place an additional $1000 in government securities or cash with the broker the next day. Losses are payable throughout the life of the contract, not simply when it matures. Profits are earned the same way, daily, as they occur. If rates rise a week later, part of Lowden's security deposit is released. Even though the security deposit is not large (.15%), the variations in the deposit that can occur during a period of volatile interest rates add uncertainty to the total cost of the locked in rate achieved with financial futures contracts.

APPENDIX

Derivation of the Formula for Forward–Forward
Investment and Borrowing Rates

The principle of the formulas is that the bank passes on to the customer all the costs and earnings resulting from the transactions involved in setting up the future loan or deposit. The formulas apply to the instances where the interest is paid or collected at maturity. Where interim payments are made, the easiest approach is to set up a table of interest flows as shown in the present chapter.

Forward–Forward Investment Rate.   The bank invests $1 at rate i for a certain period, $days_i$. The bank borrows $1 at rate b for a shorter period of time, $days_b$. Because the bank has to pay interest on the borrowing at the end of $days_b$, but does not receive any income until the end of $days_i$, the bank borrows to pay that interest for the period, $days_i - days_b$. The interest amounts on the transactions are

$$\text{investment}\ \$1\ \times\ i\ \times\ \frac{days_i}{360}$$

$$\text{loan}\ \ \$1\ \times\ b\ \times\ \frac{days_b}{360}$$

$$\text{Borrowing the interest}\ \left(\$1\ \times\ b\ \times\ \frac{days_b}{360}\right)\ \times\ K\ \times\ \frac{(days_i - days_b)}{360}$$

where K is the investment rate in the forward–forward period. It is assumed the bank can borrow the loan interest at the same rate it pays the customer for its investment in the forward–forward period. All the preceding elements are put together as follows:

$$K = \frac{\left(\$1 \times i \times \dfrac{days_i}{36{,}000}\right) - \left(\$1 \times b \times \dfrac{days_b}{36{,}000}\right) - \left(\$1 \times b \times \dfrac{days_b}{36{,}000}\right) \times K \times \left(\dfrac{days_i - days_b}{36{,}000}\right)}{\left(\dfrac{days_i - days_b}{36{,}000}\right)}$$

To solve for K it is easier if the $1 terms are dropped and if the top and bottom of the equation are multiplied by 36,000. Interest rate K is equal to the forward–forward rate. The equation is

$$K = \frac{(i \times days_i) - (b \times days_b)}{(days_i - days_b) \times \left[1 + \left(b \times \dfrac{days_b}{36{,}000}\right)\right]}$$

Forward–Forward Borrowing Rate. The bank borrows $1 at rate b for a certain period, $days_b$. The bank invests $1 at rate i for a shorter period of time, $days_i$. Because the bank earns interest on the investment at the end of $days_i$ but does not have any interest expense until the end of $days_b$, the bank can invest that interest for the period, $days_b - days_i$. The interest amounts on the transactions are

$$\text{borrowing } \$1 \times b \times \frac{days_b}{360}$$

$$\text{investment } \$1 \times i \times \frac{days_i}{360}$$

$$\text{investment of the interest } \left(\$1 \times i \times \frac{days_i}{360}\right) \times J \times \left(\frac{days_b - days_i}{360}\right)$$

where J is an interest rate to be determined, and similar to the investment rate, it is assumed that the bank can invest the interest at the same rate as it charges the customer for the forward loan. Again, all the costs and earnings are spread over the number of days in the forward–forward period, ($days_b - days_i$), to determine the rate. The borrowing rate is designated as J.

Similar to the derivation of the investment rate, the loan, the investment, and the interest investment elements are collected and with the same simplifying adjustments, solved for J:

$$J = \frac{(b \times days_b) - (i \times days_i)}{(days_b - days_i) \times \left[1 + \left(i \times \dfrac{days_i}{36{,}000}\right)\right]}$$

This is the forward–forward borrowing rate.

Forward–Forward Investment Rate for Antigone

$$\frac{(10\% \times 122) - (8.5\% \times 31)}{(122 - 31) \times \left[1 + \left(8.5\% \times \dfrac{31}{36{,}000}\right)\right]} = 10.43\%$$

CHAPTER TWELVE
LEADS AND LAGS

Companies lead and lag payments to change their foreign currency exposure and to finance operations. The Lead is one of the basic options for covering an exposure. Its use has been demonstrated in previous chapters. The Lag is an option that eliminates risk when the delay matches a flow in the opposite direction. A German company puts off paying an invoice in dollars for 30 days because it has a receivable in dollars at that time. A Lag extends exposure, however, if there is no matching flow. A payable may be postponed if the company thinks the payable currency will fall against its own. A receivable will be delayed if the company believes the foreign currency will rise in value. The present chapter shows the way to determine how much a currency must rise or fall to make the Lag a worthwhile venture.

Leading and lagging accelerate currency movements in the foreign exchange market. Sterling is a good example. When the value of the pound becomes suspect, British firms lead their foreign currency payables, selling pounds, buying the foreign currency. At the same time, these firms lag their foreign currency receivables. Companies on the other side of the English channel hold off buying pounds, but cash in their sterling receivables quickly. These actions create an imbalance in the supply of and demand for sterling in the foreign exchange market and push the value of the pound lower. When people think sterling has reached bottom, the lag is reversed; overseas firms now buy the pounds that they had held off buying before, and British firms sell their foreign currency receivables for sterling. By so doing, the pound is strengthened.

Leading and lagging provide financing. In this context it is practiced most frequently by the subsidiaries of multinational firms. Lagging a payment to an affiliate allows you to use the money now at the expense of the affiliate. Asking your affiliate to lead its payment to you has the same effect. On the other hand, if you allow another subsidiary to lag its payment to you or if you pay early, you provide financing to that subsidiary now and deprive yourself of funds. Moving funds in this fashion enables a multinational company to do some of its financing without using a bank. The present chapter looks at the exchange and exposure implications of this type of financing.

LEAD

There is more than one way to lead a payable or a receivable. Besides the Lead option used in previous chapters, another way to lead a future payable is to borrow that currency in the external money market and pay the supplier now with the borrowed funds. The loan is repaid by buying the foreign currency forward. This is symbolized as

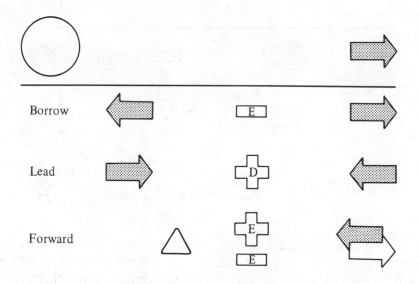

This method of leading is more advantageous than a Forward if the external interest rate of the foreign currency is less than the domestic interest rate of that currency. Even if the company has decided not to cover the payable, it is still worthwhile to execute the borrow and lead.

There is an analogous way to lead a receivable—have the customer pay early. Rather than converting to home currency on the spot date, invest the foreign currency. Arrange today to sell the maturing investment forward. The illustration of this option:

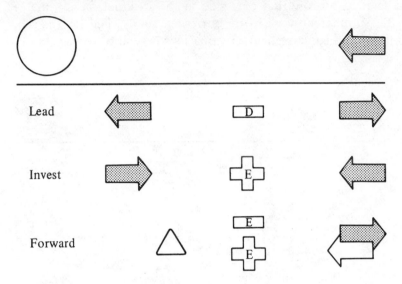

This option is also designed to take advantage of any difference between domestic and external interest rates of the foreign currency. To the extent that there is a positive difference, this option will be better than the Forward. Again, even if the firm has decided not to cover the receivable, it is worthwhile executing the lead and investment portions of it.

This option is called *Lead–F*. It benefits those firms who do not have access to the external market in their own currency. The illustration of the receivable exposure shows an external plus and an external minus for the foreign currency. The plus and minus essentially cancel out, at a cost of $\frac{1}{4}$% to $\frac{1}{2}$%.* The remaining elements are (1) a cost in the domestic money market of the foreign currency and (2) an earning in the external money market of the home currency. No other option produces this comparison if the company cannot access its external money mar-

*The $\frac{1}{4}$% to $\frac{1}{2}$% is the spread between the borrowing rate and the investing rate.

ket directly. It is desirable to have the comparison so that the company can choose from all money markets. The purpose of having more than one covering option is to find the best combination from all possibilities. The following chart shows the money market used for each currency in each option:

Option	Home Currency	Foreign Currency
Forward	External	External
BSI	Domestic	External
Lead	Domestic	Domestic
Lead–F	External	Domestic

With the addition of Lead–F all, the possible combinations of the money markets are used. If the firm has direct access to its external market, the Lead will do the same job as Lead–F.

The desirability of adding Lead–F to the set of covering options is shown by the following example. Danish firms are not permitted to borrow or deposit funds in the external kroner money market. Sørenson Brewing A/S has an invoice due for DM5 million in 30 days. The interest rates prevailing are

Danish kroner external $14-14\frac{1}{4}\%$
domestic $18-18\frac{1}{4}\%$
Deutsche mark external $4-4\frac{1}{4}\%$
domestic $5-5\frac{1}{4}\%$

All the options available to Sørenson are the following:

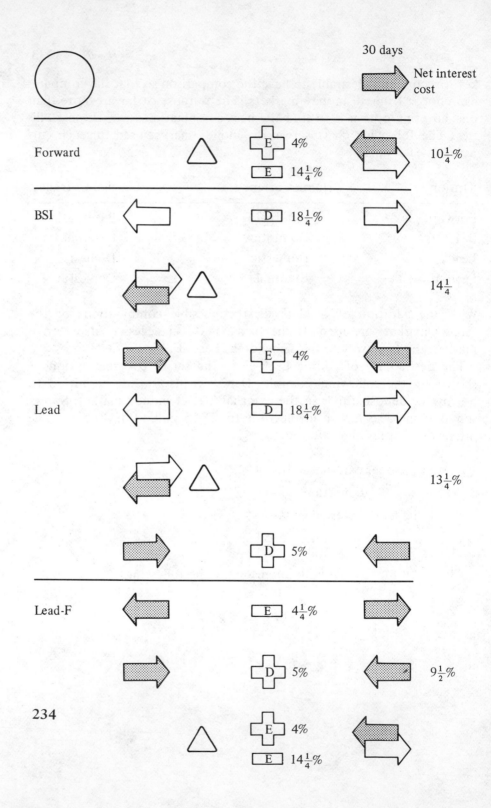

30 days

Net interest cost

Forward $10\frac{1}{4}\%$

E 4%

E $14\frac{1}{4}\%$

BSI $18\frac{1}{4}\%$

$14\frac{1}{4}$

E 4%

Lead D $18\frac{1}{4}\%$

$13\frac{1}{4}\%$

D 5%

Lead-F E $4\frac{1}{4}\%$

D 5% $9\frac{1}{2}\%$

234

E 4%

E $14\frac{1}{4}\%$

The illustration shows that Lead–F is superior to the Forward by the difference between the domestic and external money market rates for Deutsche marks. Lead–F allows Sørenson to cover its mark payable at the least cost. The combination of the external kroner market and the domestic mark market is better than the market combinations produced by the other options.

CALCULATIONS

Discount. Up to this point the discount for advancing payment has been expressed in the same terms as money market interest rates. This is not the usual practice. Trade terms that allow a discount for early payment are commonly quoted in terms of a *flat* rate, a reduction of a certain percentage of the invoice. This rate is based on the interest rate in the seller's country and on custom in the industry. An invoice may read, "$1\frac{1}{2}\%$ discount if paid in 30 days." If the bill is for $1, the amount paid is

formula: $1 – ($1 × flat rate)

example: $1 – ($1 × .015) = $.985

When the company pays early, it earns this discount at the beginning of the period. This is different from a money market investment where interest is received at the end of the period. Similarly, when a receivable is accelerated, the premium is paid to the customer at the beginning of the period. This contrasts with a loan where interest is paid at the end. When the discount is quoted flat, adjustments are necessary to make it comparable to the money market interest rates it is being compared to. The discount is put on a per annum basis and is adjusted to reflect the interest payment at the beginning rather than at the end of the period. The formula that calculates this true interest rate (I_t) from a flat discount is

$$I_t = \frac{\text{flat discount} \times \dfrac{360}{\text{days in discount period}}}{1 - \text{flat discount}}$$

Example. A flat $1\frac{1}{2}\%$ discount if paid in 30 days.

$$I_t = \frac{.015 \times \dfrac{360}{30}}{1 - .015} \times 100 = 18.27\%$$

The derivation is given in the Appendix.

Finding the discounted amount actually paid can be done using the flat rate or the true interest rate.

$$\$1 - (\$1 \times \text{flat rate}) \quad \text{or} \quad \frac{\$1}{1 + \left(I_t \times \dfrac{\text{days}}{360}\right)}$$

The two expressions are equivalent. The proof is given in the Appendix.

The right-hand expression is the one used in the Points formula to match up the principal plus interest flow of a loan or investment with the exposed flow.

Lead–F. Lead–F can be compared to the other options as follows:

Interest Cost/Earning =
± interest rate on borrowing or investment
± true interest rate of lead
± interest cost/earning of the forward

Points =
forward points
± points for lead and borrowing or investment (Points–F)

The calculation for finding Points–F is a modification of the points formula developed in Chapter 5. In that formula the foreign interest rate is used in the denominator because we want to match up the principal plus interest from the money market operation with the foreign currency exposure. A smaller amount than the future flow is borrowed or invested. Here, we want to match up the principal of the money market operation with the amount involved in the lead. If the exposure situation is a foreign currency outflow in the future, the amount paid early is

$$\frac{1}{1 + \left(I_t \times \frac{\text{days}}{360}\right)}$$

The amount received from leading a receivable is given by the same expression; it is the amount that is invested.

The formula for Points–F is developed from the following considerations:

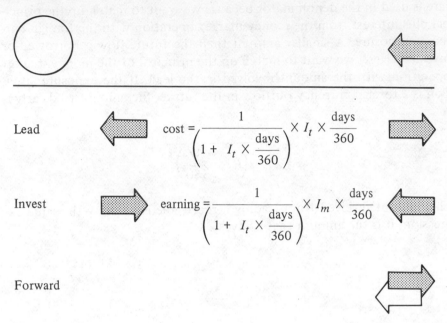

Lead

$$\text{cost} = \frac{1}{\left(1 + I_t \times \dfrac{\text{days}}{360}\right)} \times I_t \times \frac{\text{days}}{360}$$

Invest

$$\text{earning} = \frac{1}{\left(1 + I_t \times \dfrac{\text{days}}{360}\right)} \times I_m \times \frac{\text{days}}{360}$$

Forward

where I_m is the investment or borrowing rate. Combining the cost and earning gives

$$\frac{(I_m - I_t) \times \dfrac{\text{days}}{360}}{1 + \left(I_t \times \dfrac{\text{days}}{360}\right)}$$

This expresses the cost and earning in foreign currency units. To express them in home currency units, multiply by the spot rate:

$$\text{Points –F} = \frac{\text{spot} \times (I_m - I_t) \times \dfrac{\text{days}}{360}}{1 + \left(I_t \times \dfrac{\text{days}}{360}\right)}$$

where I_t takes the place of I_f in the points formula and I_m takes the place of I_h. This formula applies to a payable situation as readily as it does to receivable exposures.

There is the additional consideration in the calculation of points for the Lead-F option. The principal plus the interest from the investment or loan will not be the same as the amount of the original exposure. In the vast majority of cases this will have no effect on the comparison of options. The Appendix illustrates the issue and shows how it can be resolved.

PROBLEM

This problem is designed to use the calculations and apply the principles just discussed. Sørenson Brewing A/S has just received an invoice for FF 5 million payable in 30 days. Sørenson's French supplier offers 1% off the bill if paid in 10 days. External French franc rates for 30 days are $10\frac{3}{4}\%$–11%, local kroner rates are 18–$18\frac{1}{4}\%$, the bank lending spread is $\frac{1}{2}\%$ on both; FF/Dkr spot is 133.30–50, the one month points are 33–40. Use the four options to determine which is the best for covering Sørenson's French franc exposure now. Work the problem before referring to the solution.

SOLUTION

The options for this exposure situation are the same as those for Sørenson's Deutsche mark exposure discussed earlier in the chapter. There is nothing new about the calculations of points and interest cost/ earning for the Forward and BSI. For the Lead it is necessary to find the true interest rate from the flat rate. This is shown in connection with the discussion of Lead-F. For Lead-F the given information is:

Option	Spot	Net Interest Cost/Earning			Points	Locked-In Future Rate
			I_t	I_m Net		
Lead–F	133.50	Lead-Invest		$11\frac{1}{2}\%$		
		Forward			40	
		Total				

To find I_t: The problem states that there is a discount of 1%. A flat discount of 1% is equivalent to an interest rate of 12.12% if the bill is paid now.

$$I_t = 12.12\% = \frac{.01 \times \dfrac{360}{30}}{1 - .01} \times 100$$

This earning, compared with the cost of $11\frac{1}{2}\%$, gives a net interest earning of .62%. To find Points–F:

$$\text{Points–F} = 7 = \frac{133.50 \times (.115 - .1212) \times \dfrac{30}{360}}{1 + \left(.1212 \times \dfrac{30}{360}\right)}$$

The points for the Forward are converted to an interest rate by ICE-1:

$$\text{ICE-1} = 3.60\% = \frac{.40}{133.50} \times \frac{360}{30} \times 100$$

The known and calculated elements for Lead–F are now:

	I_t	I_m	Net	Points
Lead–Invest	12.12	$11\frac{1}{2}$	+ .62%	7
Forward			–3.60%	40
Total			–2.98%	33

The completed matrix for Sørenson Brewing A/S is as follows:

Option	Spot	Net Interest Cost/Earning			Points	Locked-In Future Rate
		I_h	I_f	Net		
Forward	133.50			-3.60%	40	133.90
BSI	133.50	18.75	10.75	-8	88	134.38
Lead	133.50	18.75	12.12	-6.63%	73	134.23
Lead–F	133.50			-2.98%	33	133.83

The option that combines the cost in the external kroner market with an earning in the domestic franc market is the least expensive way of covering the franc exposure.

LAG

Cranbery Ltd. is an Australian mining company. It wants to delay an upcoming yen payment for another month because it believes the yen will fall against the dollar during that time. A Japanese sister company is expecting those funds, however, and will want to be compensated for the delay. Cranbery is effectively borrowing from its Japanese affiliate for a month. The Australian company will be able to use the funds it does not pay out to buy yen. The treasurer of Cranbery wants to determine whether it is worthwhile to gamble on delaying the payment. Will the expected change in the exchange rate be enough to offset the costs of the lag?

The flows for the Lag are symbolized in the following diagram.

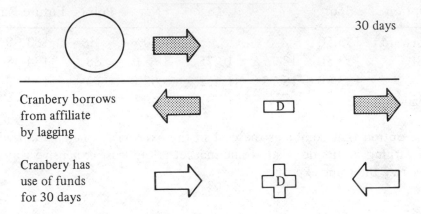

The symbol for the Lag is the same as for borrowing. The Japanese company will charge Cranbery the cost of replacing those funds in the Japanese market; hence there is a symbol for a domestic cost. It is presumed that Cranbery will use the Australian dollars locally. The earning may be from a money market investment, the postponement of bank borrowing for another month, or it may be used to pay another supplier. Against this cost and earning the treasurer must balance the number of Australian dollars he would pay out today to buy yen against the number he expects to pay out in 30 days. To be as well off in 30 days as today, any cost in delaying the payable must be compensated for, by an exchange gain. If there is an earning, the company can afford an exchange loss. The treasurer wants to calculate the future break even exchange rate at which an exchange gain (loss) compensates a cost (earning) from delaying payment.

The break-even rate is calculated by converting interest costs and earnings into points. In this situation the full amount of the payable is available for use; hence there is no discount factor.

The points calculation* to find the break-even rate is

$$\text{points} = \text{spot} \times (I_h - I_f) \times \frac{\text{days}}{360}$$

The points are then added to or subtracted from spot, depending on whether there is an earning or a cost from lagging the payment. As an example, use these numbers in the Cranbery situation: domestic yen interest rate is 11% and domestic dollar interest rate is 7%, spot ¥/A\$3.7660, per 1000 yen.

$$\text{points} = 3.7660 \times (.07 - .11) \times \frac{30}{360} = 126 \text{ points}$$

Since this is a cost to Cranbery the company must recover through an exchange gain and pay out fewer Australian dollars in the future. The ¥/A\$ rate at which the company covers the transaction must be at least 3.7534 (3.7660 – .0126), compared to spot of 3.7660. Cranbery can arrange for the cover anytime between the present and 30 days, hopefully at something like 3.7400.

*A modification of this formula is given in the Appendix. It takes account of the conversion of the lagged foreign currency at a rate different from spot.

Lagging a receivable is very similar to lagging a payable. Let's assume now that Cranbery has an imminent receivable from New Zealand. Because the affiliate in Wellington is in need of funds Cranbery is willing to delay the inflow of New Zealand dollars.

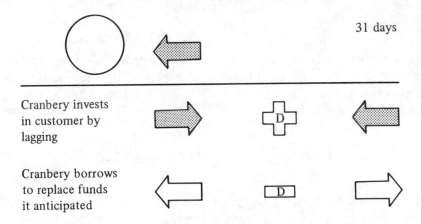

The Australian firm receives its money in 30 days. The New Zealand firm is able to use the funds for working capital or to delay borrowing from the bank for another month. Cranbery expected to receive money and must now forego the use of it. The cost to Cranbery can be either an earning foregone from investment of the funds or the cost of a bank loan. Why may Cranbery agree to the lag if it needs funds for its own operations? The New Zealand affiliate may be near the limit of its bank credit lines, and Cranbery has ample credit facilities.

Before agreeing, the treasurer will check the exchange implications of this Lag. If the New Zealand dollar is expected to rise against its Australian counterpart, the treasurer may be willing to suffer a small cost in the delay. If the opposite is expected, Cranbery will want to be compensated through interest earnings. The break-even rate is calculated just as before.

As an example, let the New Zealand dollar interest rate be 13% and the Australian dollar interest rate be 7%; spot is NZ$/A$.8925.

$$\text{points} = .8925 \times (.07 - .13) \times \frac{31}{360} = 46 \text{ points}$$

This is an earning for Cranbery Ltd., since the New Zealand firm is paying more than the cost of borrowing. Cranbery can afford to lose a little in the exchange rate and still be as well off in 31 days as the firm is today. Losing on a receivable means the firm would receive fewer Australian dollars; therefore, the points are subtracted from spot. The break-even rate is .8879, below that Cranbery is worse off; above that, it is better off than today.

The conventions for adding and subtracting points to find the break-even rate are:

Lag	Receivable Exposure	Payable Exposure
Cost	Add the points	Subtract the points
Earning	Subtract the points	Add the points

With a receivable exposure the objective is to maximize the number of home currency units per unit of foreign currency. If there is a cost to lag, then the break-even rate must be higher, and must represent more home currency units. If there is an earning through the delay, money gained there can be used to compensate a loss due to a lower exchange rate.

The objective in a payable exposure situation is to pay out the fewest number of home currency units. If there is a cost to the lag, the firm will be just as well off if it pays out even less of its own currency. On the other hand, if the firm earns from the delay, the earning will compensate for a higher exchange rate.

Lag When Customer/Supplier Won't Cooperate

If Cranbery's Japanese affiliate will not go along with the delay in the yen payment and the Australian company feels strongly about a fall in the value of the yen, there is an alternative. The treasurer can borrow external yen from the company's bank for one month to pay off its affiliate. By this action Cranbery has created an exposure for itself in Japanese yen in 30 days. The company counters the cost of the yen loan with earning from its own funds that had been set aside to purchase the yen. The differences between this and the previous method of lagging are (1) the cost is external yen interest rather than domestic, (2) this method does not depend on the cooperation of the supplier and thus may be easily practiced outside multinational companies, and (3) this method forces Cranbery to increase the level of bank debt on its balance sheet.

A foreign currency receivable can be lagged in a similar fashion. If the customer cannot be persuaded to delay the inflow, the company can simply let the foreign currency flow in and invest it in the external money market. This will be done when the company feels strongly that the foreign currency will rise in value since an exposure is created. The company will borrow funds in its own market to replace the inflow.

The calculation of the points and the break-even rate in the cases just presented is the same as shown previously.

Lag-F

Lag-F is an option that combines the Lag with a Forward. As opposed to the Lag, this option covers an exposure. After the treasurer of Cranbery Ltd. looks at the exposure created in New Zealand dollars, he decides he doesn't like it. Rather than refusing to finance the affiliate in Wellington for a month, the treasurer decides to cover the New Zealand dollar exposure with a one-month forward contract. The transaction looks like like this:

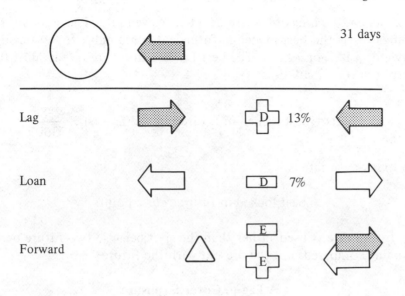

The costs and earnings of the Lag, Loan, and Forward are combined to find the overall effect. If the end result is a cost to Cranbery, the treasurer will insist on additional compensation from his counterpart in Wellington before he goes through with the transaction.

Lagging a Future Flow

Today a company decides to lag a payable due in one month. The company wishes to fix the costs and earnings of the operation now rather than wait. To do this, the company arranges for a forward–forward deposit with its bank for a period starting one month from to-day. Likewise, the supplier who is due the money will arrange a forward–forward loan with his bank. Otherwise, lagging a future flow is the same as lagging a flow due tomorrow. However, the standard for comparing the well-being of the company shifts to the future. Previously the spot rate has been used as the standard. The spot rate was adjusted for costs and earnings to arrive at a break-even rate. The standard for a future flow is the best locked-in future rate obtainable today through a Forward, a BSI, or a Lead. The best Locked-in future rate is substituted for spot in the calculations.

$$\text{points} = \text{best locked-in future rate} \times (I_h - I_f) \times \frac{\text{days}}{360}$$

The break-even rate is

$$\text{best locked-in future rate} \pm \text{points}$$

The future rate is used rather than the spot because two future periods are being compared, not the present with the future.

A Lag to Cover Exposure

Most of the discussion has been devoted to the Lag that extends exposure rather than covers it. If the delay of a receivable or payable matches a flow in the opposite direction, the Lag covers exposure. But there are cost and earning implications to this way of covering a future exposure. The cost/earning of covering that future exposure is the value of today's flow plus the interest cost and earning from moving it to the future.

Lagging a present flow is not necessarily the best way of covering the future flow. Earning may be greater if the imminent receivable were converted at spot and the future flow were covered by a Forward or a BSI. All the options should be considered. Chapter 13 examines multiple flows more closely.

J. TODD, INC.

The case of J. Todd, Inc. illustrates the working of intercompany financing and exposure management through leads and lags. J. Todd, Inc. manufactures and sells paper and wood products in the United States,

Canada, England, and Ireland. The affiliates in each country have both manufacturing and sales responsibilities. Each country specializes in producing a particular product, but all the products are sold in every country. This system creates a network of payments between the affiliates.

Each subsidiary handles its own exchange exposure and short-term financing needs. Corporate policy is to cover exposure unless there is an identifiable trend in the market or unless the cost of cover is high. The interpretation of "trend" and "high" is left to the country treasurers. A daily communique informs each treasurer of the financing and exposure positions of all others. Today's cable indicates that the English treasurer is in need of working capital. Business is strong, but expansion is being hampered by the government's restriction on bank borrowing. The Canadian treasurer reports an overly liquid situation for the next four weeks. The Irish situation is normal. The American international treasurer shows a need for working capital during the next month. The situation is not like the British one; bank credit is readily available in the States. The U.S. affiliate also records an outflow of Canadian dollars in two days and an outflow of pounds sterling in one month.

Exchange and capital controls are not a restricting influence in Canada, the United States, or England. American firms have been effectively cut off from borrowing in the Eurodollar market, however, because of high reserve requirements imposed on the banks who make such loans. This raises the cost of such loans above domestic levels.

A way to resolve the situations in Canada, the United States, and England is for the American treasurer to lag the payment to the Canadian affiliate (thereby reducing Canadian liquidity and increasing U.S. liquidity) and lead the payment to the English (thus increasing UK liquidity). The American treasurer's concern is that these options do not leave the company in the States worse off than if the exposures were addressed by other means. With this criterion in mind, the treasurer will ask the following questions: "How much should the American affiliate charge the English firm for leading the sterling payment? How much is J. Todd, Inc. willing to pay the Canadian unit for a delay in payment to it?"

The two questions will be handled separately, first England, then Canada. The initial step is to examine all the possible ways of handling the exposure and accomplishing the financing objective. The possible options are in the RESPONSE section below, followed by a RESPONSE ANALYSIS. The SOLUTION section illustrates the viable options. Exchange and interest rates are provided and the reader is asked to calculate the prices of the options. With this information it is possible to answer the questions.

RESPONSES

1. BSI.
2. Lead–F.
3. Lead.
4. Forward.
5. Lag-F.
6. Lag.
7. Spot.

RESPONSE ANALYSIS–ENGLAND

A. *If you chose 1, 3, 4*: These are the basic options for covering exposure and should be considered for all situations involving a future foreign currency flow.

B. *If you omitted 2*: This option should be included along with the Forward, the BSI, and the Lead because it was mentioned in the case that U.S. firms had been effectively cut off from the Eurodollar market by high reserve requirements. Only this option will allow J. Todd the possibility of comparing rates in the Eurodollar market and the resident sterling market.

C. *If you chose 5*: This option does cover the sterling exposure; however, it does not address the need to provide financing to the English affiliate. It worsens the English liquidity situation.

D. *If you chose 6*: This option will neither cover the sterling exposure nor assist the English desire for increased working capital; it would deprive them of it for another month.

E. *If you chose 7*: This is not sufficient to cover an outflow in one month. It must be combined with transactions that cover time, as in the BSI and the Lead.

SOLUTION–ENGLAND

Sterling exposure 32 days

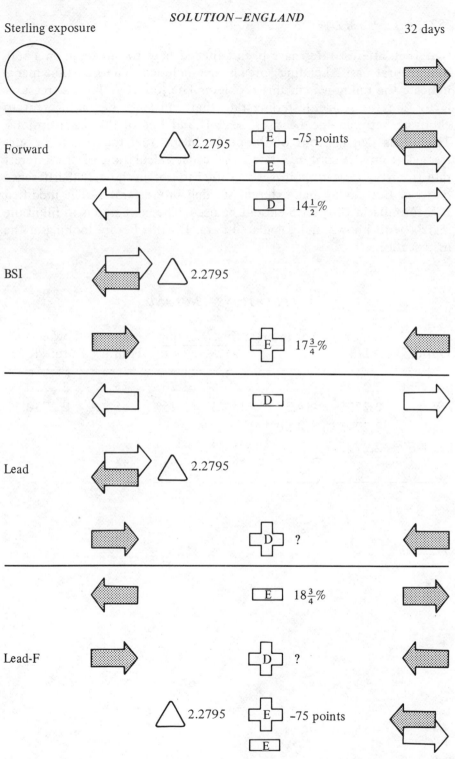

White, U.S. dollars; gray, pound sterling

Sterling interest rates have been adjusted here to put them on a 360-day accural basis. Lending spreads are included. The question marks indicate the unknowns in this problem. The job of J. Todd's treasurer is to find the resident sterling rate that will leave her indifferent to choosing between the Lead or Lead-F and one of the other options. The minus sign in front of the points means that they are to be subtracted from the spot £/$ rate. The usual calculation of the interest rate from the forward points is modified to obtain the actual difference between Eurodollar and external sterling interest rates. The modified ICE formula in Chapter 5 should be used. The next step is to fill in the matrix with known and calculated data. Do this before looking at the next section.

CALCULATIONS—ENGLAND

Option	Spot £/$	Net Interest Cost/Earning I_h	I_f	Net	Points	Locked-In Future Rate
Forward	2.2795			+3.76%	75	2.2720
BSI	2.2795	−14.50	+17.75	+3.25%	65	2.2730
Lead	2.2795	−14.50	?			
Lead–F	2.2795		−18.75			
				+3.76%	75	

The net interest cost/earning for the Forward is calculated with the following formula:

$$\text{ICE} = \left(\frac{\text{points}}{\text{spot}} \times \frac{360}{\text{days}}\right) \times \left[1 + \left(I_f \times \frac{\text{days}}{360}\right)\right] \times 100$$

$$3.76\% = \left(\frac{.0075}{2.2795} \times \frac{360}{32}\right) \times \left[1 + \left(.1775 \times \frac{32}{360}\right)\right] \times 100$$

The calculation gives the actual difference between the Eurodollar rates and external sterling interest rates represented by the points. The reason for using this formula is that the treasurer of J. Todd, Inc. will be setting an interest rate for the English company and needs to know the actual interest difference in the Forward.

From the information in the matrix it is possible to calculate the resident sterling rate that the English company must pay to induce J. Todd, Inc. to lead its payment. The possible responses are given in the next section.

RESPONSES—ENGLAND

1. 18.26%; on the English accural basis, 18.51%.
2. 17.75%, (18%).
3. 18.24%, (18.49%).
4. 18.75%, (19.01%).

RESPONSE ANALYSIS—ENGLAND

A. *If you chose 1*: This number was calculated by taking the net interest earning of the Forward, the best option, and adding it to the cost of borrowing dollars in the Lead. If the English affiliate pays 18.51%, J. Todd, Inc. will be as well off as it could be under any option at this time; that is the objective.

B. *If you chose 2*: This number was calculated by taking the net interest earning of the BSI and adding it to the cost of borrowing dollars in the Lead. Since the BSI is not the best option, this would result in asking too little from the English firm.

C. *If you chose 3 or 4*: These are calculated from Lead-F and BSI and Lead-F and the Forward. The known cost and earning of Lead-F gives a net cost of 14.99%. This is higher than the net cost the company starts out with in the Lead, 14.50%. Response 3 fails to capture all of the benefits to the American company; response 4 overcharges the English, but to the benefit of no one.

The Canadian situation is the next to be solved. How much is J. Todd willing to pay the Canadian firm for a delay in payment to it? Start again by examining all the possible ways of handling the exposure and financing objectives. The options are repeated in the response section, followed by an analysis, the illustrated options, and calculations.

RESPONSES

1. BSI.
2. Lead-F.
3. Lead.
4. Forward.
5. Lag-F.
6. Lag.
7. Spot.

RESPONSE ANALYSIS–CANADA

A. *If you chose 6*: This option will provide J. Todd with the required working capital by using the liquidity of the Canadian affiliate. This option leaves the company with an exposure.

B. *If you chose 5*: This option uses the Canadian liquidity to augment working capital in the United States. Additionally, the exposure created by the Lag is covered.

C. *If you chose 1, 2, 3, 4*: These options address exposures that are in the future. The Canadian dollar outflow is immediate.

D. *If you omitted* 7: This is the simplest way to cover an exposure in two days. The spot rate is the basis of comparison for any other option used for the Canadian dollar exposure.

SOLUTION–CANADA

Canadian dollar exposure   32 days

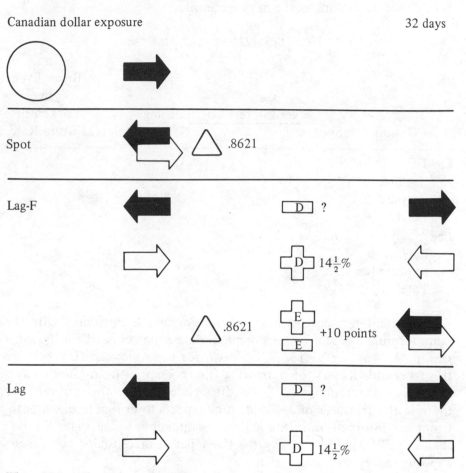

White, U.S. dollars; black, Canadian dollars

The interest rates include bank lending spreads. The question marks indicate the interest rates that the treasurer of J. Todd must find to determine the rate to pay the Canadians. The reason the Lag is included as one of the options is that the treasurer expects a fall in the Canadian dollar in the coming month. She is forecasting a rate of C$/US$.8500 and wants to see what effect that will have on the price she is willing to pay to the Canadians. The next step is to calculate the interest rate for Lag-F and the interest rate for the Lag given the expected C$/US$ rate. Do this before looking at the next section.

CALCULATIONS–CANADA

| Option | Spot | Net Interest Cost/Earning | | | Points | Break Even or Locked-In Future Rate |
		I_h	I_f	Net		
Lag-F	.8621					
Lag/invest		+14.50	?			
Forward				−1.32%	+10	
Total						
Lag	.8621					
Lag/invest		+14.50	?			
Expected				+15.79%	−121	
Total						

The net interest cost/earning for the Forward is calculated with the same formula as used for the pound sterling exposure, and for the same reason. An earning of $14\frac{1}{4}\%$ is shown for the American firm because this represents its cost of borrowing funds. That is the amount it saves by lagging. The number 121 is the difference between the spot rate and the rate the treasurer of J. Todd, Inc. expects to prevail in one month. From the information in the matrix it is possible to calculate the rate that J. Todd is willing to pay the Canadian affiliate under two cases—exposure covered or uncovered.

Exposure Covered. The U.S. firm is willing to pay the Canadians 13.18%, the difference between the saving from not borrowing and the cost of covering forward. Viewed another way, the lag/invest portion of the operation will generate an earning of 1.32%, equivalent to 10 points, set against the forward cost of 10 points, leaving J. Todd, Inc. paying the same amount to buy Canadian dollars future as spot.

Exposure Uncovered. The U.S. firm could afford to pay the Canadian affiliate 30.29% in interest, if the treasurer is right about the movement of the Canadian dollar. Since that rate is clearly in excess of Canadian rates, the U.S. treasurer may offer 13.18%, yet leave the exposure uncovered.

APPENDIX

Conversion of a Flat Discount to a True Interest Rate

To convert a flat discount into an equivalent annual rate, the discount is prorated from the discount period over one year. It is very similar to the way points for one month are adjusted to come up with an annual percentage.

$$\text{percent discount per annum} = \text{flat discount} \times \frac{360}{\text{days in discount period}} \times 100$$

The adjustment to reflect interest payment at the beginning of the period increases the percent discount per annum because it is better to have money today than tomorrow. You can invest the money today and have even more tomorrow.

$$\text{true interest rate } I_t = \frac{\text{percent discount per annum}}{1 - \left(\text{percent discount per annum} \times \dfrac{\text{days in discount period}}{360} \right)}$$

Example. A flat $1\frac{1}{2}\%$ discount if paid in 30 days.

$$\text{percent per annum} = .015 \times \frac{360}{30} \times 100 = 18\%$$

$$I_t = \frac{.18}{1 - \left(.18 \times \dfrac{30}{360} \right)} \times 100 = 18.27\%$$

The formula shown in the body of the present chapter is found by substituting the expression for "percent discount per annum" in the formula for the "true interest rate." The effect is to express I_t strictly in terms of the flat discount.

Proof of Equivalence of the Expressions

$$1 - (1 \times \text{Flat Rate}) \quad \text{and} \quad \frac{1}{1 + \left(I_t \times \dfrac{\text{days}}{360} \right)}$$

From the earlier part of the chapter it has been shown that

$$I_t = \frac{\text{flat rate} \times \left(\dfrac{360}{\text{days in discount period}} \right)}{1 - \text{flat rate}}$$

Let's abbreviate "days in discount period" to days and "flat rate" to f. Substitute the expression for I_t in the expression

$$\frac{1}{1 + \left(I_t \times \dfrac{\text{days}}{360} \right)}$$

The result is

$$\frac{1}{1 + \left(f \times \dfrac{360}{\text{days}} \times \dfrac{\text{days}}{360} \right)}{1 - f}$$

This is simplified to

$$\frac{1}{1 + \dfrac{f}{(1-f)}} = \frac{1}{\dfrac{1-f+f}{(1-f)}} = 1 - f$$

And $(1 - f)$ equals $1 - (1 \times f)$.

The Forward Calculation in the Lead-F Option

The amount of the forward contract in the Lead-F option is not the same as the amount of the exposure. This affects the comparability of the forward with the other elements of the Lead-F option. The reason for the difference and the resolution of this difference are shown. Previously, when dealing with a foreign currency loan or investment, the amount at maturity of the transaction was made equal to the amount of the exposure. The principal amount of

$$\frac{1}{1+\left(I_f \times \dfrac{\text{days}}{360}\right)}$$

was invested or borrowed at rate I_f. The principal and interest at maturity equals the amount of the exposure, 1.

$$\text{principal} \quad + \quad \text{amount of interest} = 1$$

$$\frac{1}{1+\left(I_f \times \dfrac{\text{days}}{360}\right)} + \frac{1}{1+\left(I_f \times \dfrac{\text{days}}{360}\right)} \times I_f \times \frac{\text{days}}{360} = 1$$

This is seen more readily by rewriting the equation as

$$\frac{1}{\left(1+ I_f \times \dfrac{\text{days}}{360}\right)} \times \left(1 + I_f \times \frac{\text{days}}{360}\right) = 1$$

In the lead-F option we chose to match up the lead amount, thus leaving the money market transaction unmatched. Because of this the principal plus the interest at maturity does not equal 1.

$$\text{principal} \quad + \quad \text{amount of interest} \neq 1$$

$$\frac{1}{1+\left(I_t \times \dfrac{\text{days}}{360}\right)} + \frac{1}{1+\left(I_t \times \dfrac{\text{days}}{360}\right)} \times I_m \times \frac{\text{days}}{360} \neq 1$$

The amount at maturity differs from 1 because I_t and I_m are not the same interest rate. When the investment rate I_m is higher than the rate on the lead I_t, principal plus interest will be greater than 1. When the investment rate is lower, the option would not be considered, it will be immediately apparent that it is inferior to the Forward. When the borrowing rate I_m is lower than the true discount rate I_t, principal plus interest will be less than 1. When the interest rate for borrowing is higher than the discount on the lead, the option will not be considered.

The adjustment of the forward points is easy; multiply the points by the ratio

$$\frac{1 + \left(I_m \times \frac{\text{days}}{360} \right)}{1 + \left(I_t \times \frac{\text{days}}{360} \right)}$$

The result will make the points comparable to the other elements of Lead-F, which are based on the amount of the exposure.

Earlier in the chapter it was stated that this adjustment has little effect on the comparison of Lead-F to the BSI, Forward, or Lead.

Examples.

1. From the Sørenson Brewing problem, $I_t = 12.12\%$, $I_m = 11.50\%$, and the forward points are 40.

$$40 \times \frac{1 + \left(.1150 \times \frac{30}{360} \right)}{1 + \left(.1212 \times \frac{30}{360} \right)} = 39.979$$

There is no real change in the result.

2.   The difference between the rates are not large in the first example, nor were the number of points large. But let I_t = 20% and I_m = 5%, and the forward points are 1000.

$$1000 \times \frac{1 + \left(.05 \times \dfrac{30}{360}\right)}{1 + \left(.20 \times \dfrac{30}{360}\right)} = 987.7$$

The difference between the given and adjusted forward points is not large in this example, either. The difference will widen as the number of days increases. In commercial practice, however, 90 days is normally the longest period over which a lead occurs. An adjustment would be made in those instances where the differences between Lead–F and the other options is small and where differences in interest rates are large, or if the period of the lead is long.

Modification of the Points Calculation for the Lag

The points calculation for the Lag can be modified to account for the conversion of the lagged foreign currency at a rate different from spot. This illustration of the flows will clarify the situation.

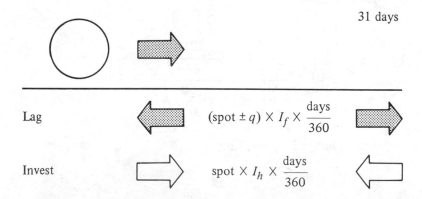

31 days

Lag   (spot $\pm q$) $\times I_f \times \dfrac{\text{days}}{360}$

Invest   spot $\times I_h \times \dfrac{\text{days}}{360}$

It is assumed that the amount of the payable is 1. Cranbery will then invest the number of home units given by the spot rate, as that is the number it would be paying out to buy yen. At the end of one month Cranbery pays the principal amount of the payable plus a premium for keeping the funds for an additional month. Cranbery buys this principal plus interest, not at the spot rate, but at a rate that is unknown today. We can call that rate spot $\pm q$, where q is the number of points representing the difference between today's spot rate and the rate of conversion of the outflow. The points calculation then looks like

$$\text{points} = (\text{spot} \pm q) \times I_f \times \frac{\text{days}}{360} - \text{spot} \times I_h \times \frac{\text{days}}{360}$$

This can be simplified to give

$$\text{points} = \text{spot} \times (I_f - I_h) \times \frac{\text{days}}{360} \pm q \times I_f \times \frac{\text{days}}{360}$$

The number of points that q represents is not known. A likely candidate would be the points difference between the spot rate and the expected rate in one month. Let's see how the modification works with the situation of Cranbery's payable of Japanese yen. The spot rate ¥/A\$ is 3.7660, $I_f = 11\%$ and $I_h = 7\%$, days = 30. The treasurer expects a rate of 3.7400 in 30 days, a weakening yen.

$$\text{points} = 3.7660 \times (.11 - .07) \times \frac{30}{360} - .0240 \times .11 \times \frac{30}{360} = 123$$

Rather than a 126-point cost, the treasurer, given his expectations, would have a cost of 123 points. The break-even rate changes to 3.7537 from 3.7534. This is not terribly significant given the divergence of the treasurer's expectations from the break-even rate. Various values can be tested to see how sensitive the break-even rate is to different expectations of future rates. In general, unless the number of days is large and the expected rate diverges greatly from the spot rate, the modification is not necessary to make the decision to lag.

CHAPTER THIRTEEN
MULTIPLE EXPOSURES

"Multiple exposures" describes situations where a company has more than one flow in the same foreign currency or has flows in different foreign currencies. In some cases time and money are saved by dealing with more than one exposure at the same time. There are other instances where it is beneficial to deal with each exposure independently.

MORE THAN ONE CURRENCY

A major Dutch trading company has an inflow of dollars in 31 days and at the same time an outflow of the equivalent amount in French francs. There is a temptation to solve both exposures at one time by doing a $/FF Forward, or some other option, without any reference to the home currency. However, this strategy does not always yield the best results for the company. The reason is that the best option for covering the dollar inflow may be a $/DG Forward, whereas the best option for covering the franc outflow may be a FF/DG Lead. If the options are analyzed only in terms of the dollar and franc the optimal combination is missed.

Example. A Dutch trading company has a U.S. dollar receivable exposure and French franc payable exposure. The amount of the payable

264

and receivable is the same; they are both due in 31 days. For this illustration only two options are considered, Forward and Lead; the principle applies equally to all others.

The rates for the example are:

	Guilders	Francs	Dollars
External	$9-9\frac{1}{4}\%$	$10-10\frac{1}{4}\%$	$14-14\frac{1}{4}\%$
Domestic	$6-6\frac{1}{4}\%$	$11-11\frac{1}{4}\%$	$12-12\frac{1}{4}\%$

For bank loans, a spread of 1% is added.

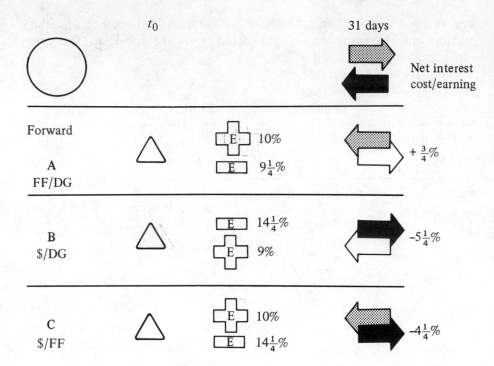

266

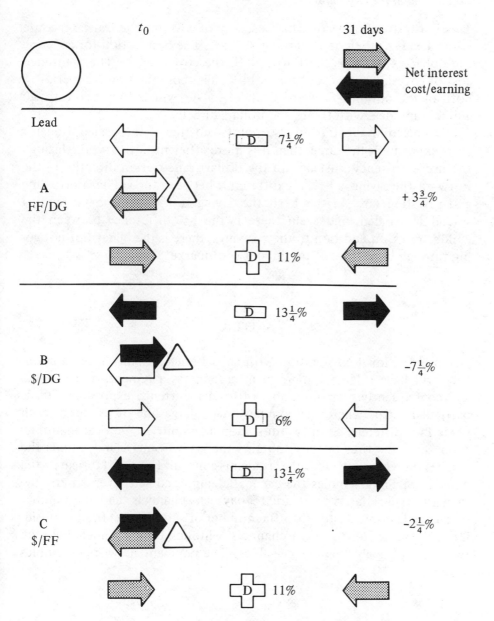

t_0 31 days

Net interest cost/earning

Lead

D $7\frac{1}{4}\%$

A
FF/DG

$+3\frac{3}{4}\%$

D 11%

B
$/DG

D $13\frac{1}{4}\%$

$-7\frac{1}{4}\%$

D 6%

C
$/FF

D $13\frac{1}{4}\%$

$-2\frac{1}{4}\%$

D 11%

White, Dutch guilders; gray, French francs; black, U.S. dollars

This illustration shows that the best way of covering the franc exposure is the Lead–A; there is an earning of $3\frac{3}{4}\%$. The best option for covering the dollar exposure is the Forward–B, the cost is $5\frac{1}{4}\%$. The combined cost of covering both exposures is $1\frac{1}{2}\%$. This combination is superior to both of the options, Forward–C and Lead–C, which do not go through guilders and deal with francs and dollars directly.

The preceding illustration also points out that if the best option for each exposure is the same, then it is more efficient not to work through the home currency; instead, do the dollar/franc option directly. In the Forward the saving is $\frac{1}{4}\%$, the difference between the guilder borrowing and investing rate. In the Lead the saving is $1\frac{1}{4}\%$; one bank lending spread is avoided, and again there is the $\frac{1}{4}\%$ difference between the guilder rates. In addition to these savings, there is the benefit of not going through both sides of the guilder spot market.

NETTING

A multinational corporation with subsidiaries in many foreign countries will have a large volume of intercompany payments and receipts and consequently a large number of foreign currency exposures. This is particularly true where the company has a large line of products, each made in a different country but sold in all countries. Or a car manufacturer buys the tires in Italy, obtains the glass from Ireland, builds the engines in Germany and the transmissions in France, fabricates the body in Spain, assembles the car in Belgium, and sells everywhere. Between six subsidiaries there are 15 payment channels, and the number of channels grows faster than the number of subsidiaries; for 12 subsidiaries, there are 66 payment channels. Through each channel there are two flows, payables and receivables. The payment network resembles a web:

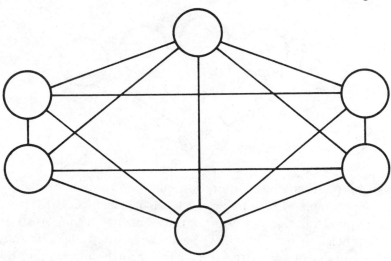

A way to rationalize this web is a netting system. It covers all of the exposures of the subsidiaries at one time. Each subsidiary submits to a central point—usually regional headquarters—the amount, the currency, and the destination of its intercompany payments due in five days. The payments are netted and each subsidiary is charged or credited in its own currency at its local bank. The money is cleared through a bank working with headquarters. An example of how the net works can be shown with two subsidiaries.

Austria owes Belgium BF 14,000,000.
Belgium owes Austria AS 18,750,000.
A common currency is used to compare the different payables.
Austria owes Belgium BF 14,000,000 = $500,000, $/BF 28.00.
Belgium owes Austria AS 18,750,000 = $1,500,000, $/AS 12.50.
Net: Belgium owes Austria $1,000,000.
Belgium is charged BF 28,000,000.
Austria is credited AS 12,500,000.

The Belgian francs are credited to a headquarters account; headquarters executes a spot transaction selling francs to buy schillings and then credits the Austrian subsidiary.

A netting system reduces the payments network of six subsidiaries from 15 payment channels to six:

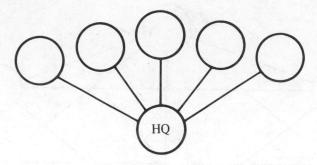

The saving a multinational corporation can reap from a netting system can be considerable. The number of foreign exchange transactions is reduced (from 15 to 6 in our example). Rather than having Austria buy francs and Belgium buy schillings, headquarters executes one transaction. The corporation saves the spread between the buying and selling rates. The number of money transfers is drastically reduced; therefore, so is the company's cost for transfers. The amount of time money spends in transit is cut by a netting system. This allows more efficient use of the funds the company has and reduces interest expenses. Experience with these systems shows that about $100,000 can be saved on an annual volume of $50 million. The information obtained from a netting system increases headquarter's knowledge of the corporation's financial structure and enables it to identify opportunities for lagging payments to improve liquidity positions of the subsidiaries. Because the period of time between the receipt of information and the net is so short, there are few opportunities for adding to liquidity by leading.

A netting system is not a substitute for exposure management. The only items to be included in the periodic net are those that the company decided not to cover by other options. And as pointed out in Chapter 1, the mutual indebtedness of the Austrian and Belgian subsidiaries does not necessarily constitute zero exposure for the corporation, even if the amounts were the same.

A number of banks offer computerized netting systems to corporations, assist the corporations in negotiations with government authorities, and offer the use of their branch networks to facilitate the flow of funds.

MORE THAN ONE FLOW IN THE SAME CURRENCY

Aspinwall Ltd., a Canadian textile concern, borrowed Swiss francs a number of years back. It is repaying the loan in quarterly installments of principal and interest. The firm's directors have decided they wish to cover the last four payments all at once. They feel the Canadian dollar is currently at a high point vis-à-vis the franc. The chances of doing much better are not very strong. The assistant treasurer is instructed to execute this program as soon as possible. The Lead and the Lead-F are not feasible options since the loan agreement with the bank prohibits prepayment.

Aspinwall's assistant treasurer calls the bank for the latest rates:

Period	Exchange Rates	Interest Rates	
		Domestic Dollars	External Francs
Spot SF/C$	.7214–16		
Three months (90 days)	148–152	$14\frac{3}{8}\%$	$5\frac{3}{8}\%$
Six months (182 days)	268–278	$14\frac{3}{8}$	$5\frac{5}{8}$
Nine months (272 days)	396–406	$12\frac{1}{2}$	$5\frac{1}{2}$
Twelve months (366 days)	512–532	12	$5\frac{1}{2}$

A few calculations are made:

Option	Net Interest Cost	Option	Net Interest Cost
Three months		*Nine months*	
Forward	8.43%	Forward	7.45%
BSI	9.00%	BSI	7.00%
Six months		*Twelve months*	
Forward	7.62%	Forward	7.25%
BSI	8.75%	BSI	6.50%

The assistant treasurer reports back to the directors that he covered the three- and six-month installments with forward contracts but covered the last two quarters with the BSI option. The firm borrows Canadian dollars for two separate periods—9 months and 12 months. It sells the proceeds of both loans spot for Swiss francs and invests the francs in the external market for 9 months and for 12 months. When questioned about using a different option to cover the last two quarters, the assistant treasurer points out that it is cheaper because the shapes of the interest rate yield curves for domestic Canadian dollars and external dollars are different. The following graph is presented:

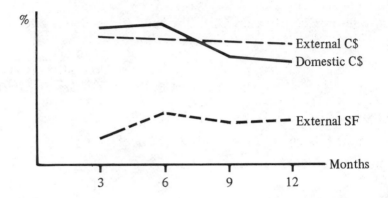

The gap between the interest rates in the two external markets is thinnest for the first two periods; hence the Forward is best there. The gap between the interest rates in the franc external and dollar domestic markets is narrowest in the last two periods; hence the BSI is best there.

Because the shape of interest rate yield curves in domestic and external markets are not always the same, each foreign currency exposure in a series should be analyzed independently.

PAYABLE AND RECEIVABLE, SAME CURRENCY, DIFFERENT TIMES

A trading company or an intermediate processing firm imports and pays for goods at one time and sells and receives payment later. JSW

Ltd. imports cotton into Hong Kong for reexport to Japan and Korea. Most of the trade is denominated in U.S. dollars. A typical cash flow scenario for the Hong Kong firm looks like:

It is unlikely that the same option will be the best for both exposures since the relative advantage of the options switches in going from the payable to the receivable. Consider JSW's situation and the covering options:

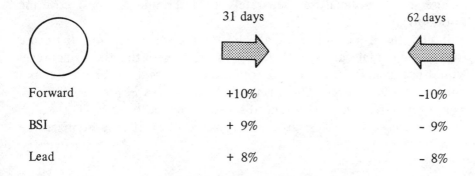

	31 days	62 days
Forward	+10%	–10%
BSI	+ 9%	– 9%
Lead	+ 8%	– 8%

The Forward is the best option for covering the payable, but the Lead is the best option for covering the receivable. The wide spread between the external interest rates that was desirable in covering the payable is not desirable for covering the receivable. Similarly, the narrow spread between domestic interest rates that makes the Lead the best option for covering the receivable makes it the least desirable way to cover the payable exposure.

The rates that Aspinwall Ltd. faces lead to different results for an outflow and subsequent inflow of foreign currency:

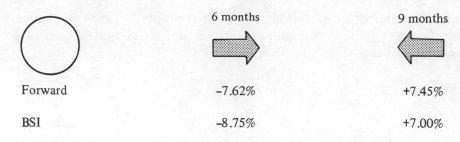

	6 months	9 months
Forward	−7.62%	+7.45%
BSI	−8.75%	+7.00%

The Forward is the best option for covering both exposures because the interest rate differential in the external money markets narrows more slowly in the longer periods than does the differential between external francs and domestic Canadian dollars.

The message is that each foreign currency flow that constitutes an exposure should be analyzed separately to determine the best covering option for it.

Should the same option be the best for both exposures, there are some savings that can be realized by covering them together. Aspinwall would not execute two separate forward contracts to cover the six- and nine-month exposures. The firm would do a *forward–forward swap*. This swap differs from the one discussed previously only in the fact that it starts in 182 days rather than in two days. It is symbolized the same way:

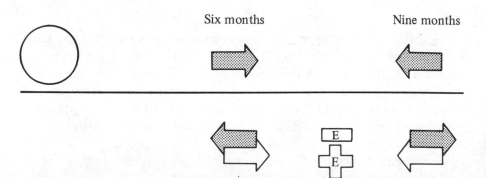

The reason for the swap is the same as before. It saves going through both sides of the spot exchange market when the desired operation involves time only. The sole feature to be worked out is the pricing of the forward–forward swap. Aspinwall Ltd. is working with these rates:

SF/C$ spot	.7214–16
Six months	268–278
Nine months	396–406

It is helpful to think of the forward–forward swap as being composed of two swaps: (1) spot to nine months and (2) spot to six months. The flows at nine months are the tail of the first swap in which the foreign currency is borrowed and the home currency invested. According to the rules formulated in Chapter 9, this swap is done at 396 points. The flows at six months are the tail of the second swap in which the foreign currency is invested and the home currency borrowed. This swap is done at 278 points. The difference between the two, 118, is the forward–forward swap points. The contracts are priced at .7492 for six months and .7610 for nine months. This is an earning because Swiss interest rates are lower than the Canadian. To calculate the interest earning represented by 118 points, the six month contract rate, not the spot rate, is used.

PROBLEM

Some weeks have passed and JSW Ltd. now finds that it is in a similar position, payable in 31 days, receivable in 62. Now, however, the Forward is the best option for covering both dollar exposures. The rates are

US$/HK$ spot	4.8090–10
One month	320–300
Two months	610–590

What are the points and interest cost/earning of the forward–forward swap? Work the problem before looking at the solution.

SOLUTION

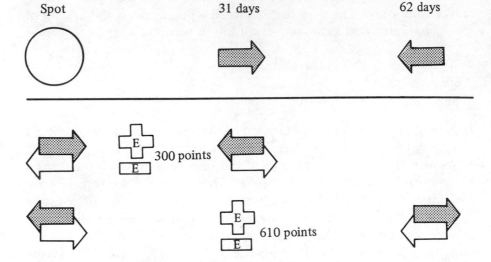

Spot   31 days   62 days

White, Hong Kong dollars; gray, U.S. dollars.

In the one-month swap U.S. dollars are invested and Hong Kong dollars borrowed; hence the swap is done at 300 points. This is an earning since the way the points are written indicate that U.S. interest rates are higher than those in Hong Kong. In the two-month swap U.S. dollars are borrowed, and Hong Kong dollars are invested at 610 points. This is a cost because of the higher U.S. interest rates. The forward–forward swap, one month against two months, is done at a cost of 310 points. The net interest cost is

$$7.53\% = \frac{.0310}{4.7790} \times \frac{360}{62 - 31} \times 100$$

Since the two swaps that constitute a forward–forward swap are the reverse of one another, once the appropriate points have been determined for one swap, the other will be found on the opposite side of the market.

If it is found that the BSI is the best option for both the payable and receivable, there are savings if some of the operations are combined. The combination of two BSI options yields, not surprisingly, two forward–forward money transactions of the type discussed in Chapter 11. There is no need for a spot exchange since the exposure has a time dimension only. The Lead and Lag options are treated similarly.

PAYABLE AND RECEIVABLE, SAME CURRENCY, SAME TIME

The situation shown below does not constitute an exposure for JSW Ltd. The dates are the same and the amounts are the same also.

The import–export firm can easily allow the inflow to offset the out-flow. However, there may be a more worthwhile way for the firm to operate. A few pages earlier it was noted that different options are often appropriate for payable and receivable flows at different times because the relative advantage of the options shifts in going from covering a payable to a receivable, and vice versa.

This idea also applies with even more vigor to payables and receivables that flow at the same time since the possibility of a change in the shape of the interest rate yield curves is eliminated. An example with the following rates illustrates the point:

	Domestic	External
Hong Kong	$5-5\frac{1}{4}\%$	$7-7\frac{1}{4}\%$
United States	$13\frac{3}{4}-14\%$	$14-14\frac{1}{4}\%$

The Forward and Lead options are used to illustrate.

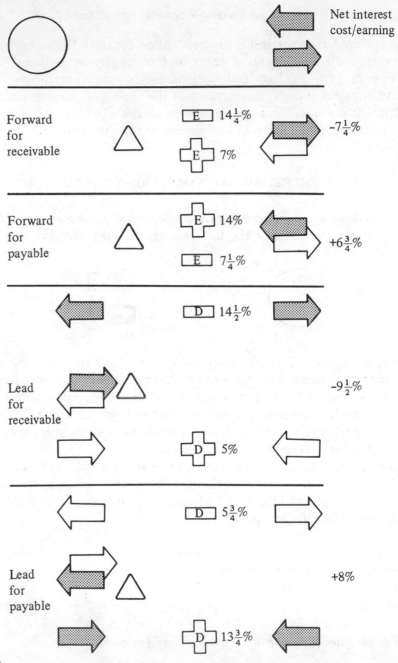

Net interest
cost/earning

Forward
for
receivable

E 14¼%

E 7%

−7¼%

Forward
for
payable

E 14%

E 7¼%

+6¾%

D 14½%

Lead
for
receivable

−9½%

D 5%

D 5¾%

Lead
for
payable

+8%

D 13¾%

278

By covering the receivable with the Forward and the payable with the Lead, JSW Ltd. earns $\frac{3}{4}$%. Execution of these options when the two flows cover each other (1) earns the firm US\$3750 on US\$2 million over 90 days, (2) decreases the availability of bank credit for other uses, and (3) does not change the debt structure of the firm's balance sheet since current liabilities remain unchanged—accounts payable are reduced by the same amount short term bank debt is increased.

CHAPTER FOURTEEN
TIME OPTIONS

A number of foreign exchange and money market techniques are grouped together in this chapter because they relate to the time element in exposure. The facets of time to be considered are:

- Length, from very short to very long. How to deal with exposures that are before spot and those that are two years after spot, where there is no market.

- Uncertainty of time. Is the payable due in 30, 35, or 40 days? If the ship delivering the goods is fighting its way to port through stormy seas, no one can pick a definite date for its arrival. Yet, foreign exchange and money market contracts are made for a specific date.

- Unwillingness to pay the price of time. The firm wants to cover its exposure, but interest rates are so high at the moment that the cost is prohibitive.

- Broken time. How do you figure out the price of a forward contract which is not one month, two months or any other standard period, but is 39 days? And likewise, how much does it cost to borrow for 39 days when all you know is the interest rate for 30 days and 60 days?

The settlement convention in the foreign exchange and Eurodollar markets is a factor in all time calculations involving the U.S. dollar.

CLEARING HOUSE FUNDS AND FEDERAL FUNDS

In the early nineteenth century most financial transactions in the United States were executed by check. When the Bank of New York received a check from a customer of Irving Trust, it sent a messenger over to Irving to exchange the check for the equivalent amount in gold or bank notes. The system worked well with only a few banks in town. By 1853 New York City had over 50 financial institutions, and settlement by messenger became unwieldy. In that year the banks in the city formed the New York Clearing House. Representatives of the banks met every day to present one another with their checks. If after all the checks were tallied, Bank of New York owed Irving Trust $1 million, Bank of New York would hand over to Irving $1 million in gold or bank notes.

The volume of checks at the Clearing House grew rapidly. Because of this, banks couldn't predict how much gold and bank notes would be needed each day. They were bringing too much one day and not enough the next. The solution was to tally the checks one day and exchange the equivalent in bank notes and gold the day after. The checks were called *clearing house funds;* gold and bank notes were *good funds.* In 1914 the Federal Reserve System was established. Banks were (and still are) required to keep money on deposit with the Federal Reserve Bank. The good funds—gold and bank notes—were replaced by the deposits that banks kept with the Federal Reserve. Rather than hand over gold to another bank on the day after the checks were cleared, banks instructed the Federal Reserve Bank to charge their account and credit the account of the other bank the day after. *Federal funds* became synonomous with good funds.

Instructions concerning the settlement of dollars (from overseas transactions) are carried by international cable. In the early 1900s this system was subject to delay and breakdown. This precluded settling these transactions on the same day with good funds. Since the clearing house system was established for settling domestic checks, it was readily extended to settling international dollar payments.

This convention exists today. Eurodollar loans and investments are made in clearing house funds. The dollars delivered in foreign exchange transactions are also clearing house funds. On the other hand, if a company wishes to invest in the domestic U.S. money market, it must use Federal funds, or good funds. The dollars received from selling Deutsche marks can be invested in U.S. Treasury bills (T bills) the next day, but not sooner. On the other hand, a company's obligation to deliver dollars on the fourth day of the month to purchase sterling can be satisfied by delivering Federal funds on the fifth day. Federal funds and clearing house funds are interchangeable with a one business day gap, and with notification to the receiving party.*

Does the company that receives dollars from the sale of Deutsche marks lose interest for a day because it cannot invest in T bills until tomorrow? No, the firm can establish an investment program in Federal funds that is equivalent to a clearing house investment starting today.

---

*A bank is expecting Sloat & Company to pay in clearing house funds on the fifth day. Sloat does not deliver and says nothing. The bank is missing $1 million in clearing house funds. To cover its obligations, the bank borrows $1 million for one day. Even though Sloat pays in Federal funds the following day, the bank will charge for the cost of its borrowing.

The two investment alternatives are shown in the following diagram:

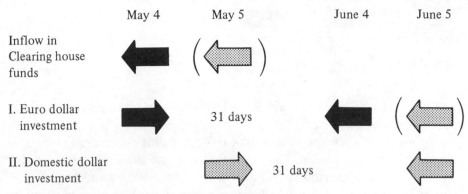

Black, Clearing house funds; gray, Federal funds.

The parentheses indicate that the Federal funds flow is linked with the receipt of the clearing house funds; it is not independent of it.

On June 5 under investment programs I and II the company has earned 31 days of interest and has an inflow of Federal funds. These are equivalent investment programs. The company decides which program to implement on the basis of the interest rates in the external and domestic markets.

Because of the relationship between clearing house and Federal funds, the Eurodollar market shows some abnormal interest rates in two particular periods: one-day deposits from Thursday to Friday and three-day deposits from Friday to Monday. If a company has clearing house funds available for an investment on Thursday, it can either place the funds in the Eurodollar market for one day, or place the funds in the domestic money market starting on Friday for three days. They are equivalent investments.

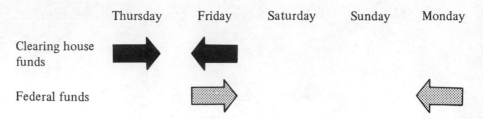

The interest rate which is paid for a Thursday–Friday investment in the Eurodollar market reflects the domestic opportunity. The rate for clearing house funds always adjusts to the opportunity represented by the market for Federal funds. The Federal funds rate does not adjust to the clearing house opportunity. This is a market convention. Let's say a company can earn 10% a day for three days if the money is invested in the domestic money market. For the one-day Thursday–Friday investment in the Eurodollar market to be equivalent, it must pay 30% for that one day. The one-day rate for clearing house funds on Thursday–Friday is 30%, three times the Federal funds rate.

If a company wishes to borrow clearing house funds from Friday to Monday, it pays interest for three days. An equivalent way of satisfying the same need is to borrow in the domestic market for only one day, Monday–Tuesday. The market for clearing house funds recognizes this opportunity and adjusts its rate accordingly. The interest rate for borrowing over the weekend in clearing house funds is one-third of the rate for borrowing Federal funds for one day. If that rate is 10%, the weekend rate is $3\frac{1}{3}\%$. An investment or loan that runs from Thursday through Monday will be made up of one day at 30% and three days at $3\frac{1}{3}\%$; the average for the four days is 10%.*

*Because of the way bank reserves in the United States are calculated, New York banks can save reserves when they borrow clearing house funds for the weekend. Lending clearing house funds from Thursday to Friday also saves reserves. This alters their effective rates for borrowing and lending for these periods. In the market this is reflected by a weekend rate somewhat greater than one-third and a Thursday-Friday rate somewhat less than three times the day-to-day rate.

The impact of the clearing house–Federal funds technicality on Euro-dollar rates can be significant. Consider an investment that begins on a Wednesday but ends on a Friday one month later. Throughout the month the interest rate has averaged 10% a day, but the last day is 30%. If there are 31 days in the month, 30 days at 10% and one day at 30% gives a rate of 10.65% for 31 days. The day before the one-month rate was 10%. Seeing that rate without knowing that the investment matured on a Friday could definitely distort your view of interest rate developments.

QUESTIONS

Assume that the supply and demand for one-month Eurodollars remains constant and that the normal rate is 10%. What elements will affect the one-month rate in the following situations? What will be the net effect on the rate?

1. A loan begins on a Friday and ends on a Monday.
2. A loan begins on a Friday and ends on a Friday.
3. A loan begins on a Thursday and ends on a Wednesday.
4. A loan begins on a Tuesday and ends on a Friday before a three-day weekend, (Monday is a holiday).

RESPONSES

1. Interest rate for the first day(s) of the month is low.
2. Interest rate for the first day(s) of the month is high.
3. Interest rate for the last day(s) of the month is high.
4. Interest rate for the last day(s) of the month is low.
5. Interest rate for the first day(s) of the month is normal.
6. Interest rate for the last day(s) of the month is normal.

RESPONSE ANALYSIS

Question 1

A. *If you chose 1*: The first three days of the month are worth $3\frac{1}{3}\%$ a day. The rest of the days in a 30-day month average to 10%; the month as a whole is priced at 9.33%.

$$\frac{(27 \times 10\%) + (3 \times 3\frac{1}{3}\%)}{30} = 9.33\%$$

B. *If you chose 4*: The last three days of the month are low ($3\frac{1}{3}\%$); however, the last four days average to 10% since Thursday–Friday is 30%. As a result, there is no effect on the rate if the loan ends on Monday.

C. *If you chose 6*: The last four days of the month can be considered to be normal since their average is 10%—30% for Thursday–Friday and $3\frac{1}{3}\%$ for Friday–Monday.

D. *If you chose 2*: Money borrowed starting Friday does not carry the high rate; it is money borrowed from Thursday to Friday that has a rate three times normal.

Question 2

E. *If you chose 1 and 4*: The first three days of the month are low, $\frac{1}{3}$ of the normal rate; the last day of the month is high, three times the normal rate. The result of a Friday start and Friday end is a *neutral* run, with two clearing house–Federal fund technicalities canceling one another out. A neutral run of days is also one that is not affected at all by technicalities.

F. *If you chose 5 or 6*: Any period that starts or ends on a Friday does not begin or end with normal rates. As noted in item E (above), the interest rate for the month is normal because the technicalities cancel.

Question 3

G. *If you chose 2:* The rate from Thursday to Friday is high, but when the following three days are added on, the run of four days from Thursday to Monday averages 10%.

H. *If you chose 5:* You were thinking of the first four days of the one-month period that do average to 10%. The first day, however, is three times the normal rate.

I. *If you chose 6:* If there are no holidays during a week, loans that end on Monday through Thursday do not need to have their rates adjusted for clearing house funds settlement practices.

Question 4

J. *If you chose 5:* If there are no holidays during the week, loans which begin on Monday through Thursday do not need to be adjusted for rate due to market technicalities.

K. *If you chose 3:* The rate from Thursday to Friday is even more than three times the normal rate, it is four times the normal rate. The interest rate for the month is 11%. Another way of calculating the adjustments to the normal rate is to look at the number of days in the clearing house transaction and compare it with the number of days in the equivalent Federal funds transaction. In the present example:

	June			July			
Tues	Wed		Fri	Sat	Sun	Mon	Tues
	30 days					H	
		33 days					

The comparable opportunity in Federal funds runs for 33 days; since that in clearing house funds runs only 30 days, the clearing house fund rate is adjusted upward.

$$\frac{33 \text{ days}}{30 \text{ days}} \times 10\% = 11\%$$

In general, the formula for making the adjustment upward or downward is

$$\frac{\text{Federal fund days}}{\text{Clearing house fund days}} \times \text{normal rate} = \text{adjusted rate}$$

SUMMARY

The following table summarizes the adjustments:

Start	End	Adjust
Friday	Mon–Thurs	Down
Mon–Thurs	Friday	Up
Friday	Friday	None

A holiday in the middle of the week has a similar effect on the previous days as the weekend does on Friday.

Impact of the Clearing House–Federal Funds Technicality

An awareness of influence of this market technicality is important for the firm with continual funding requirements. One-month money that has cost 12% for the last eight days is not suddenly a bargain at $11\frac{1}{2}\%$, when the Friday start should have meant a rate of $11\frac{1}{4}\%$. One-month rates have in fact increased by $\frac{1}{4}\%$. The influence of a Friday end or Friday start diminishes as the period becomes longer. With high dollar interest rates, however, even the six-month period is adjusted by $\frac{1}{8}\%$ when the neutral run is 12%.

The clearing house–Federal funds technicality also affects forward points where the dollar is one of the currencies involved. Assume dollar interest rates are higher than Deutsche mark rates. Points for any period will be greater if the month ends on a Friday than on any other day. The number of points will be smaller if the period starts on a Friday. The opposite will be true where dollar interest rates are lower than those of another currency.

Earlier in the present chapter it was noted that clearing house funds are the convention in the foreign exchange market although Federal funds can be obtained (or sold) in an exchange transaction. To obtain Federal funds on the spot day, the bank borrows clearing house funds for one day—from the day before spot to the spot date. The cost of the money market transaction is wrapped into the exchange price. It is better to let the bank borrow because there is no lending spread. The following illustration shows the flow of funds.

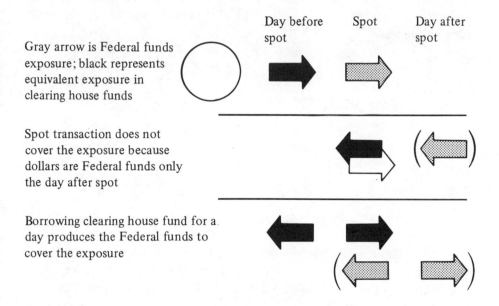

Gray arrow is Federal funds exposure; black represents equivalent exposure in clearing house funds

Spot transaction does not cover the exposure because dollars are Federal funds only the day after spot

Borrowing clearing house fund for a day produces the Federal funds to cover the exposure

Notice that all of the flows cancel with the exception of an outflow of home currency spot.

A Swedish company has a bill to pay in the United States, and the American firm has specified payment in Federal funds on the fifth day of the month. The Americans asked for Federal funds so they could invest in the U.S. money market on the same day that payment was received. Besides, if a choice exists, it is better to receive Federal funds on the fifth day than clearing house funds; an extra day of interest can be earned. The Swedish foreign manager specifically requests its bank to deliver Federal funds against payment of Swedish kroner. For this the company will pay more kroner. The spot is \$/Skr4.1555–70; the one-day rate for dollars is $13–13\frac{1}{4}\%$. The additional cost for Federal funds is calculated as

$$\text{Formula:} \quad \text{Spot} \times \text{interest rate} \times \text{time} = \text{points}$$

$$\text{Example: } 4.1570 \times .1325 \times \frac{1}{360} = 15$$

The 15 points are added to the spot rate. The Swedish firm buys Federal funds at 4.1585.

EXPOSURES TODAY, TOMORROW, AND THE DAY AFTER SPOT

The European area treasurer of Bailie Industries Ltd. in Toronto often walks in the mornings to find a cable saying that dividends from one of the overseas subsidiaries are available to be remitted immediately. JSW Ltd. in Hong Kong deals in such volume that at least once a month a foreign currency payment slips by and must be paid today or tomorrow. The spot date is too late. Antigone Shipping buys a foreign currency to provide for the expenses of its ships in foreign ports. From time to time a ship arrives two days earlier than the date on which the currency was bought. Parker & Company decided some months ago not to cover its upcoming Swiss franc loan payment, but rather to wait until the spot day to buy the francs. The payment is now three days away, and the treasurer hears from a reliable source that in the afternoon the

Federal Reserve is going to announce a lower discount rate. The measure is intended to spur the U.S. economy but will very likely weaken the dollar, at least temporarily. The treasurer wants to buy now. The Hooper Company's (Chapter 7) cash flow schedule looks, in part, like this:

	17	18	19	20	21
DM	2	2	-2	-3	1

The numbers with a minus sign indicate outflows of millions of marks; those without a sign indicate inflows. How will the day-to-day position of the company be handled? The problem common to these companies is the need to act quickly and to rearrange funds for short periods of time, and the spot date is too late for many of them to act. There are foreign exchange and money market rates for periods of 1, 2, 3, 6, and 12 months that start from the spot date. There are also markets for shorter periods of time, closer to the spot date, called *short-date markets*. These exchange and money markets consist of three separate one-day quotes around the spot day and quotes for one and two weeks. These markets differ from those previously discussed because the periods are shorter and because they do not all start on the spot date.

The quote from today to tomorrow is called *overnight* (O/N); today is the starting day. The quote from tomorrow to spot is called *tom-next* (T/N); tomorrow is the starting day. The quote from spot to the day after spot is called *spot-next* (S/N), spot is the starting day. The quote from spot to one week is called *spot-a-week* (S/W), spot is the starting day. The following diagram illustrates this idea.

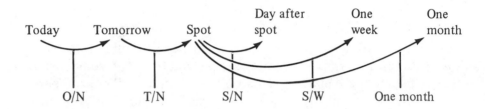

Tom-next and spot-next quotes are available for nearly all traded currencies. For the less active currencies, the tom-next market tends to dry up in the afternoon. Overnight quotes do not exist for all currencies. One governing factor is the time at which banks are required to settle their books for the day. In Zurich it may be 8 a.m., in Amsterdam 11 a.m., in New York 2 p.m., and in London 2 p.m. The ability to make an overnight quote also depends on where in the world a bank is in relation to the country of the currency it is dealing with. A U.S. dollar transaction, no matter where in the world it is made, will involve a movement of funds between two bank accounts in the United States. Likewise, a sterling transaction anywhere gives rise to a transfer of funds in London and guilders, a transfer between two accounts in The Netherlands, and so on. An overnight U.S. dollar/sterling transaction is made in Brussels at 2 p.m. There is one hour to transfer funds in London and six hours to transfer them in New York, because of the time difference. Overnight $/¥ is quoted in Tokyo, but not in London. Overnight sterling deposits can be made in Paris, but at 9 a.m. in New York it is too late. A local bank will be able to provide information on what overnight markets are available in any time zone. Of course, it is always possible for a company to do more if someone is willing to start working very early in the morning.

Options

Covering an exposure the day after spot or one week after spot is exactly the same as one month. The same options are available to corporations. Covering an exposure today or tomorrow involves the same considerations as covering an exposure 30 or 60 days in the future, but some options are not the same. The objective of the options is the same—find the most efficient combination of external and domestic money markets. The BSI is very similar to the option used to cover future exposures. The combination of a spot and a swap is also used to cover today's and tomorrow's exposures, although it is not called a "Forward." In relation to the spot date it is backward. There is no concise terminology; it is sometimes called "spot over tomorrow" and "spot over today." For an exposure today or tomorrow, the Lead has little practical value. On the other hand, a Lag will move the exposure to the spot day where it can be covered with a spot contract. The basic options for covering an exposure tomorrow are illustrated as follows:

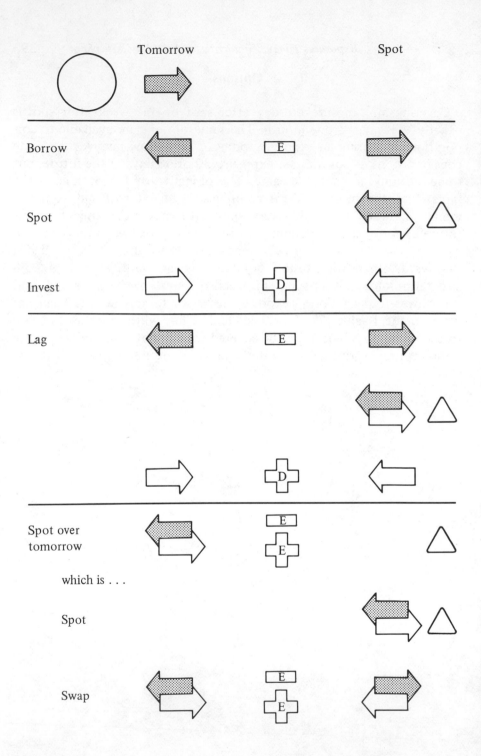

BSI: Gray is borrowed from tomorrow to spot. The inflow from the loan covers the payable. The maturing loan is paid off by a purchase of gray on the spot date. The white funds available to buy gray tomorrow are invested for a day. The maturing white investment is used to pay for the spot purchase.

Lag: The company puts off paying its gray supplier for a day and is charged the supplier's cost of borrowing for a day. The delayed exposure is covered with a spot contract. The white funds not disbursed tomorrow are invested for a day.

Spot over tomorrow: Just as a bank put together a spot and a swap to produce a Forward, it puts together a spot and a swap to cover an exposure tomorrow. One price, including both elements, is given to the customer. The white currency is disbursed tomorrow, and the price of the contract includes an earning for white in the price, just as it includes a cost for the gray.

Comparing the options is the same as with a future exposure.

Example. France is white, the United States is gray, spot $/FF 4.0120–35, French domestic interest rates are 10%, dollar domestic interest rates are 15%, external rates are 13%, and the number of points for one day is $4\frac{1}{2}-3\frac{1}{2}$.

The matrix for comparing the options is as follows:

Option	Spot	Net Interest Cost/Earning I_h	I_f	Net		Locked-In Rate
BSI	4.0136	10	13	-3%	$3\frac{3}{8}$	$4.0138\frac{3}{8}$
Lag	4.0135	10	15	-5%	$5\frac{5}{8}$	$4.0140\frac{5}{8}$
Spot over tomorrow	4.0135			-4.04%	$4\frac{1}{2}$	$4.0139\frac{1}{2}$

The best option for covering the exposure tomorrow is the BSI; it is the least costly.

The points for day-to-day transactions are generally rounded to the nearest $\frac{1}{8}$ or $\frac{1}{4}$. The reason for such precision is that $\frac{1}{8}$ or $\frac{1}{4}$ point for one day has considerable implications for the related interest rate differentials. In the present case $\frac{1}{4}$ point a day is the equivalent to $\frac{1}{4}\%$ per annum difference between French and U.S. interest rates.

The calculation of points is the same.

$$\text{Points} = \frac{4.0135 \times (.10 - .13) \times \dfrac{1}{360}}{1 + \left(.13 \times \dfrac{11}{360}\right)} = .000334 = 3\frac{3}{8}$$

For one- or two-day transactions it is not necessary to use the bottom half of the expression; very little is changed by omitting it. If it is omitted in the present case, the result is .0003342; if it is used, the result is .0003344. On $1,000,000 the difference is 5¢.

The interest cost/earning of spot over tomorrow is calculated with ICE-1.

$$\frac{.00045}{4.0135} \times \frac{360}{1} \times 100 = 4.04\%$$

The left side of the points quote, $4\frac{1}{2}$, is chosen because it is the price for the swap—borrowing foreign currency, lending home currency. This is the swap required to cover the payable exposure tomorrow. But the side of the spot rate $/FF4.0120–35 for buying foreign currency (dollars) is on the right, 4.0135. The points and the spot rate do not line up as they do when the transaction is on the other side of spot. The reason is that the swaps required to cover an exposure tomorrow and an exposure in one month are different. The following diagram illustrates this.

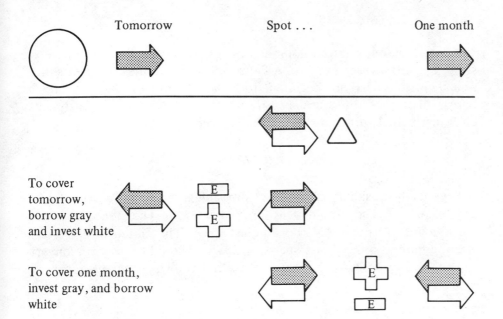

The convention for points before spot is

SWITCH THE POINTS

then the same rule applies:

LOW TO HIGH: ADD
HIGH TO LOW: SUBTRACT

Example:
$\$/FF\ 4.0120 - 4.0135$
$O/N\qquad 4 - 3$
$T/N\qquad 4\frac{1}{2} - 3\frac{1}{2}$

Quote for tomorrow:
$4.0120 \qquad 4.0135$
$\qquad 3\frac{1}{2} \qquad\qquad 4\frac{1}{2}$

Quote for today:
$4.0123\frac{1}{2} - 4.0139\frac{1}{2}$

$4.0120 - 4.0135$
$\qquad 3 \qquad\qquad 4$
$+\quad 3\frac{1}{2} \qquad + \quad 4\frac{1}{2}$

$4.0126\frac{1}{2} - 4.0143\frac{1}{2}$

A quote for today is the combination of the spot rate, the tom-next swap, and the overnight swap. A bank will combine these elements into a single price. For a loan beginning today and ending on the spot date, a bank will average the overnight rate with the tom-next rate to give the customer a single interest rate for the two days.

PROBLEM

The Dutch subsidiary of Sloat & Company is receiving $3,500,000 today, Thursday. The advising telex arrived at 9 a.m. The money is from a slow-paying customer and was due last week. The Dutch company can use the money today in its operations. What is the best way of converting the dollars to guilders? The money and foreign exchange rates are:

	Money Rates		Exchange Rates
		Domestic	
	Eurodollar	Guilder	$/DG 1.9100–10
O/N	$38\frac{1}{2}$–$38\frac{3}{4}$ %	$10\frac{1}{2}$–$10\frac{3}{4}$ %	15–$14\frac{3}{4}$
T/N	5–$5\frac{1}{4}$	$10\frac{3}{4}$–11	$8\frac{3}{4}$–$9\frac{1}{2}$
S/N	$13\frac{1}{2}$–$13\frac{3}{4}$	$10\frac{1}{2}$–$10\frac{3}{4}$	$1\frac{3}{4}$–$1\frac{1}{2}$

Bank charges 1% lending spread.

Work the problem out before looking at the solution.

SOLUTION

There are only two options for this exposure, a spot over today and BSI. The Lag is not considered since the company has already had difficulty obtaining its money.

In the pricing for spot over today, the spot rate for selling dollars is 1.9100. The overnight swap is an earning of $14\frac{3}{4}$ points and is added.

The tom-next swap is a cost of $9\frac{1}{2}$ points and is subtracted. The price for spot over today is $1.9105\frac{1}{4}$. The right side of the points quote is chosen because that swap represents an investment of foreign currency and borrowing of home currency, guilders. This is the operation needed to move the guilders purchased on the spot day to today. The reason for the switch from earning to cost is because the overnight is Thursday–Friday, and tom-next is the weekend. This is reflected in the dollar interest rates. The dollar interest rate switches from being higher than guilders on Thursday to being lower over the weekend. The interest earning is 2.47%. The calculation is

$$ICE\text{-}1 = \frac{.000525}{1.9100} \times \frac{360}{4} \times 100 = 2.47\%$$

In the pricing for BSI, the spot rate for selling dollars is 1.9100. The result of the spot transaction is an outflow of dollars four days from today and an inflow of guilders at the same time. The dollars that come in today from the customer are invested at $38\frac{1}{2}\%$ for one day and 5% for the next three days; the average interest rate for four days is $13\frac{3}{8}\%$. The maturing investment offsets the outflow from the spot transaction. Guilders are coming in on Monday but are needed today, so they are borrowed for four days. The average cost is $11\frac{15}{16}$, including lending spread. The earning from this option is $1\frac{7}{16}\%$, or three points.

The matrix comparing the two options:

| Option | Spot | Net Interest Cost/Earning | | | Points | Locked-In Rate |
		I_h	I_f	Net		
Spot over today	1.9100			+2.47%	$5\frac{1}{4}$	$1.9105\frac{1}{4}$
BSI	1.9100	11.9375	13.375	+1.4375%	3	1.9103

The spot over today option produces 787.50 more guilders for the company than the BSI.

An Aside. Consider the way the points switch in this problem from an overnight (Thursday–Friday) dollar discount to a tom-next (Friday–

Monday) dollar premium. This reflects the difference in dollar interest rates for the two periods. If the \$/DG spot rate is expected to move very little during the week, money can be made by buying dollars spot on Tuesday (delivery Thursday), swapping the dollars from Thursday to Friday at an earning of $14\frac{3}{4}$ points, and then selling the dollars spot on Wednesday (delivery Friday).

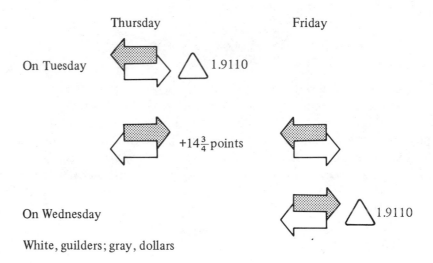

White, guilders; gray, dollars

The profit is $14\frac{3}{4}$ points; on \$1 million this is DG 1475. In a featureless market or when a central bank is holding the dollar spot rate in a narrow range, the price of the dollar is bid up by those wishing to profit from this opportunity. Under the same conditions money can be made on Wednesday by selling dollars spot, value Friday. The weekend swap earns $8\frac{3}{4}$ points. Dollars are repurchased for delivery Monday. On Wednesday the dollar spot rate is pushed down. In the rare times when the market is featureless, the phonemena of a strong dollar on Tuesday and a weak dollar on Wednesday can be observed.

PROBLEMS

A number of situations requiring short-date solutions were given at the beginning of this section. They are capsulized in the following list as problems, possible responses are listed, and an analysis of the responses follows.

1. The treasurer of Bailie Industries Ltd. in Toronto receives a cable saying that dividends from one of its overseas subsidiaries is available to be remitted immediately.

2. Antigone Shipping is informed that the ship due to dock in Hamburg in two days arrived today and needs money to pay the crew and to resupply the vessel. Antigone bought the marks, but delivery is not for two days.

3. Parker & Company has decided that it needs to cover a Swiss franc loan payment that is three days from today.

4. The Hooper Company's cash flow schedule looks, in part, like this:

	17	18	19	20	21
DM	2	2	−2	−3	1

millions of marks
−2 outflow
2 inflow

Do one problem at a time.

RESPONSES

1. Overnight swap.
2. Overnight loan.
3. Overnight deposit.
4. Tom-next swap.
5. Tom-next loan.

6. Tom-next deposit.
7. Spot.
8. Spot-next swap.
9. Spot-next loan.
10. Spot-next deposit.

RESPONSE ANALYSIS

Bailie

A. *If you chose 7, 1, and 4*: This combination will convert the foreign currency to Canadian dollars. It is the same situation as the Dutch subsidiary of Sloat & Company. The only problem may be the time difference between Toronto and the city where the currency is sitting; New York is not a problem, but Zurich is; if the money is in Zurich, 7 and 4 are the only possible actions.

B. *If you chose 7, 2, and 5, 3 and 6*: This combination will convert the foreign currency to Canadian dollars today. Canadian dollars are borrowed overnight and tom next; the foreign currency received today is invested overnight and tom next.

C. *If you chose 8, 9 or 10*: These options do not relate to the present problem because they are in a different time period.

Antigone

D. *If you chose 7*: A spot contract is redundant in this situation since the marks have been purchased.

E. *If you chose 1 and 4*: These two swaps will move the spot contract from the spot day to today.

F. *If you chose 2 and 3, 5 and 6*: The marks can be borrowed for two days, and the spot contract previously made covers the repayment. There would not be an actual deposit in this case. There would be an opportunity gain since the marks have been made available today, but home currency is not disbursed for two days.

Parker

G. *If you chose 1, 2, 3, 4, 5, or 6*: The overnight and tom-next operations do not apply to a spot-next exposure, just as they do not apply to a one-month exposure. The spot date is the starting point for all transactions beyond it in time.

H. *If you chose 7 and 8*: A spot and spot-next swap cover the Swiss franc exposure.

I. *If you chose 7, 9, and 10*: Swiss francs are purchased spot and invested for one day. The home currency that is available on the third day is borrowed for a day to pay for the spot purchase of francs.

Hooper

J. *If you chose 7*: A spot contract is not required in this case since there is a time exposure only. Hooper is not open, in this period, to any risk from a change in the value of the mark against dollars.

K. *If you chose 3, 6, and 10*: The cash flow schedule can be evened out by depositing DM2 million overnight, 17 to 18; depositing DM4 million tom-next, 18 to 19; depositing DM2 million spot-next, 19 to 20; and by borrowing DM1 million from 20 to 21. This last transaction is not included in the responses.

L. *If you chose 1, 4, or 8*: You would also have to chose 3, 6, and 10. The swap of Deutsche marks for dollars (or another currency) will generate an inflow of dollars to be invested. This will be more profitable than simply depositing the marks only if domestic dollar interest rates are higher than external dollar rates.

UNWILLINGNESS TO PAY THE PRICE OF TIME

In Chapter 8 we saw that Van der Zorn, the silver manufacturer, is faced with a situation where all the options at his disposal for selling French francs produce a locked-in future rate outside the European Monetary System (EMS) limits. Since the spot rate is within the limits, it is the time cost that causes the future rate to be outside. The alternative in Chapter 8 is: place confidence in the EMS structure and cover the exposure only if there is a sign that the established limits are not holding. There is another alternative for those firms who want to cover the exchange risk but are willing to live with interest rate risk. Rather than selling francs forward for three months, sell forward for only one month. As that contract matures, swap it forward for another month. And as that contract matures, swap it forward for another month. The exposure at three months is covered by a one-month forward plus two one-month swaps. The expectation is that the time cost of three one-month contracts is less than one three-month contract. The rates are:

FF/DG spot	46.36–41
One month	15–13
Two months	36–32
Three months	76–71

and the EMS upper limit is 45.88. The cost of the one-month swap is cheaper than the cost of the three-month swap on a per annum basis— 3.88%, compared to 6.55%. Three one-month swaps would be 45 points whereas the three month swap is 76 points. There is no guarantee, however, that the one-month swap will stay at 15. The reason for the difference in points now is that the interest rate differential between French francs and Dutch guilders is narrower at one month than at three months. This is illustrated by a graph of the yield curves:

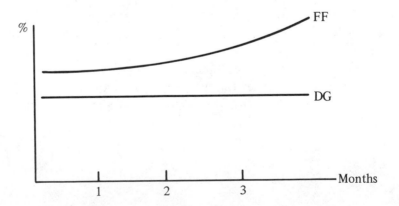

A possible strategy for Van der Zorn is to sell the francs one month forward at 46.21, hope that the yield curve structure is the same at the end of one month, and then roll the contract forward at a cost of 15 points—46.06 would be the new rate (46.21 – .15). At the end of the second month, with the yield curve structure still the same, Van der Zorn rolls the contract forwward at a cost of 15 points—45.91 would be the rate at which the exposure is covered. This is three points better than the EMS limit of 45.88. The risk of this strategy is that as time passes, guilder interest rates fall and/or franc interest rates rise, thus increasing the interest differential at one month. Instead of covering at 15 points per month, Van der Zorn may find itself covering at 30 points a month after the first month. If the interest rate shift is parallel, nothing changes; if a shift brings the rates closer together, the cost of cover is reduced.

What alternatives does Van der Zorn have if the interest differential of the external interest rates begins to widen? At the end of one month the firm can implement Borrow–Invest or Lead options that use domestic money markets. A spot is not needed since an exchange transaction has been made. Domestic interest rates are subject to different influences than are external rates and do not always move with them. The firm need not even wait until the end of one month; it can execute its options on a forward–forward basis. The following diagram illustrates the possibilities open to Van der Zorn:

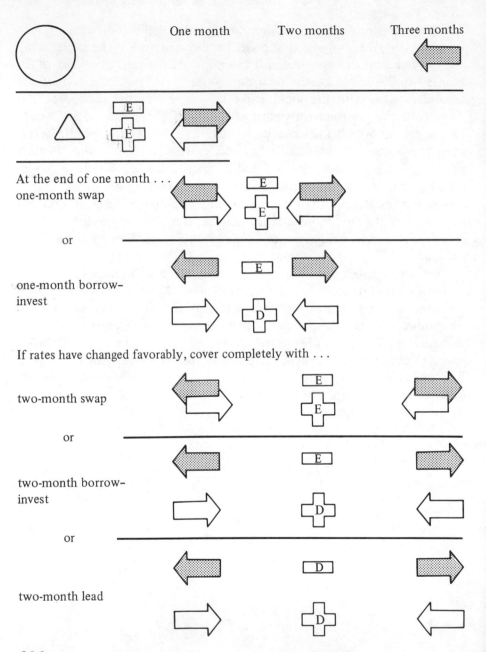

One month Two months Three months

At the end of one month . . .
one-month swap

or

one-month borrow–
invest

If rates have changed favorably, cover completely with . . .

two-month swap

or

two-month borrow–
invest

or

two-month lead

306

All these options can also be arranged at the end of the first week on a forward–forward basis. A judgment about interest rate movements is the basis for extending the cover for one month or two. The criteria for choosing an option are the same.

Those companies who feel comfortable taking risks on interest rate movements can implement such a strategy more fully than just shown. The BSI, and Lead options, unlike the Forward, separate the borrowing and the investment. It is possible to borrow one currency for six months but to invest the other for only two months, or vice versa. The particular plan followed will depend on the company's forecast of interest rates for the two currencies. Consider a six-month exposure situation where sterling is borrowed and dollars are invested. If dollar interest rates are forecast to drop, dollars would be invested for six months. If sterling rates are forecast to fall, the optimal strategy would be to borrow short term a week or month at a time. There is no way of establishing now if this is better than completely covering the exposure. A break-even interest rate for the sterling borrowings after the first month can be established and updated as the months go by. Let sterling interest rates today be

One month	16%
Two months	17%
Six months	18%

First month

Six-month today 18% × 6 months = 108
One-month today 16% × 1 month = −16
                                  92 ÷ 5 months = 18.4% = break-even rate

If the firm can borrow at an average rate below 18.4% for the next five months, it will have borrowed sterling more cheaply than if it had borrowed at 18% for six months.

Second month

```
Five-month break-even  18.4% × 5 months = 92.0
One-month today        15.5% × 1 month  = 15.5
(rates have fallen)                       76.5 ÷ 4 months = 19.125% =
                                                   break-even rate
```

If the firm can borrow at an average rate below 19.125% for the last four months, it will have borrowed sterling more cheaply than if it had borrowed at 18% for six months.

The calculation is overly favorable to borrowing on a month-to-month basis because it does not take the monthly interest payments into account. If money is borrowed from month to month, interest is paid on that basis. If money is borrowed for six months, it is paid at the end of six months or at the end of three months and six months. The more often interest is paid, the higher is the effective interest rate. Money borrowed for six months, one month at a time at 16%, is equivalent to borrowing at 16.54% with interest paid at the end of six months. Money borrowed for six months, one week at a time at 16%, is equivalent to borrowing at 16.63% with interest paid at the end of six months. The cash flow of the interest payments on short-term borrowings over long periods of time can have a substantial effect on the cost. The Appendix (at the end of the chapter) gives the formula and assumptions for the interest rate adjustment.

Rolling Forward Contracts

The risk of a movement in interest rates has been described. There is, however, another risk—a radical change in the spot rate between the time the forward contract is established and the time to roll it. This is not an exchange risk in the traditional sense, but one that is due to the convention for pricing swaps in the foreign exchange market. The convention is to use the current spot rate as the basis for the swap. A radical movement in the spot rate can create adverse cash flows for the bank, and the bank will charge the customer to finance these flows. The following example illustrates the issue:

A forward was done at FF/DG 46.21. One month has passed and the new spot rate is FF/DG 46.21–25 and the new one-month points are 15–13. The offsetting contract with the customer will be at 46.21, and the new contract will be at 46.06. Assuming the bank covers its exposure with another bank at the same rates, the flow of guilders at the bank will be as follows (all contracts are in terms of FF 100, so that flow will not be shown):

	Today	One Month
Old contract with customer	−46.21	
Old contract with other bank	+46.21	
New contracts with customer	+46.21	−46.06
New contracts with other bank	−46.21	+46.06

But if the French franc strengthens dramatically to 50.21 and if the swap is the same and the bank keeps the old contract rate for the customer, then:

	Today	One Month
New contracts with customer	+46.21	−46.06
New contracts with other bank	−50.21	+50.06

Today the bank has a net cash outflow of four guilders per 100 francs and does not recapture them for a month. The bank is obliged to finance this shortfall for a month, so it includes the finance charge in the number of points charged to the customer. The calculation is

$$\text{number of guilders financed} \times \text{interest rate} \times \text{time} = \text{points}$$

$$4 \quad \times \quad .06 \quad \times \quad \frac{30}{360} = 2$$

The bank will charge the customer two additional points:

New contract with customer	+46.21	−46.04

Should this pricing convention cause the adjustment to be very large, the corporation always has the alternative of the Lead or the Borrow–Invest. Had the French franc weakened dramatically, the adjustment would have been in favor of the corporation.

EXPOSURES IN THE FAR FUTURE

Cornie Construction Company has a contract to build a large desalinization plant in Saudi Arabia. The project will take four years from start to finish. Cornie is being paid in Saudi riyals; its expenses are denominated in dollars, yen, Swiss francs, marks, sterling, and riyals. Beyond one year the market for Saudi riyals is almost nonexistent. How is Cornie going to deal with its exposure beyond one year?

Antigone Shipping is buying a vessel in Japan. A five-year yen loan from the Japanese export agency will finance the vessel when it is delivered in 12 months. Antigone is somewhat concerned about the yen exposure since most of its revenues are in dollars and the yen is currently at a low point against the dollar. Beyond one year the market for yen is very thin. How is Antigone going to deal with its exposure beyond one year?

The exposures of these two companies cannot be covered since the markets do not extend as far in the future as the exposures. Partial cover is possible. Both Cornie and Antigone can purchase the currencies they require one year in the future and roll the contracts forward to meet the currency obligations. This means that Cornie will buy all the dollars, pounds, marks, and other currencies that it needs for the last three years of the contract. Antigone will buy the total principal and interest amount required to pay off the loan. How far ahead the currencies are purchased depends on the companies' views of interest rate movements.

Principal plus interest for Antigone is ¥5 billion, payable in semi-annual installments. The company buys this amount one year forward. At the end of one year Antigone rolls forward ¥500 million for six months and ¥4500 million for another year. At the end of the next year

Antigone rolls forward ¥500 million for six months and ¥3500 million yen for another year. This continues. The exchange risk is covered, (except for adjustments due to the swap pricing convention), but Antigone is forced to carry the interest rate risk. Antigone is not confined to the foreign exchange market; a contract may be more advantageously rolled forward with a Borrow–Invest or a Lead; loan and investment maturities can be mismatched. By the same token it is not necessary to wait until the contract matures; forward–forward transactions can be arranged. Exposures in the far future should not be neglected simply because they cannot be completely covered. The exchange risk can be covered, even though the time exposure cannot be.

Currency Swaps and Parallel Loans

An American distiller is increasing the range of its products by buying a company in Scotland. The payback on the investment is estimated to be 10 years. An English electrical supply firm wishes to restructure the liabilities of its American subsidiary to include long-term debt. The company is considering a maturity of 10 to 12 years. Both firms have enough cash in their own currency to carry out the operation but the transactions require a foreign currency. If the dollars are converted to sterling by the distiller and the pounds to dollars by the electrical company, there is an exchange risk. In 10 years there is no guarantee they will get back the amount of their currency they put in. The dollar and sterling exchange and money markets do not extend to these maturities for the large amounts required. Covering the exposure by conventional means is not possible.

The two firms can avail themselves of a currency swap or a parallel loan for 10 years. A *currency swap* is like any other swap, only longer, and is generally made between two corporations rather than between a bank and a corporation. From the American distiller's point of view, it lends dollars and borrows sterling. From the electrical company's point of view, it borrows dollars and lends sterling. The arrangement is evidenced by exchange of currencies today and a reverse exchange in 10 years. The exchange rate on the two contracts is the same. The difference in interest rates between the two currencies is settled by an annual payment rather than by a difference in the prices on the two contracts. The interest rates may be set at the beginning of the transaction for the entire 10 years, or there may be a provision to vary the rates at certain intervals.

The net interest payment between the two companies depends on whether British or American interest rates are higher, and on the exchange rate between dollars and pounds on the day the payment is made. The convention that the payment depends on the exchange rate was established by the Bank of England. If the sterling interest rate is set at 12% and the dollar rate at 10%, and the initial amounts swapped are $10 million and £5 million—at the end of one year the American owes the English company £600,000 and the English owes the American company $1 million. If £/$2.00 on the interest payment date, then $1 million = £L500,000 and the American pays the English firm £100,000. If £/$1.80 on that date, then $1 million = £555,556 and the American pays only £44,444. The interest payment will be made by the English firm if the exchange rate goes to £/$1.50. The offset to the change in interest payment for the company in England is an increase in the value of its overseas investment in sterling terms.

Generally the swap is arranged by a bank who acts as a broker between the two parties and collects a fee for the service. Banks also act as intermediaries in the transaction if one company feels uncomfortable assessing the credit risk posed by direct agreement with the other company. The advantages of a currency swap to the companies are that it (1) gives them access to long-term financing, (2) covers the principal exposure resulting from that financing, (3) does not affect the balance sheets of the companies, (4) is generally cheaper than borrowing from a bank or in the bond market, and (5) provides a good return on surplus funds.

The *parallel loan* accomplishes the same objectives as the currency swap, but not quite as neatly. Under the loan arrangement the American company lends dollars directly to the subsidiary of the English firm in the United States or Canada. Ten years later the subsidiary repays the loan. In the United Kingdom an English firm lends sterling directly to the subsidiary of an American firm. Ten years later the subsidiary repays the loan. Both the American and the English firms loan out their surplus funds, and both of their subsidiaries are funded. Each firm has lent out its own currency and will receive that same amount after 10 years. The interest rates on the loans may be set at the beginning for the entire period or may be reviewed and changed periodically. An additional feature of the parallel loan is a "top-up" clause to ensure the equivalence of the two loan amounts as exchange rates change. For example, when the loan agreements were signed, spot £/ 2.00 and $10 million equal £5 million. Two years later spot £/$1.80 and $10 million no longer equals £5 million, but £5,555,556. The English company is obliged to increase its loan to the American subsidiary in the UK by £555,556. The top-up adjustments are usually triggered by movements of 2% or more in the exchange rate.

The insulation from the effect of exchange rate movements is not as great with the parallel loan as with the currency swap. Also, a parallel loan arrangement has the affect of increasing the size of a company's balance sheet because both the borrowing and investment are reflected.

Most of the currency swaps and parallel loans that are put together are between U.S., Canadian, and British companies. The similarity of the legal systems is conducive to their arrangement.

DATE OF THE EXPOSURE IS UNCERTAIN

Foreign exchange contracts specify delivery of currencies on a definite date, like September 5, not somewhere *around* September 5. In the Eurocurrency markets most loans are for fixed periods and must be repaid on a definite date. But Cornie Construction has ordered a dozen bulldozers from Switzerland for its project in Saudi Arabia. The ship is scheduled to arrive, be off loaded, and the documents cleared by November 12. The treasurer knows, however, that the port is often jammed and that document clearance can take from 2 to 12 days. How can he be certain of the date of payment? If he is not certain of that date, how can he be certain of the cost of the Swiss machinery in riyals, the currency the company is being paid in? There is uncertainty on the income side also because the riyal progress payment depends on the completion of certain stages of the project. At the completion of stage VI the German subcontractor will be paid. The flowchart says that completion day is December 13. Completion on the target day is the exception rather than the rule. For what day should the marks be bought? How can a price be locked in?

The problem of uncertainty is not unique to the construction industry. Firms that utilize large one-of-a-kind machine tools experience delays in delivery time. This is normal given the nature of the equipment. However, when the tools are ordered from a foreign supplier it is difficult to know exactly when to arrange cover.

Cez Cie. is a French firm that ships perfumes to an affiliate in Spain. It is paid in pesetas in various amounts throughout the month. The company can predict the overall inflow for three months, but its one-month forecasts are only 80% accurate.

Option contracts are well suited for situations where the date of the exposure is uncertain, but the company wants to lock in the exchange rate. The option contract fixes the price of exchange of two currencies today, for delivery during a specified *period* in the future. The company is able to choose the day in the period it wants delivery. The company also has the option of staggering delivery throughout the period—take delivery of 300,000 francs on the fifth day, 500,000 on the ninth, and 400,000 on the fifteenth. The one option the company does not have is not to take delivery.

Pricing an Option Contract

An option contract is priced so that the customer sells at the lowest rate and buys at the highest rate during the period. Assume rates are

SF/SR spot	2.0900–15
One month forward rate	2.0840–65
points	60–50

The points indicate that Swiss franc interest rates are higher than riyal rates. For buyers of francs this means there is an earning if francs are bought for delivery one month from today rather than today. Cornie Construction wants to buy francs with riyals sometime during the next month. The two possible rates are SF/SR 2.0915 and SF/SR 2.0865. The bank will charge the higher rate because when pricing an option contract it holds onto any earning which could result during the period. The bank acts as if it bought the francs and sold riyals spot and day after day lends the francs and borrows the riyals until Cornie needs them. In this case the bank earns because franc interest rates are higher than riyal rates. But the bank does not know how long it will be able to earn. Cornie can walk in the next day and ask for the francs. If this happens there is no earning and any benefit the bank gave to Cornie would be a loss to the bank.

The bank also takes the worst case approach for the seller of francs. Given the exchange rates the seller of francs receives fewer riyals in the future than today. This is a cost to the seller. A company selling franc sometime during the next month would be quoted a rate of 2.0840, the lowest rate. The bank charges the customer all foreseeable costs during the option period. The bank acts as if it sold francs and bought riyals spot and then day after day borrows francs and lends riyals until the customer is ready to deliver francs. In this case the bank has a daily cost because franc interest rates are higher than riyal rates. And further it assumes that the customer will not deliver the francs until the last day of the last day of the period. If this happens the bank incurrs a full month of interest costs.

An option contract may be taken out for one week in the month of May, which is six months away, or for the period March 15 to April 15, which is three months away, or for the months of June, July, and August, which are seven months from today. In theory, option periods may be as long as the number of months a particular market extends. Practically, an option period longer than three months may involve additional costs for the customer. Banks are not able to offset customer option contracts by making option contracts with other banks. The risk of changes in interest rates over extended periods requires an additional margin for the risk. Because of the way option contracts are priced, it is advisable to try to narrow the option period as much as possible.

If Cornie Construction Company arrives at the end of the option period and finds that the bulldozers have not yet cleared port, it can roll the option contract to another period in the same fashion that a fixed-date contract is swapped forward.

PROBLEM

The treasurer of Cornie Construction now estimates that the German subcontractor will finish stage VI between December 18 and January 18. Today is October 16. The rates are as follows:

$/DM spot	1.7325–35	$/SR spot	3.3605–20
One month	96–86		250–230
Two months	177–167		470–450
Three months	258–248		750–725

What rate can Cornie fix for delivery of Deutsche marks between December 18 and January 18? Work out the answer before looking at the solution.

SOLUTION

The first task is to find the forward rates DM/SR for two months and three months. It is not necessary to find the cross rates for spot and one month since they are not used:

DM/SR two-month rate	1.9300–1.9343
DM/SR three-month rate	1.9228–1.9274

Cornie is buying marks for the one-month period between December 18 and January 18; the price will be 1.9343. The other possibility is 1.9274; the three-month rate is cheaper than the two-month rate. This earning will not be passed on because the bank is taking the risk that the project is completed on December 20, thereby depriving it of the opportunity to earn the 67-point difference between December 18 and January 18. If the treasurer of Cornie was able to narrow the option period to January 3–18, the rate would be 1.9310; the company would save 33 points. Later in this chapter the calculation of nonstandard periods is shown.

Options That Overlap

Cez Cie. has the following estimated inflow of pesetas from its sale of perfumes in Spain during the fall season. During a given month there may be 5 to 10 separate payments.

September	1,500,000
October	2,500,000
November	3,000,000
Total	7,000,000

But in each month it is sure of only 80% of the total, the other 20% may come in the following or previous month, depending on the weather in Madrid. The inflows per month known with some certainty are:

September	1,200,000
October	2,000,000
November	2,400,000
Total	5,600,000

The company is not sure when 1,400,000 will come in during the three-month period.

Given the following rates, Cez Cie. would execute four option contracts to cover its peseta exposure at fixed rates today, July 30. Spot is August 1.

Pts/FF spot   6.1405–45, per 100 pesetas
One month   50–55
Two months   80–85
Three months   100–105
Four months   110–115

The option contracts are:

Sale for September 1–30   Pts 1,200,000 at 6.1455
Sale for October 1–31   Pts 2,000,000 at 6.1485
Sale for November 1–30   Pts 2,400,000 at 6.1505
Sale September 1–November 30   Pts 1,400,000 at 6.1455

Each time a peseta payment arrives, the rate for that month is used until that month's option is complete, and then the rate of the overlapping option is used. By combining many small inflows in this fashion, Cez obtains a better rate from its bank than it would on each small flow taken individually. Exchange risk is covered, and it is easier for the firm to use only 4 rates of exchange in accounting for its sales rather than 40.

Alternatives to the Option Contract

The way in which option contracts are necessarily priced by banks has led to two alternative practices. Corporations are reluctant to give up all the earning or absorb all the cost involved in taking an option contract.

The First Alternative.   If Cornie is more concerned with covering its exposure at the least cost rather than fixing exactly the rate of exchange, the company can buy the marks for the last day of the period, January 18. If it needs them earlier, the company can execute a swap. The front end of the swap fulfills the commitment to deliver marks, and the back end of the swap offsets the forward contract made earlier. Cornie earns for part of the period; under the option contract there was no earning. This is illustrated in the following diagram:

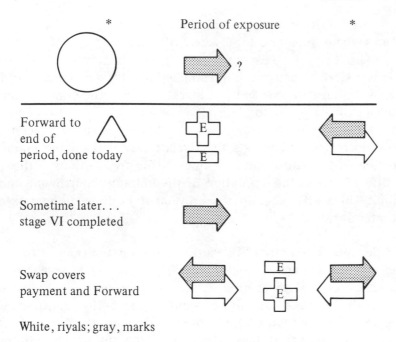

White, riyals; gray, marks

If mark interest rates are higher than riyal rates, Cornie has an earning from today to the end of the period; this is offset by the cost of the swap for part of the exposure period. The risk for Cornie is that mark interest rates rise and riyal rates fall so that the cost of the swap exceeds the initial earning from the Forward. However, because the period of earning is much longer than the period of cost, the movement in rates would have to be large for all earning to be eliminated.

If mark interest rates are lower than riyal rates, Cornie Construction has a cost from today to the end of the period; this is offset by the earning of the swap for part of the exposure period. The company pays only the time costs from today to the completion of stage VI rather than for the whole period. The company takes the risk that the interest rate levels reverse between today and the time it comes to do the swap. If mark interest rates shift above riyal rates, the swap costs. This is added to the initial cost of the Forward. This alternative is not attractive in situations where the interest rates are close together.

This alternative can be executed also with the BSI option. Let's assume Cornie is a German construction company like the subcontractor. Then it borrows external riyals and can invest marks in the domestic market to the end of the period of possible exposure. If stage VI is completed before, the company borrows marks at domestic interest rates to pay the subcontractor and invests the riyals received from the employer. Evaluation of the known interest rates in the two options is the same. The difference is in the evaluation of the unknown borrowing and the possibility of a difference in the movement in domestic and external mark interest rates.

The Second Alternative. Execute an option contract. If the ship arrives prior to the end of the option period, and if a swap between today and the end of the period earns, the company should execute a swap to fulfill today's commitment and let the option contract run to to the end of the period (the end of the swap and the option contract will cancel each other). If the swap costs, call the option. This alternative allows the company to reduce its costs for part of the option period. With this arrangement the company has no risk; it can only improve on the option contract made. On the other hand, the earning or cost reduction may not be as great as the first, albeit riskier, alternative. In evaluating which method to use to cover an exposure with an uncertain date, a company must be explicit about its interest rate assumptions for the currencies involved and the amount of risk it is willing to take to make money.

Call Money

There is no equivalent in the money market to the option contract. There is no instrument that guarantees price and a choice of the maturity date. The call market does allow the investor or borrower flexibility on the maturity date. "Call" means that the investor has the choice of when to withdraw funds and the borrower has the choice of when to repay. There are different notice periods in the Eurocurrency market concerning when money can be withdrawn or repaid.

Call—notification before 10 a.m.
Call one day—notification before 12 noon, previous day.
Call two days—notification before 12 noon two business days.
Call one week—notification seven days.

The call rate changes from day to day; the simple call is based on the overnight rate, call one day on the tom—next interest rate, and so on.

For the construction company that has covered its exposure and then discovered that it will be a couple of days before the money is required, the call market offers an alternative to making separate transactions each day to borrow or invest funds.

BROKEN-DATE EXCHANGE AND MONEY TRANSACTIONS

Exposures do not, as a rule, conveniently fall on the one-month date or the three-month date so that the standard period rates can be used. Nor does a company want to wait until the time of the month comes around when a standard period contract will cover its exposure. Once the decision is made to cover, action is taken. This section is about calculating the points for broken-date forwards and the interest rates for broken-date loans and investments. The term "odd-date" is used synonymously with "broken-date."

Broken-Date Exchange

Points are based on interest rate differentials. Because these differentials are not the same from period to period, the number of points for two months is not two times the number of points for one month. Six-month points are not six times one-month points. Therefore, to find the number of points between the one-month date and the two-month date, interpolate between one and two months rather than between spot and two months. For example:

£/Esc spot   113.45–75
One month   par–50
Two months   50–150
Three months   80–180

The points for one and one half months are 25–100. More precision is desirable. In one month there are 31 days; in two months, 61 days, and the Portuguese company wants to buy pounds 48 days from the spot date. The first 31 days cost 50 points; that is known. To find the cost of the last 17 days, calculate as follows:

Determine the value of the days in the period in which the date of the transaction lies.
 Number of points between 31 days and 61 days–100 (150 – 50).
 Number of days between one month and two months–30 (61 – 31).
 Average value of the days in the period–3.33 points (100 ÷ 30).
Multiply by the number of days into the period.
 Number of days into the period–17 (48 – 31).
 Number of points for 17 days–57 (17 × 3.33).
Add this result to the points for the prior period.
 Number of points for 48 days–107 (50 + 57).
The rate for buying pounds 48 days from spot is 114.82.

Try doing one. With the same £/Esc rates, at what price would the Portuguese company buy pounds 72 days from spot? The number of days in the three-month period is 92.

Answer. Value of the days in the period in which the date of the transaction lies:

$$\frac{\text{points}}{\text{days in period}} = \frac{180 - 150}{92 - 61} = .9677 \text{ points}$$

Multiply by the number of days into the period:

Number of days into the period—11 (72 – 61).
Number of points for 11 days—11 (11 × .9677).

Add this result to the points for the prior period:

Number of points for 72 days—161 (150 + 11).
The rate for buying pounds 72 days from spot is 115.36.

If the period in which the broken date lies has a day or days with un-usually high or low interest rates, an adjustment to the procedure is made. For many currencies abnormal rates are caused by an important tax date or other seasonal feature. Where this occurs the average value of the days in the period is misleading. One procedure is to take the un-usual days out and find the average value without it. Put the unusual days back in if they fall before the date of the transaction. Let's recon-sider the example where a Portuguese company was calculating the rate for buying pounds 48 days from spot. Assume that days 40, 41, and 42 are traditional tax collection days in Portugal. Both domestic and external money market rates are generally 10% above normal for the three days because the banking system is drained of liquidity by the tax payments. The additional 10% differential between sterling and escudo interest rates on those three days means that the number of points on those days will be 3.15 higher than the average.

$$113.45 \times .10 \times \frac{1}{360} = 3.15$$

The average value of the days in the one to two-month period is 3.33, so these days will have a value of 6.48. Now to find the average of this period without those days:

$$\frac{100 - (3 \times 6.48)}{30 - 3} = 2.98 \text{ points}$$

Without the tax days, the average value of the points in the one- to two-month period is 2.98, rather than 3.33 as previously calculated. To find the value of the 17 days:

$$14 \text{ days} \times 2.98 \quad 41.72$$
$$\underline{3 \text{ days}} \times 6.48 \quad \underline{19.44}$$
$$17 \text{ days} \qquad\qquad 61.16 \text{ points}$$

The number of points for 48 days, with unusual tax dates, is 111; without the unusual dates the number of points is 107. The difference to the company is $\frac{1}{4}$% per annum.

Quotations involving the U.S. dollar where the start or end date of the period is a Friday require special attention. During a one-month period U.S. dollar interest rates follow the up–down pattern shown in the following diagram because of the clearing house–Federal funds technicality. For the dollar, a one-month rate of 10% means that the number of Fridays and number of weekends in the month are the same. For other currencies, a one-month interest rate of 18% means most of the days in the month are 18%. (The exception were noted earlier.)

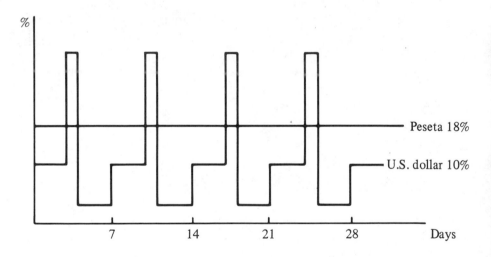

One-month points are $45\frac{1}{2}$ with a spot $/Pts66.10 and an interest differential of 8%. A Spanish firm wants to buy dollars 18 days from the spot date. The eighteenth day is a Friday. For 17 days the dollar interest rate averages 10%, but on the eighteenth day it is 30%. The points for the first 17 days are 25.

$$\frac{17}{31} \times 45\tfrac{1}{2} = 25$$

The eighteenth day is $2\tfrac{1}{4}$ points with the dollar at 30% and the peseta interest rate at 18%. These points are subtracted from 25 because the dollar interest rate is higher than the peseta rate on this day. The number of points for 18 days is $22\tfrac{3}{4}$.

Another way of looking at this is to say that the dollar interest rate for one month averages to 10%, but the dollar interest rate for 18 days is 11.11%. Twenty-two and three quarters points can be found by using 18% less 11.11% as the interest differential in the points formula. The ability to make these adjustments supposes a knowledge only of Euro-dollar interest rates. The interest rates for the other currencies can be obtained by expressing the swap points in percentage terms as illustrated in Chapter 10.

The procedures outlined here provide a baseline rate only. A bank cannot readily find an offset for a broken-date exchange transaction. Because of the time risk the bank takes in covering an 18-day transaction by a two-week or one month contract, a risk margin will be added by the bank to protect itself. Different banks take different views of this risk so that the quoted rates for broken dates differ.

Broken-Date Money Transactions

Broken-date money transactions are loans and investments for non-standard periods, like 22 days, or 1 month and 3 weeks, or 2 months and 2 days. Interest rates are normally quoted for 1-, 2-, 3-, 6-, 9-, and 12-month periods. The rates quoted are the average of the interest rates for every day in the period. One month at 5% means that on the average every day of the 30 is worth 5%. Two months at 6% means that on the average every day of the 60 is worth 6%. The only way for the average of two months to be 6% when the first month is 5% is for the last 30 days of the two-month period to be worth 7%.

When dealing with broken-date loans and investments, the first step in finding the appropriate rate is to determine the individual period interest rates that make up the overall average. Having done this, the interest rate for a nonstandard date is calculated by weighting the individual rates.

Example.   Wie Textiles Ltd. wants to borrow Deutsche marks for one and one-half months. The interest rate for one month is 5%, and the rate for two months is 6%. The average value of each day in the first month is 5%. The average value of each day in the second month is 7%. A transaction for one and one half month is weighted as

One month at 5%
One half month at 7%

The weighted average is 5.67%; this is the cost of borrowing marks for one and one-half months. The rate is calculated as

$$\frac{(5\% \times 30 \text{ days}) + (7\% \times 15 \text{ days})}{45 \text{ days}}$$

Calculate this one: Wie Textiles also wants to invest sterling for 80 days. What is the investment rate if resident sterling rates for the standard periods are:

One month (30 days) $14–14\frac{1}{4}\%$
Two months (61 days) $14\frac{1}{2}–14\frac{3}{4}$
Three months (94 days) $15–15\frac{1}{4}$

Answer. The average value of each day in the first two months is $14\frac{1}{2}\%$, and in three months it is 15%. To find the average value of the 33 days between the two- and three-month periods:

$$\frac{(94 \text{ days} \times 15\%) - (61 \text{ days} \times 14\frac{1}{2}\%)}{(94 \text{ days} - 61 \text{ days})} = 15.92\%$$

An investment for 80 days is then

$$61 \text{ days at } 14.50\% \qquad 19 \text{ days at } 15.92\%$$

The calculation is

$$\frac{(14.50\% \times 61 \text{ days}) + (19 \text{ days} \times 15.92\%)}{80 \text{ days}} = 14.84\%$$

The first calculation isolates the value of the period in which the broken-date transaction lies; the second calculation is a weighted average of the values of the days in the transaction.

In the same way as adjustments are made to broken-date exchange rates to account for tax dates and the clearing house–Federal funds technicality, they must also be made for broken-date interest rates. The procedure is the same; the unusual day is taken out before the average value is found.

Try this one. Wie Textiles wants to borrow Eurodollars for 45 days:

One month (30 days) $12\frac{3}{4}$–13%
Two months (61 days with a Friday end) $14\frac{3}{4}$–15%

What is the rate for 45 days?

Answer. The two-month period has an extra Friday. It is taken out since it is worth three times the daily rate. The two-month rate without the Friday end has days with an average value of $14\frac{1}{2}\%$.

$$\frac{(15\% \times 61 \text{ days}) - (45\% \times 1 \text{ day})}{60 \text{ days}} = 14\frac{1}{2}\%$$

The actual value of the period in which the broken date lies is

$$\frac{(14\frac{1}{2}\% \times 60 \text{ days}) - (13\% \times 30 \text{ days})}{(60 \text{ days} - 30 \text{ days})} = 16\%$$

A loan for 45 days is

30 days at 13% and 15 days at 16%

The calculation is

$$\frac{(13\% \times 30 \text{ days}) + (16\% \times 15 \text{ days})}{45 \text{ days}} = 14\%$$

If the two months were a neutral run, the 45-day rate would have been 14.33%.

A bank who accepts an investment or makes a loan for a broken date is not able to offset the transaction readily. An 80-day transaction will be offset with either a three-month or a two-month deal. The bank's view of the risk involved in this time gap will be reflected in the margin it requires above the baseline rate calculated. A company can expect that two banks will have different views on that risk.

APPENDIX

Adjustment for Frequency of Interest Payment

The interest cash flow of short-term borrowings over long periods of time can have a substantial effect on the overall cost of borrowing. It costs more to borrow and pay interest one month at a time for six months than to pay interest once at the end of six months. The interest paid out monthly will itself have to be borrowed. If it is on hand, an opportunity to invest is given up. The following formula assumes the cost of borrowing the interest is the same as the cost of borrowing the principal:

$$\text{adjusted rate} = P \times \left[\left(1 + \frac{R}{F}\right)^{F/P} - 1 \right]$$

where R = interest rate
$\quad\quad\,\, P$ = total period of the loan
$\quad\quad\quad\quad$ 1 for one year
$\quad\quad\quad\quad$ 2 for six months
$\quad\quad\quad\quad$ 4 for three months
$\quad\quad\quad\quad$ $12 \div X$ for X months
$\quad\quad\,\, F$ = frequency with which interest is paid
$\quad\quad\quad\quad$ 2 = semiannually
$\quad\quad\quad\quad$ 4 = quarterly
$\quad\quad\quad\quad$ 12 = monthly
$\quad\quad\quad\quad$ 52 = weekly

Example. A six-month period during which money is borrowed at 16% one month at a time:

$$\text{adjusted rate} = 2 \times \left[\left(1 + \frac{.16}{12}\right)^{12/2} - 1 \right] = 16.54\%$$

Example.   A one-year period during which money is borrowed at 10% three months at a time.

$$\text{adjusted rate} = 1 \ \times \ \left[\left(1 + \frac{.10}{4}\right)^{4/1} - 1\right] = 10.38\%$$

CHAPTER FIFTEEN
FOREIGN CURRENCY INVOICING, FINANCING, AND EXPOSURE

The currency a company uses to bill its overseas customer has a direct effect on the costs of financing the transaction and covering an exposure. It is often beneficial for an exporter to create an exposure with its invoicing policy and for an importer to do the same when it has the choice. The present chapter looks at the interrelationship between invoicing, financing, and covering. Three ancillary questions are examined—how to set the foreign currency price of a product made at home, how to ensure that all possible financing and covering options have been considered, and how to establish the risk parameters when an exposure is left uncovered.

THE SITUATION

The Carlton Corporation is a manufacturer of large-capacity computers in the San Francisco area. It recently received an order from a German steel firm to adapt one of its larger models. The German company is automating its operations and needs special features to control and monitor the various stages of the steel making process. This is the first time that Carlton has sold one of its products in Germany, and the sales force sliced the usual profit margin in half in order to gain entry into this growing market. The German firm will accept billing only in dollars or Deutsche marks. It will pay in six months when the computer is installed. The assistant treasurer of Carlton is asked to recommend the currency to be used for invoicing and the manner in which the company should finance this $5 million project.

FINANCING OPTIONS

The computer firm has access to all external currency markets and financing in the U.S. market. The German steel maker is not in a position to assist with the financing. After some research the assistant treasurer narrows the external financing currencies to dollars and marks because they are possible invoice currencies, and Swiss francs because the interest rate is low and the franc/mark exchange rate is generally stable. The treasurer finds that dollar acceptance financing is available and often cheaper than other types of dollar loans.

An *Acceptance* is a bank loan used to finance exports, imports, or the manufacture of products to be exported. The loan is in the form of a draft drawn on a bank by an exporter or an importer. The bank stamps the draft "accepted." The bank gives the exporter the amount of the draft less a discount; the discount is based on prevailing interest rates plus a bank commission. The exporter pays interest at the beginning of the loan period. The bank can sell the "accepted" draft in the U.S. money market to fund itself. The exporter's draft is easy to sell because the bank guarantees payment of the draft by "accepting" it. Acceptance financing is generally cheaper than other dollar financing because there are no reserve requirements imposed by the Federal Reserve on money raised by selling acceptances. The maximum period of time a company can finance with acceptances is 180 days. If a trade transaction covers 271 days, acceptance financing can be used for 180 days, but another type must be used for the remaining 91 days.

Two currencies of invoice and three financing currencies have been determined. The next step for the assistant treasurer is to describe all the possible combinations of financing for each invoice currency. You should take the role of the assistant treasurer and symbolize all the possible invoicing and financing combinations. Do this before looking at the next section.

The eight possibilities are illustrated as follows:

Dollar invoice

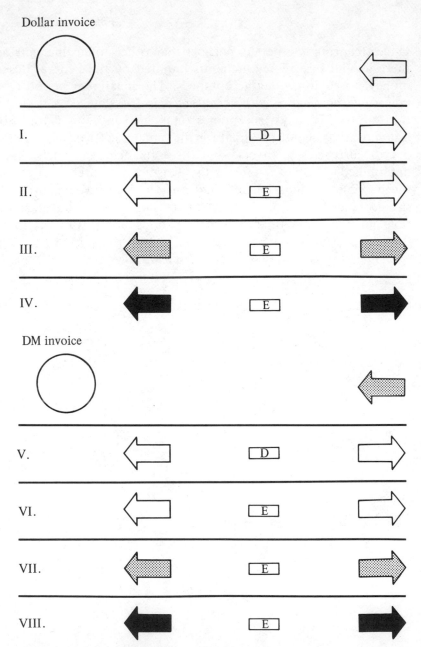

I.

II.

III.

IV.

DM invoice

V.

VI.

VII.

VIII.

White, U.S. dollars; gray, marks; black, francs

334

So far it is simply a question of listing each financing alternative beneath each invoicing alternative, using the currency of invoice as the key.

COVERING OPTIONS

Some of the combinations create an exposure for Carlton. The next task is to lay out the various ways of covering the exposed positions. Possible responses are:

1. Spot.
2. Forward.
3. Swap.
4. Borrow.
5. Invest.
6. Do nothing.

Consider each situation in turn.

RESPONSE ANALYSIS

Dollar Invoice, Dollar Acceptance Financing (I)

A. *If you chose 1, 2, 3, 4, or 5*: None of these options apply since there is no exposure in this situation.

B. *If you chose 6*: This is correct; there is no exposure to cover.

Dollar Invoice, Eurodollar Financing (II)

C. *If you chose 1, 2, 3, 4, 5, or 6*: None of these options apply since there is no exposure in this situation.

D. *If you chose 6*: This is correct; there is no exposure to cover.

Dollar Invoice, Euromark Financing (III)

E. *If you chose 1 and 2*: These two options do cover the exposure, but not in the most efficient fashion. Doing a spot and forward to cover a foreign currency loan means Carlton would pay the spread between the bid and offer side of the spot quote.

F. *If you chose 3*: The swap is an efficient way to cover the exposure created by the foreign currency loan.

G. *If you chose 1, 4, 1 and 5*: The first spot contract converts the marks into dollars to pay for the construction of computer. The BSI option covers the mark exposure. The following is an illustration of the option.

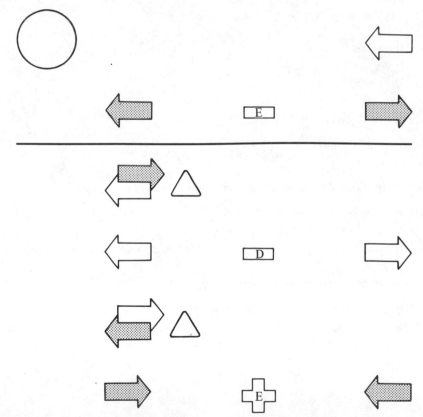

White, U.S. dollars; gray, marks

This is a feasible option but it is more costly than simply borrowing dollars through acceptances. There is a cost involved in borrowing marks and then investing them in the same external market for the same period of time (first and last lines). The cost is the bank lending spread and the difference between the borrowing rate and the investing interest rate. The two spot contracts can be eliminated since they are opposite one another.

H. *If you chose 6*: You have decided to leave an exposure uncovered.

Dollar Invoice, Eurofranc Financing (IV)

I. *If you chose 1 and 2*: See E.

J. *If you chose 3*: See F.

K. *If you chose 1, 4, 1, and 5*: The first spot contract converts the francs into dollars to pay for the construction of computer. The BSI option covers the franc exposure. See the illustration for G.

L. *If you chose 6*: You have decided to leave an exposure uncovered.

Mark Invoice, Dollar Acceptance Financing (V)

M. *If you chose 1 only*: There is no need for a spot contract itself since the borrowed dollars are used directly in the manufacture of the computer.

N. *If you chose 2*: A forward contract selling marks and buying dollars covers the exposure completely.

O. *If you chose 3*: The swap is not applicable in this situation because there is no conversion necessary on the spot date.

P. *If you chose 4, 1, and 5:* This looks like:

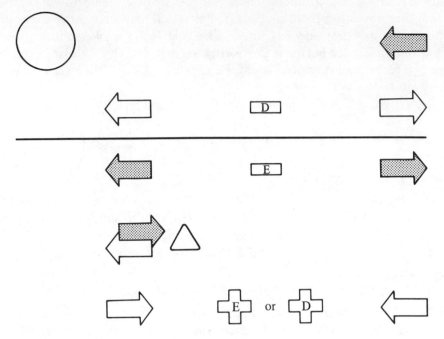

White, U.S. dollars; gray, marks

If an external dollar investment is made, this is a duplication of the forward, but with the added cost of a bank lending spread on the mark loan. If a domestic dollar investment is made, it is more costly than borrowing marks because of the spread between borrowing and investing rates in the same market.

Q. *If you chose 6:* You decided to leave an exposure uncovered.

Mark Invoice, Eurodollar Financing (VI)

R. *If you chose 1 only:* There is no need for a spot contract itself since the borrowed dollar are used directly in the manufacture of the computer.

S. *If you chose 2*: A forward contract selling marks and buying dollars covers the exposure completely.

T. *If you chose 3*: The swap is not applicable in this situation because there is no conversion necessary on the spot date.

U. *If you chose 4, 1 and 5*: This looks like:

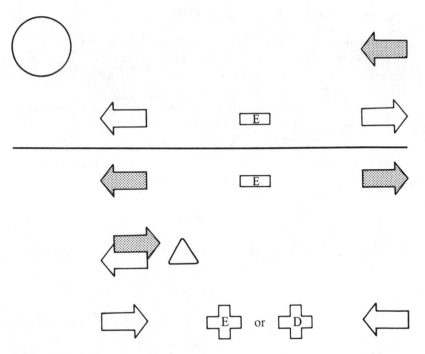

White, U.S. dollars; gray, marks

A dollar investment in external market is a cost. See S. A dollar investment in the domestic market would be advantageous if domestic rates were higher than external rates.

V. *If you chose 6*: You have decided to leave an exposure uncovered.

Mark Invoice, Euromark Financing (VII)

W. *If you chose 1*: This is the only action required—an exchange of marks for dollars on the spot date.

X. *If you chose 2, 3, 4, 5*: These actions are not appropriate in this situation because there is no time exposure and the only currency risk is on the spot date.

Mark Invoice, Eurofranc Financing (VIII)

Y. *If you chose 1 and 2*: Since this is a multiple exposure (Chapter 13), the covering options are considered independently for the marks and francs. The spot is a sale of francs and purchase of dollars; the forward contract is a sale of marks and a purchase of dollars.

Z. *If you chose 3*: The swap covers the franc/dollar exposure both spot and forward.

AA. *If you chose 4, 1, and 5*: The mark exposure is covered with a mark loan, spot, and dollar investment. The franc exposure is covered with a dollar loan, spot, and franc investment.

SUMMARY

The feasible combinations are illustrated on the following pages.

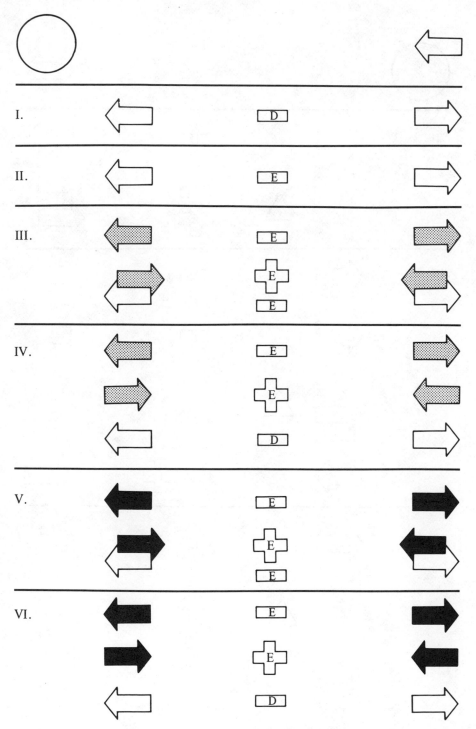

White, U.S. dollar; gray, Deutsche mark; black, Swiss franc

Mark invoice

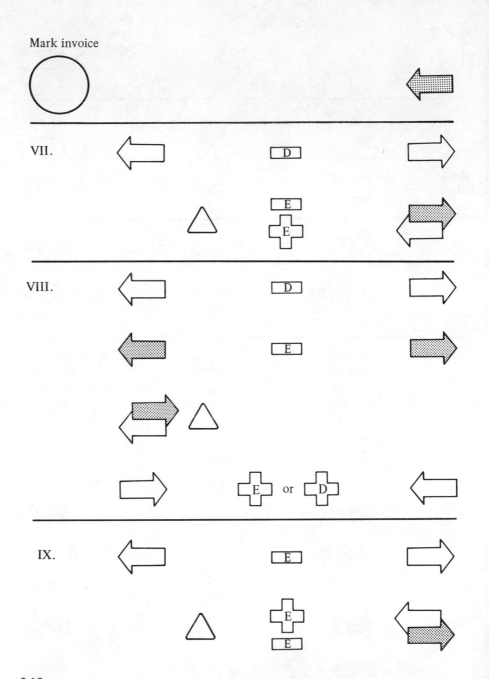

VII.

VIII.

IX.

Mark invoice

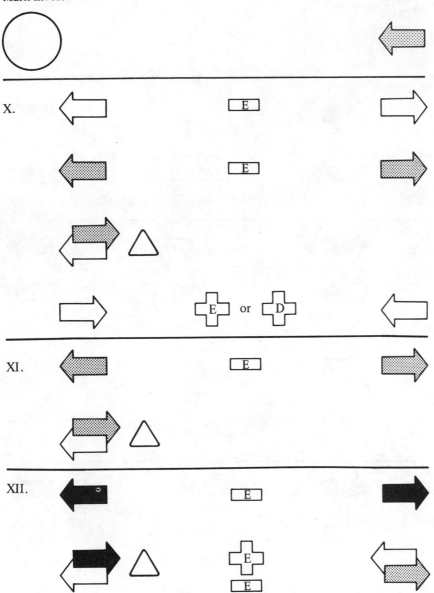

X.

XI.

XII.

Mark invoice

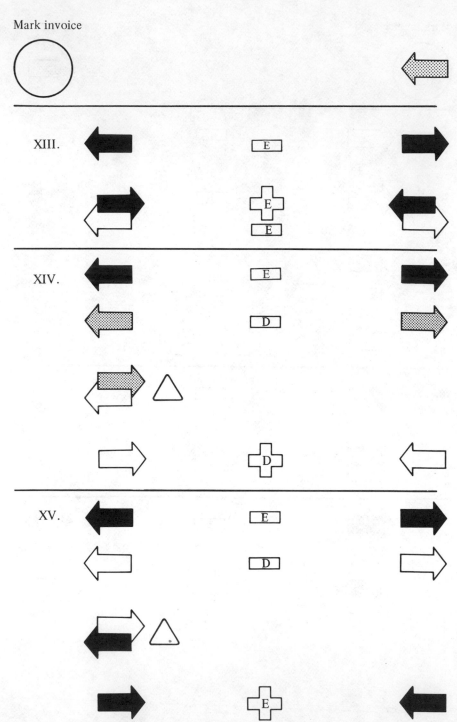

White, U.S. dollar; gray, Deutsche mark; black, Swiss franc

A branching diagram is a way of determining that all possible combinations have been considered.

For example:

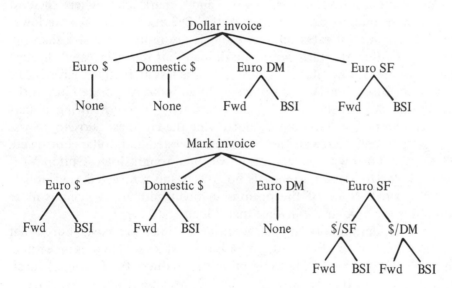

In the instances where there is a spot exchange in addition to the forward exchange, a swap is used. The preceding diagram will ensure that all the possible market combinations have been used. Unless Carlton has access to the domestic and external markets of another currency, it is not necessary to consider more financing or covering currencies. As illustrated in Chapter 10, borrowing a foreign currency in the external market and covering the exposure with a swap is equivalent to borrowing your own currency in the external money market.

ELIMINATION OF OPTIONS

There are 13 possible solutions to the problem of how to invoice and finance this computer. Many of the possibilities can be eliminated with the knowledge of only three relationships: (1) domestic dollar interest rates are lower than Eurodollar interest rates; (2) Swiss franc interest rates are lower than Deutsche mark interest rates; (3) mark interest rates are lower than dollar rates.

Consider option XI, a mark invoice and a mark loan, where the cost is the mark interest rate for six months. Because mark rates are lower than dollar interest rates options I and II are more expensive than option XI. Option III starts with a mark loan, but this is invested through the swap and Eurodollars borrowed. This is less attractive than XI. The net effect of option IV is a domestic dollar loan. As pointed out in the RESPONSE ANALYSIS, this is less attractive than borrowing dollars directly. Option V starts out by borrowing the cheapest currency, Swiss francs. Through the swap the francs are invested and dollars borrowed. The dollar borrowing is less attractive than a mark loan. Option VI is very similar to IV; a currency is borrowed and reinvested, and dollars are borrowed. None of the options involving dollar invoicing is more attractive than IX—mark invoice, mark loan.

Consider option VII, dollar acceptance financing cost, Eurodollar earning through the Forward, and a Euromark cost. There is an earning in the dollar portion of the transaction that reduces the Euromark interest cost. This option is less costly than IX because it takes advantage of the discrepancy between Euro and domestic dollar interest rates. Option VIII has the potential for doing the same as VII, but Carlton would pay two bank lending spreads, one for marks and one for dollars. The same is true for option X. This makes these alternatives more costly than either VII or XI. Option IX is less desirable than VII because domestic dollar interest rates are cheaper than external dollar rates.

The next set of options to consider involves financing with Swiss francs. Because of the multiple exposure the franc cover and mark cover are evaluated independently. From the previous discussion the only way of bettering a simple mark loan is to take advantage of the discrepancy between the external and domestic dollar markets, a cost in the domestic and earning in the external dollar market. Options XII and XV are such a combination. The combination of XIII and XIV produces the opposite effect, domestic earning in dollars against external cost. If XII and XIII are combined or XIV and XV are combined, the dollar element of the solution is eliminated; the effect in both is to reinvest the Swiss francs that were borrowed and to borrow marks. The elementary set of interest rate relationships combined with the symbolized options is powerful enough to reduce the 13 possibilities to two—VII and the combination of XII and XV.

Two general rules emerge from this discussion of foreign currency invoicing and financing:

1. Invoice in the currency with the lowest interest rate. The project can be financed more cheaply because the company can borrow against the receivable, option XI. The company earns by covering the exposure forward, options VII, VIII, IX, and X. Swiss francs is the lowest interest rate currency but was ruled out by the German customer. If possible, it should be chosen. The customer will naturally prefer just the opposite, an invoice denominated in a currency with a high interest rate.

2. Finance in a currency where there is a discrepancy between the domestic and external interest rates. There are options that will enable the firm to utilize this discrepancy to its advantage, option VII.

No matter what financing or covering options are subsequently employed, a company ends up paying the interest cost of the currency of the invoice. Some betterment is possible if domestic and external money markets can be arbitraged. The cost is increased if options are combined inefficiently.

PRICING THE OPTIONS

The assistant treasurer is now in a position to consider the actual numbers for the construction of the computer and to develop the costs of the options. The production and sales departments have come up with the following pricing breakdown for the computer.

	Dollars	Marks
Labor, materials, overhead	4,675,082	8,090,230
Financing cost (13.90%)	324,918	562,270
Cost of the computer	5,000,000	8,625,500
Profit of 5%	250,000	432,625
Sales price	5,250,000	9,085,125

The exchange and interest rates are taken from *The Reuter Monitor* shown in the following photograph and reproduced with permission from Reuters Limited.

This video unit carries up-to-the minute exchange rate and interest rate information directly into the assistant treasurer's office. The banks on the system contribute a "page." A page is turned by keying in the bank's symbol. The page is shown in this photo is Bank of America, San Francisco; the symbol is BASF. Banks do not guarantee to quote the rates shown on the screen, but will generally quote rates very close to them. The *Monitor* is a handy tool for corporations who are active in the foreign exchange and money markets. It provides current rate information to allow treasury personnel to make calculations and check quotations from a bank without making a number of phone calls.

The interest rates are taken from other pages on the Monitor. For six months they are:

Dollar acceptances   11.15–12.00%
Euromarks $8\frac{3}{8}$–$8\frac{1}{2}$

Carlton's bank charges a lending spread of 1% on all Eurocurrency loans and dollar acceptances. Acceptance interest is paid at the beginning of the loan period. The quoted rate is adjusted to arrive at the true interest rate. The calculation is

$$\frac{.13}{1 - \left(.13 \times \frac{180}{360}\right)} \times 100 = 13.90\%$$

PROBLEM

Calculate the costs of options VII, XI, and the combination XII and XV. Determine the best financing currency and covering option.

SOLUTION

The least costly financing and covering option is VII, dollar acceptance financing, and a dollar/mark Forward.
    The matrix for comparing the options is:

Option	Spot	Finance Cost	Cover Net Interest Cost/Earning I_h	I_f	Net	Points	Cost of Cover and Financing
$ acceptance Fwd $/DM	1.7305	-13.90			+5.66	476	-8.24%
DM loan	1.7305	-9.50					-9.50%
SF loan	1.6010	-6.63					
Fwd $/DM	1.7305				+5.66	476	
BSI $/SF	1.6010		-13.90	+5.50	-8.40	654	
							-9.37%

The net interest earning of the $/DM Forward, 5.66%, is calculated with ICE-2. Carlton is an American company and the rate is expressed in numbers of marks.

The reason that the combination of XII and XV is not better than VII is that the transaction involves two loans, and hence two lending spreads which are only partially offset by the difference between domestic and external dollar interest rates. By invoicing in marks and covering the exposure, Carlton has reduced its finance cost on this project from 13.90% to 8.24%. This is sufficient to restore the company's normal profit margin.

INVOICE PRICING IN FOREIGN CURRENCIES

The sales department priced the computer in marks according to the spot rate of 1.7305. Because forward marks are at a premium to the dollar, this enables Carlton to finance in dollars and then earn on covering the exposure. If the sales department had used the forward rate of 1.6829 to convert the dollar price to Deutsche marks, there would have been no earning from covering forward. The best Carlton would have been able to do is take the mark loan at 9.50%. The rules for converting home currency prices to foreign currency prices are:

1. If the invoice currency has a lower interest rate than the home currency, convert at the spot rate. Covering the exposure results in an earning.

2. If the invoice currency has a higher interest rate than the home currency, convert at the future rate of the inflow. The company breaks even when it covers the exposure. Were it to convert at the spot rate, it would loose money covering the exposure. For example, Carlton's next project is a sale to England. This computer sells for $2,250,000. It will be installed and paid for in six months. The $/£ spot is 2.2500–15, and six-month points are 400–385. Say that Carlton converts the sales price at spot and quotes the English customer a price of £1 million. Carlton sells the pounds forward and receives only $2,210,000, which is $40,000 less than the dollar sales price. Carlton should sell the computer to the English for payment in six months at £1,018,100.

EVALUATING RISKY OPTIONS

Carlton's assistant treasurer has explored all the no-risk possibilities for the computer sale to Germany. She now wants to look at options that involve some risk to see if there is any way to lower the cost further. Only variations of the mark invoicing options are considered because of their inherent advantage. A matrix is developed to enable the company to analyze the alternatives:

Option	$ Acceptance	Eurofranc Loan	Eurofranc Loan with DM Cover	Eurofranc Loan with SF Cover
Exposure	$ outflow DM inflow	SF outflow DM inflow	SF outflow $ inflow	$ outflow DM inflow
Initial cost (%)	−13.90%	−6.63%	−6.63 (Loan) +5.66 (Cover) −.97	−6.63 (Loan) − 8.40 (Cover) −15.03%
Initial cost/ benefit ($)	−132,305	+37,634	+169,939	−158,719
To match or better option VII	DM spot must rise to $/DM 1.6815	DM spot cannot fall beyond SF/DM 108.96	$ spot cannot fall beyond $/SF 1.5442	DM spot must rise to $/DM 1.6717
Cover cost/earning	+5.66%	−2.78%	−8.40%	+5.66%

The figures for the initial cost (%) are taken from the matrix used to compare the cost covering options. The initial cost/benefit ($) is the amount of money this option saves or costs in comparison to option VII. A cost must be compensated for by a favorable movement of the exchange rate. An earning can be eaten away by an unfavorable exchange rate movement. The figures are based on the production cost of the computer. The break-even exchange rates are calculated from the percentage difference between option VII and the risky alternative. The formula for finding the number of points difference between spot and the break-even future rate is shown in the following example:

$$\text{Points} = \text{Spot} \times \text{percentage difference} \times \text{time}$$

$$583 = 1.6025 \times (8.24 - .97) \times \frac{180}{360}$$

The future break-even rate for the third option is 1.5442 (1.6025 – .0583). In the case of the first and fourth options the mark must rise above the indicated rate before the option becomes better than option VII. The rates for the second and third options indicate the point at which the initial advantage of the options is wiped out by adverse exchange rate movement. The cover cost/earning numbers are taken from the previous matrix. They indicate today's earning or cost form covering.

The criteria for choosing one of the four options are (1) low initial cost for a given risk, (2) good potential reward from taking the risk, and (3) impact on cost or earning that covering would have. The standard for comparing all risky options is the best covered option. These objective criteria narrow down the choices. Beyond this, examine the remaining options to determine if their success is predicated on opposite movements of the same currency. If so, deciding which way the currency will move eliminates one option. If more than one option remains the company must make a judgment on the direction and the duration of an exchange rate movement.

Carlton can eliminate the fourth option since the exposure is the same as the first, but the initial cost is higher. The potential savings from the second and third options is high. One of the three options can be eliminated by deciding whether the dollar will rise or fall in value against the European currencies in the next six months. If the dollar falls, the dollar acceptance financing is more attractive than the franc loan with mark cover. Carlton forecasts a fall in the dollar. The first two options remain. A general rise in the Deutsche mark against all other currencies would be beneficial for both options. The Swiss franc loan option is preferable since it starts out with a lower cost and can thus absorb some movement against the expected trend. The first option cannot. Another benefit is that its relative advantage is not greatly affected if it becomes necessary to cover the exposure. If the cover cost, in percent per annum, remains the same, the monetary impact decreases as time goes by. This would adversely affect the first option.

The decision to create an exposure and leave it uncovered is not final. Exposures should be monitored daily. If the facts on which the initial decision was based change, the plan of action should change also.

CHAPTER SIXTEEN
THE DEALING ROOM

At the beginning of each day a bank foreign exchange dealer checks the financial newspapers and the wire service ticker. The wire service machines spew out a continual stream of paper on such things as balance of payments figures in France, unemployment statistics for Denmark, and the consumer price indices in Belgium. The wire services also indicate the key economic announcements that are expected from different countries during the day. *The Reuter Monitor* provides news flashes and articles on the video screen. The dealer reads the news with an eye toward the position he or she is holding. There are two types of foreign exchange position—currency and swap. A currency position is established by buying and holding a currency with the intent of selling it later at a profit, or by selling a currency with the intent of buying it back later at a lower price. A swap position is built up by borrowing one currency and lending another in the foreign exchange market. If the initial transaction was a cost, the dealer hopes to reverse it through time at an earning, and vice versa.

BROKERS

The first rates of the day are received from the brokers. Brokerage houses arrange transactions between buyers and sellers, borrowers and lenders. They act purely as intermediaries between banks and do not buy or borrow for their own account. In most cities there is an agreement that banks in the city will trade among themselves only through the brokers there. These houses facilitate transactions and are centers of information. Brokers have direct phone lines to all the major banks in a city and can find a counterpart for a given bank more quickly than if that bank telephoned every other bank in the city. Brokers have information about the market that a bank may not be aware of. For example, a dealer develops an exposed position in sterling due to customer purchases and calls from other banks in France. The broker's news that Swiss banks have started buying sterling in good amounts is enough to encourage the dealer to cover his or her exposure now rather than wait.

Most broker houses are now international. The house in London has offices in New York, Paris, Singapore, and Bahrain, with open phone lines between them. Because of this international hookup, the market spot and swap rates for a given currency at the same time are the same everywhere in the world.

A TELEX TRADE

An overseas correspondent bank calls on the telex asking to be quoted. After the banks have identified each other, the telex looks like this:

HI FRIENDS SPOT AND FWD DM PLS?	The correspondent bank is asking to be quoted the spot rate and forward points for Deutsche marks. It is understood that the request is for $/DM; any other would be specified.
HALLO THERE 1.9070 77+++	The dealer responds by quoting both the rate at which he will buy and the rate at which he will sell dollars for marks.
AT 77 DOLLARS TWO MIO PLS	The correspondent offers to buy $2 million at 1.9077.
THAT'S AGREED I SELL YOU DOLLARS TWO MILLION AT 1.9077 VAL AUGUST 9 MARKS TO MY ACC DRESDNER FRANKFURT+++	The dealer agrees immediately, spells out the transaction in detail, specifies the date on which the currencies will be delivered, and asks that the marks be delivered to his account at Dresdner Bank, Frankfurt.
OK CHASE NY FOR MY DOLLIES HOW FWD PLS?	The correspondent agrees with the date of the transaction and delivery instructions. The bank requests that its dollars be delivered to its account with the Chase Manhatten Bank, New York. It then asks for the forward points.
175–170 370–350 510–490 950–920 1800–1760+++	The dealer quotes rates for $/DM swaps of 1, 2, 3, 6, and 12 months.
PARITY TKS FOR DEAL BIBI	The correspondent indicates that it views the forward rates the same way or its view is not sufficiently different to make a transaction worthwhile.
BIBI Y'ALL	

In quoting the rate to the correspondent bank, the dealer considers the current market rate, what is likely to affect the rate later on, his current dollar position, and the prospects for offsetting the deal in the market now. If the caller is a bank known for backing its views on the market with heavy purchases, this can indicate to the dealer the feelings about dollar rates in another financial center. Did that center interpret the morning's news differently or the same way he did?

The dealer goes into the local market through the broker to buy the dollars he just sold. The responsiveness of the market and the ease with which the transaction is offset gives the dealer an idea of the sentiments of other dealers about the dollar.

DEALERS AND CUSTOMERS

As the morning progresses the dealer receives calls from corporate customers. In larger banks foreign exchange advisory groups act as a liaison between the dealers and the corporate customers. These advisors provide background commentary and forecasts of market movements to the customers in addition to executing the customer's transactions. They have the time to talk and get to know the customer that a dealer does not have. When the corporation calls, the advisor or the dealer must know if the bank has set up credit limits for the customer, if the deal proposed will make the total exceed the credit limits, and if the person on the phone is authorized to deal for the company. A foreign exchange transaction involves a risk for both parties to the transaction. There are two types of risk, settlement risk and contract risk. *Settlement risk* is due to time zones. The bank delivers marks to the customer's account in Germany but does not know for another eight to ten hours if the customer will pay the dollars in New York. If the customer does not pay, the bank is left empty handed. *Contract risk* also involves the failure of one party to deliver but assumes the first party still has the currency. A forward dollar/peso contract is made for September 8. On August 2 the party due to deliver the pesos declares bankruptcy. The party due to deliver the dollars holds onto them, but since the contract was made, rates have changed and now it may not be able to buy the same number of pesos per dollar as previously contracted for. This is a loss, although less than that involved in settlement.

Because rates change quickly, a better rate will be quoted by the dealer if the corporation is able to respond to the quote quickly. Before asking for a quote, the treasurer should have a good idea of the range of rates he or she is willing to pay. If the treasurer finds the current market rate unacceptable and believes the rate is moving in his direction but does not want the bother of calling every two minutes, he can leave a limit order with the bank. A *limit order* specifies the rate, date, and amount of the contract, and the length of time that the order is valid. For example, the treasurer of Antigone decides that buying marks two months forward at 1.8750 is a good cover for the ship company's mark exposure. It will save 10% on the budgeted mark costs for the period. The market is not currently at that rate, but close. She asks the dealer to note that Antigone is a buyer of DM 3 million at 1.8750 value October 9. The order stands for the next three hours. Since the dollar has been strengthening during the morning, the order is realistic.

A corporation with a transaction of $500,000 or its equivalent in other currencies should obtain quotes from more than one bank. Quotes vary among banks depending on the dealers' views of the market, his position, what he thinks he going to happen, and his skill. A dealer who has more marks than he wants at the moment will offer a better price to a buyer of marks than one who has fewer in position than he wants. In asking more than one bank to quote, the corporate dealer should remember the following:

1. Because rates move fast, the quotes must be truly simultaneous. Calling four banks in succession for their quote results in four different noncomparable quotes; to get four comparable quotes, four phones are needed at the same time.

2. Most banks will not participate in an "auction." For example, one might ask "Bank of America is quoting me 1.9075, can you do better than that?" and them go back to Bank of America and ask if it will outbid the other bank. It is expected that a dealer will quote his finest rate at the outset; only a change in the market will lead to a change in the quote.

3. If a corporation has a large amount to buy, if the transaction is for a broken date, if the market in the currency is not large, or if it is late in the day, it does not pay to ask for competitive quotes from banks. The effect of this is to move the exchange rate without executing the transaction. The four banks will check with the brokers on market price for the transaction and try to obtain an indication of the amount doable at the price. Instead of one deal for $10 million 39 days forward, the market will perceive a transaction for $40 million for that date. It is better in these cases to go to one bank known to have experience in this particular currency and ask them for a price on the understanding that other banks will not be approached.

The size of customer transactions and their number and direction indicate to the dealer how the corporations are reacting to market developments. Input to the dealer is also provided by another dealer in the same room who is trading dollars against another currency. He indicates that Swiss francs are also being sold to buy dollars. The dealer who handles money transactions says that dollar interest rates are pushing upward, giving further reason for a strengthening dollar.

Smaller customers wanting to buy $10,000 or to sell FF 100,000 may not receive as good a rate as the larger customer. The reason for this is that the dealer cannot offset the transaction immediately in the market. The amount is so small that the dealer must accumulate a number of such transactions in this currency before he is able to offset the transaction. In the interim the exchange rate may move against him. One advantage the smaller corporation has in dealing with an active bank dealing room is that the bank always has a position in most currencies and adding or taking away a small portion of that position can be accommodated at market rates. For most currencies, a transaction of $500,000 equivalent is market size.

DEALER PROFIT

The foreign exchange dealer evaluates all the information he receives in the light of the position he has at the moment and what he wants to do with it. The decision to increase or decrease the position will depend on its size and price. The average rate at which the position was established, compared to the current market rate, is a measure of the dealer's ability to withstand swings in market rates.

The dealer ends the day with a profit. This does not mean that those he dealt with lost. As we saw, Antigone sold dollars to buy marks at 1.8750. Ten minutes later the dealer sold those dollars at 1.8775 for a profit of 25 points per dollar. Antigone did not lose on the transaction; it cut budgeted costs by 10%. The company did forego the 25 points, but it did not lose them. The dealer earned the 25 points by taking the risk of carrying an exposure and then covering at the opportune moment.

BIBLIOGRAPHY

Aliber, R. Z. "The Firm Under Pegged and Floating Exchange Rates." *Scandinavian Journal of Economics,* Vol. 78, No. 2, 1976.

Bradshaw, R. C. "Foreign Exchange Operations of U.S. Banks." *International Finance Discussion Papers,* No. 69, November, 1975.

Branson, W. H. "The Minimum Covered Interest Differential Needed for International Arbitrage Activity." *Journal of Political Economy,* November/December, 1969.

Chase Manhattan Bank. *F. X.: An Inside View of the Foreign Exchange Market.* New York: Chase Manhattan Bank, 1976.

Coombs, C. A. *The Arena of International Finance.* New York: Wiley, 1976.

Coulbois, P., Ed. *Le Change à Terme.* Paris: Editions Cujas, 1972.

Friedman, M. "The Eurodollar Market; Some First Principles." *Federal Reserve Bank of St. Louis Review,* July, 1971.

Haegele, M. J., and Wilford, D. S. "Exchange, Not Interest Rates Will Bear the Lion's Share of Shift from Dollar Assets." *The Money Manager,* December 19, 1977.

Heller, H. R. "The European Monetary System: Is It More than a New Skin on the Old Snake?" *Bank of America Management Magazine,* May/June, 1979.

Hepburn, A. "The Way to True Profit on Interest Arbitrage." *Euromoney,* July, 1974.

Heywood, J. *Foreign Exchange and the Corporate Treasurer,* 2nd ed. London: A & C Black, 1979.

Jacque, Laurenth. *Management of Foreign Exchange Risk, Theory and Praxis,* Lexington, Massachusetts: Lexington Books, 1978.

Klopstock, F. "The Euro-Dollar Market: Some Unresolved Issues." *Princeton Essays in International Finance,* 1968.

Kubarych, R. M. *Foreign Exchange Markets in the United States.* New York: Federal Reserve Bank of New York, 1978.

Lall, S. "What Does it Really Mean?—The Forward Exchange Market." *Finance and Development,* September, 1967.

Lesseps, M., and Monell, J. *Forecasting Exchange Rates: Theory and Practice.* Forecasting Study Paper No. 1. London: The Henley Center for Forecasting, March, 1977.

Lietaer, B. A. *Financial Management of Foreign Exchange.* (Cambridge, Massachusetts: The M.I.T. Press, 1971.

Makin, J. H. "The Portfolio Method of Managing Foreign Exchange Risk." *Euromoney,* August, 1976.

Mandick, D. R., Ed. *FX Trading Techniques and Controls.* Washington, D.C.: American Banking Association, 1976.

Marston, R. C. "Interest Arbitrage in the Eurocurrency Markets." *European Economic Review,* January, 1976.

Officer, L. H. "The Purchasing Power Parity Theory of Exchange Rates: A Review Article." *I.M.F. Staff Papers,* March, 1976.

Prindl, A. R. *Foreign Exchange Risk.* London: Wiley, 1976.

Riehl, H., and Rodriquez, R. M. *Foreign Exchange Markets, A Guide to Foreign Currency Operations.* New York: McGraw-Hill, 1977.

Rodriquez, R. M., and Carter, E. E. *International Financial Management,* 2nd, ed. Englewood Cliffs, N.J.: Prentice Hall, 1979.

Rosenwald, R. W. "How to Use Various Definitions of Exposures." *Euromoney,* December, 1976.

Salop, J. "Dollar Intervention Within the Snake." *I. M. F. Staff Papers,* March, 1977.

Stanton, C. P. *A Practical Guide to Foreign Exchange.* New York: Morgan Guaranty Trust, 1975.

Stoll, H. R. "An Empirical Study of the Forward Exchange Market under Fixed and Flexible Exchange Rate Systems." *Canadian Journal of Economics,* February, 1968.

Swiss Bank Corporation. *Foreign Exchange and Money Market Operations.* Zurich: Swiss Bank Corporation, 1976.

Telser, L. G. "A Theory of Speculation Relating Profitability and Stability." *Review of Economics and Statistics,* August, 1959.

Walker, T. "Foreign Exchange: What Every Contractor Should Know (But Often Doesn't)." *Worldwide Projects,* April/May, 1979.

Sources of Information and Articles

Agefi, Paris
Bank for International Settlements Annual Report, Basle
Bank of England Quarterly Bulletin, London
Euromoney, London
Financial Times, London
International Reports, New York
London Currency Review, London
The Money Manager, New York
The Wall Street Journal, New York

INDEX

367